AUTISM

How to Raise a Happy Autistic Child

JESSIE HEWITSON

First published in Great Britain in 2018
by Orion Spring
an imprint of The Orion Publishing Group Ltd
Carmelite House, 50 Victoria Embankment
London EC4Y 0DZ

An Hachette UK Company

7 9 10 8

A CIP catalogue record for this book is
available from the British Library.

ISBN: 978 1 4091 7628 2

Printed and bound in Great Britain by Clays Ltd, Elcograf S.p.A.

www.orionbooks.co.uk

ORION
SPRING

For Ellis, with all my love.

CONTENTS

FOREWORD

* * *

For many families, receiving a diagnosis of autism for their child is a life-changing moment. It can unlock access to the right support and provide an explanation for why they may be struggling to cope in nursery or in school. It's the result of a long and hard-fought journey for the support they so desperately need. But it is just the beginning.

While awareness of autism has increased, understanding of autism still has a long way to go. Alongside the relief of a diagnosis, parents often feel panic and confusion as they attempt to navigate their way towards an understanding of this disability. A quick Google of 'autism' returns millions of results, some reliable and many ill-informed. There are numerous medical journals packed full of important research, but it's lengthy and difficult to wade through the jargon. It is easy to feel confused and overwhelmed in the first years after diagnosis.

All any parent or carer wants for their child is for them to be happy and supported to achieve their potential. For parents and carers of children with autism, knowledge is power.

In this book, Jessie Hewitson, the mother of a child with autism, has done much of the hard work for you. Pairing the most-up-to-date research and information on autism with the experiences of people with autism themselves, makes for a powerful and enlightening read.

It is also an incredibly useful and accessible guide to autism, which debunks common myths and breaks down medical and educational jargon into plain English. Underpinned throughout by Jessie's own experience, this is a refreshingly honest and candid insight into the many challenges – but also the joys – of raising a child with autism.

The result is an important book that will no doubt become an invaluable source of support for any parent who suspects, or has been told, that their child has autism.

The journey that Jessie describes in this book – from the stumbling blocks she encounters trying to get a diagnosis, to the challenge of securing the right support in school – is one that will be all too familiar for parents of children with autism.

As any parent knows, when you have a child you enter a daunting new world. As well as the joy and love you feel, there is also anxiety about the road ahead. For parents of autistic children, this journey feels even more difficult and fraught with challenges. It's easy to see why. There are still far too many barriers in society preventing children with autism from fulfilling their potential.

At Ambitious about Autism our mission is to break down these barriers and make the ordinary possible for children and young people with autism. This could be making sure they have access to an education that meets their needs, to finding a job, or simply finding acceptance.

We were founded by a small group of parents in 1997 who were determined to challenge the lack of education and support for their children's needs. Starting out with a handful of students, we have gone on to expand our services to help thousands of young people. We now run specialist schools and colleges for young people with complex autism at four sites across London.

Education is key and we must keep pushing for change to ensure no child with autism is let down by the system. This begins with greater understanding and awareness of autism among teachers and classroom staff. Ambitious about Autism campaigned for basic autism training to be made a mandatory part of all teachers' initial training – and we're pleased this is now a reality. But it's crucial that all teachers, not just newly qualified ones, as well as support staff and classroom assistants, receive autism training as part of their ongoing professional development. The more school staff appreciate and value the differences in autistic children, the better their ability to offer them the support they need to succeed.

The book you are about to read is very honest about the problems that continue to exist for children with autism – many of which are rooted in a lack of understanding. But reading it will reassure parents that they are not alone, and will equip them with vital knowledge to help themselves and their children.

It is above all a book that is hopeful and ambitious about autism – something that very much resonates with our charity's work. While its practical advice does not sugar coat or shy away from any of the difficulties that await parents – this is a book that celebrates difference and champions happiness. It's a message all of us can support, whether you have a connection to autism or not. For, as the author so eloquently puts it early on, what is so brilliant about being normal?

Jolanta Lasota,
Chief Executive of Ambitious about Autism

⚹   ⚹   ⚹

INTRODUCTION

* * *

'An expert is a person who has found out by his own painful experience all the mistakes that one can make in a very narrow field.'
Niels Bohr, Danish physicist awarded the 1922 Nobel Prize
in Physics

Lots of mothers and fathers will tell you they didn't know what they were doing when their newborn baby was first handed to them. But if your child is autistic, and you aren't, then you really don't know what you're doing, and most likely won't for years.

Because you and your child are fundamentally different – in the way you think, how you perceive the world, how you communicate and how you play. All the while, though, you're both likely to be thinking you're the same.

To put it a different way: imagine you are a British person married to a fellow Brit; brought up in this country and used to the culture, food and language. You then have a child together and discover, when the child is five years old, that they are actually from, say, France. A different culture. They find some of your food disgusting, they speak another language. It's a hell of a shock, but eventually it makes sense: this is why you felt so at sea and found it hard to communicate with them. You knew on an intuitive level there was a difference, but you couldn't put your finger on it.

You blame the fact they're French. That's the reason I can't play with my baby, or soothe them, you tell yourself. You also blame yourself: how did I not realise for all these years that my own child came from a different country? You start to imagine what it must have been like for them to have a parent who didn't understand their experiences were so different.

But the problem isn't that they are French. The problem is the not realising your child is French, as well as not knowing much about France. Once you take language classes things get a lot better.

This happened to me when my son was diagnosed at the age of two. I thought autism was the reason he wasn't happy and I hated it. I felt it had robbed my child of the life I wanted for him.

Gradually, though, I realised he was unhappy not because he was autistic, but because the people around him didn't have a clue about autism. My husband and I only knew the horrible stereotypes. We didn't know what he needed.

It is this knowledge gap that needs to be tackled, not the autism. I'm hoping this book will speed up this process, by giving you a lot of what you need to know in one place. By telling you it's going to be OK. It's the book containing everything I wish I had known from the very beginning – information it has taken me years to gain, sometimes by learning some very hard lessons.

The other key message of this book is: what is so brilliant about being 'normal'? We use the word 'average' as an insult in every context except when a child is developing differently. Then, suddenly, it's the thing to aspire to.

Let's not aim for average. Let's aim for happiness. It may not be easy to achieve when your child has a different brain nationality to your own, but you've come to the right place to start figuring out how to get there.

A few notes about writing this book

I realised halfway through that I had made a mistake. I was writing a book about autism by interviewing non-autistic people – it seemed as ridiculous as interviewing only men for a book about feminism. The penny dropped after I spoke to a few autistic adults. I started again, this time making autistic adults central to the book. I am so pleased I did. Not just because it was the right thing to do, but because this way I got the best advice and insight.

I also wasn't aware of the role language plays in the discussion of autism. This changed when I saw my son reading an article about autism in the kids' newspaper we subscribe to. I felt panicky when he turned the page and I saw the headline – I was worried the piece would talk about 'autism sufferers' and leave him feeling like he had a disorder. It didn't – gold star *First News*.

So, message received: language matters very much; the words we choose reflect our unconscious bias. In my writing, I now refer to autistic people as precisely that – autistic people, not people with autism. People *with* autism have a medical condition (as if you can somehow separate the autism from the person); autistic people's autism is part of who they are. Similarly, I reject the notion of autism as a calamity or a medical disorder, so I have steered clear of terms such as 'impairment', 'disorder', 'severe' autism, or people being 'at risk of' autism. Terms such as 'high-functioning' and 'low-functioning' are also misleading, as I explain later in the book. In direct quotes, however, I have used people's own terminology.

*   *   *

1

DEFINING AUTISM

*   *   *

'Nature never draws a line without smudging it.'
Winston Churchill, frequently quoted by Lorna Wing

Until I started researching this book I had never actually read the criteria for the diagnosis my son received back in 2012. When I did, I was horrified. According to the ICD-10, the World Health Organization's International Statistical Classification of Diseases and Related Health Problems – the diagnostic manual most commonly used by UK doctors – childhood autism is:

A disorder that is usually diagnosed in early childhood. The main signs and symptoms of autism involve communication, social interactions and repetitive behaviors. Children with autism might have problems talking with you, or they might not look you in the eye when you talk to them. They may spend a lot of time putting things in order before they can pay attention, or they may say the same sentence again and again to calm themselves down. They often seem to be in their 'own world'. Because people with autism can have very different features or symptoms, healthcare providers think of autism as a 'spectrum' disorder. Asperger syndrome is a milder version of the disorder. The cause of autism is not known. Autism lasts throughout a person's lifetime. There is no cure, but treatment can help.

It adds:

Type of autism [is] characterized by very early detection (< 30 months), social coldness, grossly impaired communication and bizarre motor responses.

Had I read this definition when my son was being assessed, I'm sure I would have felt total panic. Back then, I too looked at what he wasn't doing compared with non-autistic children the same age, and thought this was the problem. I saw autism as a disorder, and being non-autistic as the goal.

While my knowledge of autism at this stage was limited, the medical profession doesn't have the same excuse. You would think at the very least its definitions should be objective. But this one is not – it contains several value judgements. Describing someone as 'socially cold' is a highly offensive way of describing social difference, as is labelling particular motor responses 'bizarre' and communication 'grossly impaired'.

I wonder if the gravely portentous declaration that 'there is no cure, but treatment can help' will come back to haunt the compilers of the ICD-10 in years to come. In a couple of decades, we may be as amused-horrified to read those words as we are today to see the sexist *Mad Men*-style ad campaigns of the 1950s.

Increasingly the medical view of autism as a disorder or impairment is being challenged. Take, for example, the man responsible for the iPhone in your pocket. With his single-mindedness, attention to detail and ability to think differently, the late Steve Jobs is seen by many autistic people as a kindred spirit. You wouldn't call him impaired, would you? In fact, you'd probably say he functioned at an envy-inducing level. Or what about the many autistic people who have found their significant other, started a family and are leading happy, fulfilled lives – are they socially cold? The clinical definition is meaningless for them.

To try to highlight how skewed the medical take on autism is, take a look at the definition of homosexuality in the ICD-9, compiled in 1977:

Exclusive or predominant sexual attraction for persons of the same sex with or without physical relationship.

Doesn't sound too bad? It is listed under 'Sexual deviations and disorders', which are defined as:

Abnormal sexual inclinations or behavior which are part of a referral problem. The limits and features of normal sexual inclination and behavior have not been stated absolutely in different societies and cultures but are broadly such as serve approved social and biological purposes. The sexual activity of affected persons is directed primarily either towards people not of the opposite sex, or towards sexual acts not associated with coitus normally, or towards coitus performed under abnormal circumstances ... It is preferable not to include in this category individuals who perform deviant sexual acts when normal sexual outlets are not available to them.

This view of homosexuality – particularly that last hilarious get-out clause – now seems just embarrassing, yet it was there in black and white in the WHO's manual until 1990, when it was dropped from the newly minted ICD-10.

While the current edition's definition of autism is misguided in many ways, and will hopefully be reworded when the next one appears in coming years, it is mainly wrong because it measures autism against a non-autistic benchmark and finds it lacking. Since autistic people are not of the usual order, not normal, then they must be disordered, abnormal.

If the compilers of the ICD-11 are looking for a fairer definition, they could do worse than consider this take, offered by Nick Walker, an autistic author, aikido teacher and psychology professor in the US, on his blog www.neurocosmopolitanism.com:

Autism produces distinctive, atypical ways of thinking, moving, interacting, and sensory and cognitive processing. One analogy that has often been made is that autistic individuals have a different neurological 'operating system' than non-autistic individuals.

He adds that while autism is still widely regarded as a disorder, 'this view has been challenged in recent years by proponents of the neurodiversity model, which holds that autism and other neurocognitive variants are simply part of the natural spectrum of human biodiversity, like variations in ethnicity or sexual orientation' – which have been pathologised in the past.

Amen to that. In fact, rather than trying to pin down what autism is, I think it's more helpful to say what it *isn't*. It isn't a barrier to having friends, getting married, having a happy, fulfilled life, evolving or changing, learning, being close to your parents, caring about other people, having a job, being good at sport, feeling empathy or emotions (quite the opposite: autistic people can feel emotions very intensely). But then neither is it a passport to understanding the mysteries of mathematics or computing, nor the key to making millions at a Las Vegas blackjack table.

While autistic people are at a considerable disadvantage because they live in a sense-overloading world that doesn't understand and rarely makes allowances for them, arguably what disadvantages them most is being constantly defined by what they can't do, rather than what they can.

A history of autism in seven people

Hans Asperger

In the 1930s, the Austrian paediatrician Hans Asperger (1906–1980) began notic-ing a particular set of characteristics among children he was studying in Vienna. He called the condition 'autism psychopathy', using a word first coined in 1910 by the Swiss psychologist Eugen Bleuler to describe the tendency among his schizophrenic patients to become detached, interacting not with their immedi-ate environments but with their interior worlds.

Asperger's views on autism were decades ahead of their time. He believed autism was common and heritable; that it needed to be adapted to, rather than cured; that it was a lifelong condition requiring special forms of support from family, schools and the community. He identified what would come to be known as the 'spectrum theory', the idea that autism impacts people in differ-ent ways, leaving some unable to speak and others capable of discoursing at length about their special and very specific interests – such as the 'little profes-sors' at his clinic.

He also recognised that having exceptional talents in some areas did not preclude a child from having profound difficulties in others. He kept tabs on one boy, Fritz V, long after he had left the clinic. Fritz V had shown 'a very severe impairment in social integration' and at school 'quickly became aggressive and lashed out with anything he could get hold of (once with a hammer)'. The boy showed an astonishing facility for mathematics, how-ever. He gained a place at university, on his way to becoming an assistant professor of astronomy, and discovered a mistake in the work of Isaac Newton.

There has always been doubt over Asperger's role in the Nazi party. Re-search published in 2018 shows he was far more involved than previously thought and willingly selected disabled children to be euthanised, though there is no evidence that he signed a death warrant for any of the autistic children at his school. It had been reported that he was a passionate defend-er of difference, but the truth appears to be far more complex and disturbing.

In 1944, he published a paper on his work on autism, but the conflagration in Europe meant it went largely unnoticed. A lot of his early work was also lost when his school-clinic was bombed towards the end of the Second World War. The war arguably delayed the understanding of the autism spectrum and left its definition to another doctor, one with a very different view of autism.

Leo Kanner

Born during the days of the Austro-Hungarian empire in what is now Ukraine, Leo Kanner (1894–1981) was a child psychiatrist who relocated to the US in 1924. There, at around the same time as Asperger but about 4,000 miles away, he too was beginning to identify autism in the children he was observing.

In 1943, while working at the Johns Hopkins Hospital in Baltimore, Maryland, Kanner published his seminal study on autism, coincidentally using the same word as Asperger to describe the condition. Although he was not yet aware of Asperger's work, the younger man referenced Kanner's paper in his own the following year.

Kanner based his findings on observations of 11 young people – among them Donald Triplett, written up as 'Case 1', the first person in the world to be diagnosed as autistic. Kanner noted that the youngsters seemed to inhabit their own private worlds, ignoring people around them, including their own parents, and were able to amuse themselves for hours by flapping their hands in front of their faces. Autism, he concluded, was a rare and serious condition with a narrow definition. By the 1950s, he had only diagnosed 50 cases of 'true autism'.

While Kanner and Asperger had identified similar characteristics in their subjects, their interpretations were hugely different. Kanner saw autism in a negative light, and his recommendation to parents who brought their children to see him was to send them away to institutions and forget about them. He assumed autistic people were beyond help, uneducable. Because they were sent to institutions, where they were taught nothing, this view stayed unchallenged for decades.

Kanner was in part responsible for the theory of the 'refrigerator mother'. In 1949, he suggested autism may be related to a 'genuine lack of maternal warmth', observing that the children 'were left neatly in refrigerators which did not defrost. Their withdrawal seems to be an act of turning away from such a situation to seek comfort in solitude.' In a 1960 interview he went further, bluntly condemning parents of autistic children as having happened 'to defrost enough to produce a child'.

The psychoanalyst Bruno Bettelheim, a professor of psychology at the University of Chicago, born in Vienna three years before Asperger, took this idea and ran with it. Thanks to him the refrigerator mother theory became mainstream, accepted by the medical establishment and public alike. Yet when Bettelheim died it was discovered that his expertise in psychoanalysis amounted to three introductory classes in psychology, and that his claims to have met and been praised by the father of psychoanalysis, Sigmund Freud, were false.

As a result of Kanner's observations and Bettelheim's now discredited theories, autism became linked with shame and stigma, with autistic children continuing to be sent to institutions and mothers being told it was all their fault. Kanner later backtracked, claiming his work had been hijacked by Bettelheim.

In the early 1970s, the British psychiatrist Michael Rutter carried out research looking at non-identical and identical twins where one sibling was autistic. This proved a genetic component to autism for the first time.

Lorna Wing

A better understanding still was developed in the 1970s by the British psychiatrist Lorna Wing and her assistant, the British psychotherapist Judith Gould. While Wing respected Kanner for having identified autism, she doubted his conclusion that it was rare and set out to prove otherwise. As the mum of an autistic daughter, Suzy, she also knew that the refrigerator mother theory was, in her words, 'bloody stupid'.

It was Wing who stumbled upon Hans Asperger's work. In the late seventies, while looking into the incidence rate of autism, she unearthed his 1944 paper, written in German. Her husband, John Wing, a German speaker, was the first to translate it into English.

Asperger's paper chimed with Wing's research and led in the 1980s to the formulation of her 'spectrum theory' of autism. The autistic children Asperger had observed in the 1930s were for the most part more in line with their non-autistic peers, while those being studied by Kanner had more complex needs. The pair, she surmised, had identified the same condition but at different points on a continuum. Autism, she concluded, was a spectrum, meaning the condition was likely to be anything but rare.

She also introduced the term 'Asperger syndrome', to indicate autistic children with little or no communication delay and no cognitive difficulties. Asperger syndrome was given formal recognition a decade later when it was included in the International Classification of Diseases.

If the story of autism so far sounds like something Hollywood might have conjured up, perhaps it won't surprise you to see Tom Cruise stepping into shot. In 1988, the film *Rain Man* came out, starring Cruise as the brother of an autistic savant, played by Dustin Hoffman. It won four Oscars and brought autism to the attention of the world, where previously only a small number of professionals knew about it.

These two incidents – Wing's realisation that autism was far more prevalent than previously thought and the success of *Rain Man* – is one explanation for the spike in diagnoses that occurred in the 1980s and 1990s. For most of the twentieth century, autism had indeed been very rare – then suddenly it wasn't. In a short space of time, most people knew of someone with a diagnosis.

Andrew Wakefield

In 1998, a British gastroenterologist, Andrew Wakefield, claimed there was another reason for this sudden rise in diagnoses: the MMR (measles, mumps and rubella) vaccine, which he concluded was causing autism. His controversial study, published in *The Lancet*, was widely publicised. Sensationalist newspaper headlines screamed that an 'autism epidemic' had been triggered by the triple MMR vaccine.

Wakefield's study was found to be fraudulent, however, and he was reported to have been paid more than £435,000 by lawyers acting on behalf of parents who believed their children had been harmed by the vaccine. In 2010, he was found guilty of serious professional misconduct and struck off the medical register. The final nail in the coffin for Wakefield's claims came in 2014, when a review of more than 1.2 million children established no link between the triple MMR vaccine and autism.

Neither Wakefield nor those journalists looking for a disaster angle understood that the increase in diagnoses was a good thing. Thanks to the work of Hans Asperger, Lorna Wing and Judith Gould, children and adults were at last having their differences and difficulties recognised, and beginning to get the support they needed. There was never an epidemic; autism was instead being recognised as a common part of the human condition for the first time. The latest estimate by America's Centers for Disease Control and Prevention puts the number of autistic children at one in 68.

Jim Sinclair

The spike in diagnoses during the 1980s and 1990s saw an accompanying spike in panic among parents. Autism conventions were held to discuss the urgent need to find a cure; mothers and fathers spoke about the tragedy of having a child with autism. Those children rarely, if ever, got podium space to share their thoughts.

One autistic man, Jim Sinclair, described by the author Steve Silberman as 'the Martin Luther King of the autism rights movement', had attended such conventions. He had had enough. In 1993, he requested to speak at the International Conference on Autism in Toronto. There, before an audience of parents and professionals, he delivered his now-famous 'Don't mourn for us' speech, an anti-cure perspective on autism.

He told the conference: 'You didn't lose a child to autism. You lost a child because the child you waited for never came into existence. That isn't the fault of the autistic child who does exist, and it shouldn't be our burden. We need and deserve families who can see us and value us for ourselves, not families whose vision of us is obscured by the ghosts of children who never lived. Grieve if you must, for your own lost dreams. But don't mourn for *us*. We are alive. We are real.'

This speech was a turning point. The idea that the condition is a difference rather than a life-destroying tragedy was now part of the conversation.

Neurotypical* syndrome

In 1998, an autistic woman known as Muskie set up a website for a made-up organisation, the Institute for the Study of the Neurologically Typical, on which she posted the following satirical definition of 'neurotypical syndrome'. (*NB: Neurotypical means non-autistic.)

What is NT? *Neurotypical syndrome is a neurobiological disorder characterised by preoccupation with social concerns, delusions of superiority and obsession with conformity.*

How common is it? *Tragically, as many as 9,625 cases out of every 10,000 individuals may be neurotypical.*

Are there any treatments for it? *There is no known cure for neurotypical syndrome.*

Judy Singer

In 1998, Judy Singer, an Australian autism-rights scholar writing her sociology thesis, coined the word 'neurodiversity'. The term is a powerful one, suggesting as it does that our minds and brains in their infinite variety are part of a spectrum of human diversity. It invites us to view neurological difference in the same way as we view sexual orientation or cultural diversity.

'While the medical view stated there was one way to be, and that way is "normal" – anything that deviates from normal is a disorder or a deficit – the neurodiversity paradigm questions the assumption that there is only one right way of being,' argued Nick Walker in a talk he gave on autistic identity at the University of California, Davis in October 2014. 'In the past, it was thought that there was only one right ethnicity – everyone else was inferior or savages.'

In 2005, a charity was founded in the US with the goal of curing autism and addressing the 'global health crisis' it represented. Autism Speaks, backed by wealthy benefactors, spent millions of dollars per year funding research to achieve its aim. In 2016, it announced it was dropping the search for a cure from its mission statement and has since removed from its website and literature references to 'struggles', 'hardship' and 'crisis'.

There is now a movement among autistic adults to encourage people to accept their difference, and for non-autistic people to find out from autistic adults what autism is all about.

'Neurodiversity is a fact, like all kinds of diversity – human diversity, ecological diversity,' says Virginia Bovell, mother of Danny Hornby, a young autistic man with severe-to-profound learning disabilities. Danny's father, and Virginia's ex-husband, is the writer Nick Hornby. 'When it becomes linked to your belief systems it becomes more than that, though – it becomes a fact that's celebrated and promoted. If you were to advocate for neurodiversity, you'd be saying: "We don't need to make everyone the same. We shouldn't require autistic people to behave as if they weren't autistic."

'It's about equality of respect and equality of taking people seriously. Studies have explored how autistic people behave in certain circumstances versus neurotypicals, and how sometimes researchers have viewed in a bad light the positive attributes of autism. It's just assumed the neurotypicals are doing the right thing.

'In one study, autistic and neurotypical people were observed in an experiment involving donating money to charity. The autistic people continued to give the same way as they did when not observed, but the neurotypicals behaved more generously when they were being observed. The study was written up as if they were somehow wrong for not being governed by what others might think of them.'

Donald Triplett

Donald Triplett, Leo Kanner's 'Case 1', is now 84 and still living in Mississippi, in the same house he grew up in. He was sent to an institution at the age of the three, on the advice of doctors, and was expected to die there. His parents, however, changed their minds a year later and brought him home.

The boy they were advised to forget has forged a life, built a group of friends, has the support and acceptance of his community. He gets around town in a Cadillac, plays golf every day and enjoys travelling; he has visited more than 20 countries on his own. The authors of *In a Different Key: The Story of Autism*, John Donvan and Caren Zucker, interviewed Triplett over a number of years, writing for *BBC News Magazine* in 2016 that, 'even though he still has obsessions, and talks rather mechanically, and cannot really hold a conversation beyond one or two rounds of exchanged pleasantries . . . he is a fully fledged personality, a pleasure to hang out with, and a friend'.

They added: 'What Donald's story suggests is that parents hearing for the first time that a child is autistic should understand that, with this particular diagnosis, the die is never cast. Each individual has a unique capacity to grow and learn, as Donald did, even if he hit most of his milestones rather later than most people. For example, he learned to drive only in his late twenties.'

This is why the medical definition of autism feels so incomplete: I don't recognise my son in it, and nor does it do justice to Donald Triplett. Triplett is now a happy retiree, an active part of his community, enjoying a life very different to the one that nearly was his lot had his parents not taken him out of the institution. Had he been left, Triplett would no doubt have fulfilled the horrible definition of autism set down in the ICD-10, but he was lucky to have parents who didn't define him in medical terms alone. Who would have guessed in the 1940s that Case 1 in Kanner's report would lead a fulfilling life and now be travelling the world on his own? I certainly had no idea, back when my son was diagnosed, how well he'd be doing at the age of seven.

*   *   *

2

IS MY CHILD AUTISTIC?

* * *

'It's really important to share the idea that being different might feel like a problem at the time, but ultimately diversity is a strength.'
Carson Lee Kressley, fashion expert on the American television programme *Queer Eye for the Straight Guy*

I first heard the word autism in relation to my son when he was one and we were staying with my mother-in-law, a retired educational psychologist. I told her I was worried he wasn't happy; I felt he didn't need me.

She raised the possibility of him being autistic. I was taken aback: the thought had never occurred to me, most likely because I knew nothing about autism. So I did what everyone does in a time of crisis: I turned to the internet. On YouTube, I came across a video of an autistic boy flapping his hands at the dinner table – exactly the same hand-flapping my son did. This must be it, I thought. I had always known there was something different about him and about our relationship; it must be because he was autistic. I panicked.

I spoke to a health visitor about my son's lack of eye contact and mentioned autism. She watched him for a minute, put the cap back on her pen, handed me back his 'red book' health record, and told me he wasn't. I felt a burst of relief, but this quickly faded when we got back to the flat: I still couldn't play with him; I couldn't get him to look at me. The nagging feeling returned.

I visited the GP, who said she didn't think he was autistic but would refer him 'just in case'. We saw a speech and language therapist (SLT) who told me my son wasn't autistic but did have an attachment disorder.

Well, hearing that felt like getting hit on the head with a baseball bat. This woman, in her early twenties, had confirmed that whatever was happening was down to my shit mothering, a possibility I already worried about every hour of the day. I phoned up my mother-in-law and burst into tears. She was brilliant. She told me the SLT didn't know what she was talking about and told me to have confidence in what I thought was happening.

It is all about confidence, isn't it? So many parents know deep down that their child is autistic, and so many professionals and lovely, well-meaning friends chip away at that belief. The health visitor should have realised she wasn't qualified to answer my questions and referred me on straight away.

If she had been more knowledgeable, she would have seen the signs, which include fleeting eye contact. She might have noticed he was anxious in the unfamiliar and noisy health centre and, instead of seeking comfort from me or playing with any of the toys on offer, had zoned out. He wasn't pointing, waving, looking to my face for reassurance or copying the other children; he stayed away from them. The whole situation overwhelmed him. Really, she should have taken me seriously because parents are often right in such situations – certainly more often than health visitors who know nothing about autism, at any rate.

While many professionals were lacking in knowledge and highly patronising – and if they patronise me, a middle-class journalist, then I hate to think how they treat other parents who don't have the same privileges – others took me seriously.

About a year after that first conversation with my mother-in-law, I went to see Dr Stella Acquarone, who validated my concerns. I wish I could say I accepted my child's likely autism with equanimity. But I didn't. I felt a deep, crushing despair. Confusingly, this was combined with a sense of relief that someone else could see what I could see. I've never been in this situation before or since, where I was desperate for someone to confirm something that I desperately didn't want to be happening.

Stella taught me that my son needed me very much and that he was an extremely sensitive child. I'm so glad someone said this to me early on. While I felt guilty that I'd got him so wrong, it changed everything. She helped me start to see things from his point of view. Stella was our translator, mediating between my son's world and mine.

I find it painful to think of what life was like for my son when he was a baby, with a mum and dad who couldn't know innately what was going on for him. I think this situation can make the relationship between neurotypical parents and autistic babies and children very complex. Parents can't seem to get close to a child who appears withdrawn – so they too withdraw, to protect themselves from the pain of rejection. I imagine the autistic child finds the neurotypical parents too much, too unpredictable. They don't know how best to soothe him or her.

For these reasons, I think it's important to register the signs of autism, some of which we list below. Listen to that small voice in your head. For me, this period of knowing, then not knowing, was the absolute pits. Things only got better once we knew for sure.

Communication differences

Joint attention

Joint attention means sharing interest with someone else. A neurotypical kid might do this by pointing and demanding you attend to something they are interested in – 'Look at this train set, Mum'; 'I want *that*'; 'Come and see the cat running in the garden'.

The autistic child, however, might not make demands on your attention in the same way. They may hyper-focus on an activity, and if an adult joins in with what they are focusing on, the pair can communicate in a way that is meaningful for the child.

Language

By six months, most children will have started to babble, repeating syllables that combine a vowel and consonant, such as 'ba', 'da', 'ma' and 'gaga', swapping them back and forth with parents and siblings, urgently expressing an unintelligible sentence then waiting expectantly, with a serious expression on their face, to hear your answer.

By 12 months, the first word has usually been said; at 18 months that has increased to 6–20 words, and by two and a half a child might have a repertoire of 200 words. At three they will be saying three-word sentences and by four they may be answering who and why questions.

My son didn't really babble (I only realised this when my second son hit this stage) and said his first word – tick-tock – after he was two. Language is considered delayed if the first word is spoken after this age. Be prepared when talking to friends for them to swear blind that they didn't utter a word until the age of three (hmm), or to be told your child's delay is because they are a boy (if they are a boy) and everybody knows boys speak later.

Language delay can suggest a child's neurology is different, but equally some autistic children have no language delay. They can be precocious speakers, in fact, with some autistic children speaking in full sentences from 14 months.

It is important to recognise that speech, or lack of it, is not an indicator of intelligence. Non-autistic people often place such an emphasis on communicating that we tend to use it to judge lots of things that we shouldn't; plenty of non-verbal autistic people have lots to 'say' given the opportunity to communicate another way.

Some children appear to be developing words and then lose their language skills. It can be devastating for parents, and for the child. In these scenarios, if you have early video footage on your phone, it can help speech and language therapists work out what is going on.

Scripting

Autistic children do a lot of scripting – repeating stock phrases they've picked up – because it's compulsive, fun or soothing, or because they find spontaneous language tricky. My son loves to repeat verbatim passages from books or TV programmes.

All children learn language by copying, but autistic children often copy better. One autistic woman reports that as a child she holidayed in Wales with her family, and within two days was speaking with a Welsh accent. Even as an adult she struggles not to mirror other people's accents and phrases.

Questions and echolalia

Autistic kids may also not feel the need to ask who, what, where, when and why questions. Why questions are by far the most difficult as they're open-ended. While autistic kids may ask and answer lots of questions if they are based on a particular interest of theirs, they may avoid questions on other topics they find hard or boring. A perfectionist child, and autistic kids are often perfectionists, might panic that they may not be able to answer the question. Others might be uninterested in small talk.

Some children reverse their personal pronouns, using 'you' instead of 'I' when talking about themselves. They may also display echolalia, where they repeat verbatim words that they have overheard. This may occur immediately – for instance, they may respond to a question with the same question – or be delayed, where they use a stock phrase such as 'Do you want to have a snack?'

every time they want something to eat. Echolalia is the child's way of practising questions.

Literal language

Words will often be taken literally, which can be a source of confusion when navigating a language as idiomatic as English. 'Skating on thin ice', 'You're full of beans' and 'It's raining cats and dogs' are all phrases we use that, quite rightly, may be met with complete bafflement by an autistic child. Irony and sarcasm can also be a source of confusion. My son went through a phase of loudly exclaiming 'Not on your nelly!' when faced with something he didn't like, such as the horror of finding broccoli on his plate. He looked puzzled when the adults around him laughed. It was a phrase picked up from CBeebies that to him simply meant an emphatic 'no'. Related to this, some autistic children may be capable of reading words at a startlingly young age but may not get the meaning (this is known as hyperlexia).

Informing, not conversing

In older children, the words might be there but they aren't being used communicatively. This can come down to a difference in preference between (some) neurotypicals who love to chat and (some) autistic people who prefer not to chat so much.

'These kids sometimes engage in conversation but if you unpick the conversation, you'll notice it's different,' says Lucia Santi, head teacher of The Grove, a school for autistic children in Haringey, north London, and the mum of a ten-year-old autistic girl. 'I sometimes speak to people working with my daughter and ask them: when has she asked an open question? When have you had a reciprocal conversation? Is the conversation her answering your questions? Watch how she's dominating the game.'

Non-verbal communication

This includes things like pointing, stretching out the arms to be picked up, waving hello or goodbye, or shaking the head to say 'no', things that are typically evident at about 12 months. Younger autistic children may show an absence of non-verbal communication, or a delay in developing it. Facial expressions may be less animated.

Eye contact

Some autistic people can make eye contact, some can't. Some look at the space between the eyes, or the end of the nose. Some stare, while other autistic children's eye contact may be fleeting – they may scan a situation looking out of the corner of their eyes rather than with a direct gaze. If your child finds eye contact difficult, other kids' laser-beam gazes suddenly seem oddly intense.

Toddlers begin to interpret different facial expressions by watching other people's faces, using this non-verbal information as a guide to behaviour. They study their mother's face for cues about whether it is safe to approach a stranger, for example. But this isn't something that occurs so much with autistic children. A study in the 1980s carried out by Geraldine Dawson and Julie Osterling, of the University of Washington, analysed home video footage of birthday parties thrown for one-year-olds. They found that a lack of attention to others' faces was the most powerful predictor of a future diagnosis of autism.

Not making eye contact doesn't mean a child isn't listening or understanding. 'This may give rise to a child being described as a "daydreamer" or "in her own little world", when in fact she might be entirely present but not making the socially required non-verbal signals to indicate that she is,' writes Sarah Hendrickx in her book *Women and Girls with Autism Spectrum Disorder*. This equally applies to boys, too.

Disengagement

The first time someone mentioned that my son was disengaged was a lightbulb moment for me – I realised it was one of the reasons I struggled to play meaningfully with him.

Few things in life are more frustrating than consistently being ignored by your child who has benefited from all your love, time and energy. Surely it's not too much to ask that you at least be the centre of their little universe? Feeling ignored is maddening, hurtful and, when it happens in public, humiliating. It isn't personal – you may be in an environment in which they can't cope, or your approach is one they don't understand.

Play differences

The play pose of many autistic children will be head down, engrossed in a toy – or perhaps just one random element of it. For them it may be a solitary rather than a social activity, though if you joined them in playing with the element that they are fascinated by, they may love it.

They may play with the toy in a way the manufacturer hadn't intended, such as laying a car on its back and spinning the wheels. The play may be self-directed: this means the child follows their own agenda, taking less account of the suggestions or desires of those around them and with much less copying.

If the child is anxious, they may dominate play in order to regulate the pace of proceedings, making things more predictable and helping calm themselves. Some autistic children find it far easier to play with an adult or older child than someone their own age.

While by the age of two neurotypical children often enjoy pretend play, many autistic boys and girls with their logical, literal minds won't see the point. A broom is a broom and not a rocket ship. You may receive a look of blank incomprehension when you try to pretend otherwise.

Boys on the autistic spectrum don't usually engage in lots of pretend play, preferring instead to explore the physical aspects of toys: examining the screws on the underside of their toy fire engine, for example, rather than driving it to save people from an imaginary fire. Girls may appear to demonstrate lots of imagination but careful observation will show a rigidity in their play: teddies sat in a circle for a tea party will have to be in the same place every time, for example. They are likely to be in charge of the activity and unwilling to let other children mess up the set-up they have in mind.

Typical early indicators of autism and parental anecdotal reports relating to characteristics and behaviour, from the book *Women and Girls with Autism Spectrum Disorder* by Sarah Hendrickx. I think this works for many boys as well as girls.

* The parent feels a sense of detachment from the baby or young child – often this cannot be further articulated by the parent; it is just a feeling of the baby or child 'being in their own world'
* Atypical eye contact (either unusually limited or staring)

- ✳ A lack of attention paid specifically to people and faces – interest in people is not prioritised over objects
- ✳ Limited interest and/or response to people stimuli (smiling, voices, peek-a-boo games)
- ✳ Limited reciprocal social facial expressions and social cues (smiling, pointing)
- ✳ Limited seeking-out of people and responses from people
- ✳ Very placid, silent and peaceful babies – 'It was spooky, was almost as though she was a ghost just lying there silently without moving' (parent of a girl with autism)

Or:

- ✳ Very anxious, distressed and clingy babies – 'Intense emotions, especially distress, and an inability to be comforted by affection' (Attwood, 2012)
- ✳ Sensory preferences and intolerances:
  Small temperature tolerance range, which can result in febrile convulsions
  Clothing – texture and touch
  Physical touch – distressed by being cuddled
  Specific strong food preferences and dislikes
  Food and other intolerances and allergies

Cognitive differences

These are the differences in thinking and brain function your autistic child may have compared with non-autistic children.

Theory of mind (different perspectives)

There's a reason an autistic child won't draw your attention to the train they are playing with, according to developmental psychologists. It's because they lack 'theory of mind' – that is, the ability to understand that people have different thoughts, beliefs and knowledge to their own.

The theory was formulated in 1978 by psychologists David Premack and Guy Woodruff, who were studying the ability of chimpanzees to infer what was going on inside the heads of their trainers. In 1983, psychologists Josef Perner and Heinz Wimmer extended it to the study of child development, creating in the process what has since become a seminal experiment: the 'Sally-Anne' test. It was perhaps most famously used by Simon Baron-Cohen, Alan M. Leslie and Uta Frith two years later, as part of their 1985 study into theory of mind in autistic children.

Professor Baron-Cohen and his team studied the responses of 61 children – 20 of them autistic, 14 with Down's syndrome and 27 of them neurotypical – to a puppet play starring two dollies named, unsurprisingly, Sally and Anne. Sally had a basket and a marble; Anne had a box. Sally put the marble into her basket and then went out for a walk, leaving the basket behind. While she was gone, Anne took the marble from the basket and put it in the box. When Sally returned, the children were asked: 'Where will Sally look for her marble?'

Of the three groups of children, 12 of the 14 kids with Down's syndrome answered the question correctly (86 per cent), 23 of the 27 neurotypical kids (85 per cent), but just 4 of the 20 autistic kids (20 per cent). The other 16 believed Sally would look for the marble in Anne's box, because that's where they saw it go – why would Sally think anything different? The results suggested autistic children struggle to put themselves in other people's shoes or grasp that others have an alternative perspective, and as a result can't understand or predict their behaviour. (Interesting to note, though, that a fifth of the autistic kids could, which is a significant proportion.)

But not everyone agrees with this theory. In an article for the Autism Education Trust entitled 'What Is Autism?' – a question it takes 12 pages to answer – the autistic academic Damian Milton argued that autistic people struggle to understand the neurotypical perspective in much the same way as neurotypicals struggle to understand the autistic point of view. He calls this the 'double empathy problem.'

Professor Baron-Cohen explained to me how a lack of theory of mind affects day-to-day living. 'Without theory of mind, you will be confused by a lot of social interaction – not picking up on hints, or people's intentions, which could leave you very vulnerable to exploitation,' he said. 'It is what people call "street smarts" – being aware people are trying to deceive you or manipulate you. The classic example is when another child in the playground asks the child with autism if they will show them their wallet. The child with autism hands it over and then is surprised when the other child runs off with it. They didn't see the potential deception.'

Empathy

The ability to see a different perspective is part of what enables us to empathise, which is the ability to infer emotional experiences. Empathy is a hotly debated topic within the autism community. Baron-Cohen divides it into two components: cognitive empathy (the ability to imagine someone's thoughts and feelings, which is theory of mind) and affective empathy (responding with an appropriate emotion to what someone is thinking or feeling).

In his controversially titled book *Zero Degrees of Empathy*, Baron-Cohen argues that people with Asperger syndrome have difficulties with cognitive empathy, yet when they are told what another person is experiencing their affective empathy kicks in with no trouble – that is, they may not be able to read what you're feeling but they certainly care (zero positive empathy). He goes on to state that autistic people are the polar opposite of psychopaths, whose cognitive empathy is intact and their affective empathy reduced or non-existent – they're perfectly able to read what you're feeling, they simply don't care (zero negative empathy).

In his book *Autism and Asperger Syndrome in Adults*, Dr Luke Beardon suggests we all have potential difficulty with what he refers to as 'cross-neurological empathy', meaning that while autistic people may struggle to empathise with neurotypicals, and vice versa, it is less likely that either population will have a problem empathising with members of their own group.

While many of the autistic people I have interviewed reject Baron-Cohen's notion that they have difficulties with cognitive empathy, two autistic women agreed. One told me she can only guess at other people's emotions but that did not mean she wasn't able to be compassionate once she understood what they were feeling. The second, Robyn Steward, an autism trainer in schools, says that she did not intuitively have cognitive empathy but has taught herself how to empathise. The ability to put yourself in someone else's shoes isn't always static – many people can learn it.

Executive function

Executive function is a term for the set of mental skills that allows us to problem-solve, plan, organise, switch focus, self-regulate and control our impulses. It can affect the big things in life – holding down a job and planning a career – as well as the day-to-day tasks, such as getting washed and dressed, doing housework and cooking.

Suzy, an autistic woman and the mum of an autistic daughter, based in Northern Ireland, explains what it's like to have difficulties in this area.

'I have problems keeping focused long enough to complete tasks and tend to struggle keeping up with household chores. I can't seem to get on top of things, it's just so overwhelming. Filling forms, returning them, returning phone calls and making or keeping appointments are the other things I find very hard . . . I wish I could just bounce out of bed and do all the "normal" day-to-day things without giving it much thought, but I can't. My brain doesn't work that way.'

The weak central coherence theory (big picture versus detail)

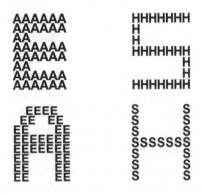

Which do you see first when you look at this image: the small letters or the big ones they make up? If you are autistic, it's likely to be the former. Put another way, autistic people will tend to see the trees and neurotypicals the wood.

This difference in autistic cognition, described as 'weak central coherence', was first spotted by Uta Frith, the pioneering German-born developmental psychologist who co-wrote the autistic theory of mind paper with Simon Baron-Cohen (her PhD student at the time). She tested it out by giving autistic children a jigsaw to piece together, except that she didn't show them the original image, and asked them to do it with the puzzle turned upside down. It turned out they were just as good at doing it that way as the right way up, suggesting they were not concerned with the broad picture.

This approach to mental processing affects the ability to understand and impart information too. For example, while most people when retelling a story tend to go for the gist and lose the detail if need be, an autistic child might re-tell the story verbatim and, when questioned on parts of the meaning, may not know.

Monotropism (the opposite of multitasking)

Monotropism describes when a person can only easily focus on a single task or interest, as opposed to polytropism, where your attention flits between many interests. The theory was put forward by three autistic researchers and academics – the researcher and campaigner Dinah Murray, the late mathema-tician and political activist Mike Lesser and Dr Wenn Lawson (formerly Wendy Lawson).

Murray explains that attention is a processing resource that people distrib-ute in different ways. Autistic people are more likely to give all their attention to one thing, while non-autistic tend to people distribute their attention broad-ly – it's more thinly spread, more available everywhere. 'With autism, when you are doing something that comes from the heart, the processing resource is unlimited,' she told me. 'But with anything else, it's hard. You have great areas of autistic people's lives that are unvisited by attention.

'When things go wrong for the autistic person – if they're pulled from their attention tunnel, for example – the shock and the distress caused will tend to be extreme, as they don't have the resources to handle things and it can take time to recover. It underlines their difficulties with emotional control.

'This is why the best advice [when trying to engage with an autistic child] is to start with what their interests are. It's idiotic to do things any other way because it won't work. Switching attention can be hard, for autistic and non-autistic people alike. It can feel like an interruption – in the same way as the neurotypical person engrossed in a TV programme finds it difficult when someone wants to talk to them about something else.'

When we're engaged in a conversation, most of us can handle the demands on our attention, which must shift constantly, from subject to subject, zipping back into the past to access memories or forward to discuss hopes for the future. This is because we are not in what Mike Lesser described, in an inter-view in 2005, as the 'attention tunnels'.

Monotropic attention, as explained by the health journalist Jerome Burne, who interviewed Lesser for the *Guardian*, is the equivalent of '[putting] all your mental eggs into one basket . . . Most of us have a mental space that is like a river delta – fairly flat with lots of connecting channels, only the water (information) is flowing both ways. The autistic style is to create psychological Grand Canyons.'

While spending time in these canyons of the mind may afford the traveller everything from intellectual insight to great pleasure, monotropism can also mean autistic people miss many of the peripheral cues about what is happening around them, so they are constantly blindsided by events. In a fast-changing environment, whether a party or a supermarket, the effect can induce overwhelming panic and meltdown.

A spiky profile

'One of the key aspects of the experience of being autistic is that of having a "spiky" or "uneven" set of abilities and capabilities,' writes Damian Milton, in a document for the Autism Education Trust. 'It is the feeling of many on the spectrum, however, that the spiky profile is often unrecognised by service providers and support workers. Verbal autistic people are often incorrectly assumed to be capable in areas in which they struggle, while those with fewer verbal skills are often incorrectly assumed to be lacking in skills, "strengths", ability or potential.'

It took me a while to get a handle on what a spiky profile means: it can be that a highly gifted software engineer struggles with getting the bus to work or bathing himself at night, or that a non-verbal child with very limited adaptive (i.e. independent) skills who people assume is cognitively disabled is fully cognisant and sensitive to their emotions and others around them. This means that people can underestimate the support some more 'able' autistic children need and underestimate the abilities of those with higher support needs.

This spiky profile can make life very difficult for some autistic people – as one person said to me: 'Why can I be successful at work and speak in public but I can't cook dinner?' Those described as high-functioning can feel a huge amount of pressure to be able to function in all aspects of their life, when at times they find it near-impossible, often when others can't see them.

What are autistic strengths?

Michelle Dawson, a researcher who works at the University of Montreal, found that autistic people are better at doing visual searches, better at remembering auditory pitch and can generally process information faster. Thanks to the work of Uta Frith, we know autistic people are far better at noticing details.

A 2015 study carried out by the University of Stirling involving 312 people found that autistic people display higher levels of creativity than non-autistic people and are more likely to come up with unusual or unique solutions to problems.

Anecdotally, autistic people can have a lack of regard for status, possessions, hidden agendas, point-scoring and spite. In an interview I did for *The Times* with the TV presenter and garden designer Alan Gardner, otherwise known as the Autistic Gardener, he told me that sometimes for his private work he quotes people a figure that is tens of thousands of pounds below their (very generous) budget.

Perhaps because of a lack of duplicity, autistic people can think the best of people until proved otherwise and are more likely to be honest.

Autism, like non-autism, comes with advantages and disadvantages. We aren't so aware of the advantages – the kindness, the honesty, the creativity – because the research, much like the medical definition of autism, has up until fairly recently focused on what autistic people can't do. What is far less explored is the many ways autistic brains work differently or better than neurotypical ones.

Parents' experiences

David Mitchell, author and father of an autistic son:
'There was no eye contact from him, and no interest in picture books, or in reading. He also had a propensity to meltdowns which might be

understandable when he was five months old but when he was two, my
wife and I began to suspect there might be an underlying issue here.'

J, from north London, mum of a seven-year-old girl:

'*I had considered my daughter's obsessive attachments to unusual items*
like a particular empty shampoo bottle and a pink plastic letter W
merely quirky and endearing. She talked about letters of the alphabet
and numbers as if they were living characters: letter A was apparently
naughty and constantly chasing other letters, while M and later W were
her favourites. She was very interested in the numbers 5 and 25, which
seemed to have been chosen arbitrarily.

'As a toddler she seemed both to need me very much and also not much
at all. She was clingy and reluctant to leave my side at toddler groups
and early playdates, but when at home together did not really seek me
out or demand things of me.'

L, who lives in Staffordshire and has a son who is 17:

'*My son developed normally until around the age of 18–20 months. He*
then stopped speaking, became extremely fussy about food and was very
stressed. He behaved differently from other children in social situations.
He stopped playing with toys and began to line everything up. His eye
contact became poor.'

N, who lives in South Yorkshire. Her son is four:

'*I noticed he was different when he was around six months old. He cried*
when held and much preferred to be left on his play mat for long periods
of time. He never put his arms up to be picked up, and would constantly
bang his heels on the floor. At 12 months he didn't babble, he just made
lots of high-pitched squealing noises. The health visitor referred him to
speech therapy. At the first session the therapist told me to "keep an open
mind" in regard to him having autism. I went home that night and
researched and I just knew.'

* * *

3

THE DIAGNOSIS PROCESS

⚹ ⚹ ⚹

*'One of my autistic friends, Mark Romoser, was diagnosed
by Leo Kanner himself. He told me, "Kanner told my
mother to put me in an institution. So she did – Yale."'*
Neurotribes author Steve Silberman

Waiting for an assessment is unlikely to be a high point of your life. We waited a year for my son to be assessed and diagnosed with autism spectrum disorder (ASD) in 2011.

By today's standards a year is lightning quick – almost four times faster than the average waiting time. Even so, it was tough. My husband and I responded in a very gender-stereotyped way: I knew early on that my son was autistic; my husband was unsure.

Our approaches to the situation – mine to roar into action to try to ease the anxiety I was feeling, a coping strategy; his to put the brakes on and hope things would be fine – worked in opposition to one another. The result, inevitably, was a lot of rowing.

The NHS assessment felt like an endurance race. Getting to the end involved telephone calls, emails, lost referrals, the chivvying along of professionals, arguments with speech and language therapists, two meetings with a community paediatrician to double-check our son suddenly wasn't autistic.

Then the big day arrived. We arrived at the NHS assessment centre in Hackney, in London: a large, airy, modern building with knackered toys in the waiting room. A female clinical psychologist played with my son while the diagnostic paediatrician, a kind Irishman in his fifties, asked us questions. He wanted to know when my son crawled, walked and started babbling, and was very skilled at maintaining eye contact while scribbling all my answers down. He observed my son, trying and failing to get his attention until a pot of bubble mixture was produced.

They went outside to confer while my son sat bashing the daylights out of an electronic drum. After all that waiting, the diagnosis came quickly: my son was officially autistic. The psychologist bluntly explained to me that my son had not been playing with her as a human being, but using her as a toy-fetcher.

I felt like Dorothy at the end of the Yellow Brick Road: weary, anticlimactic, sad. I wanted my son to be interested in people as human beings. The paediatrician, meanwhile, stuck to the facts and didn't speculate about the future, though he chose his words carefully. Hints were made that schooling would be tough.

I can understand why the medical community focuses on not giving false hope at a time when the future is unknowable, but sometimes I think clinicians could worry a bit more about giving false despair. Perhaps my son wasn't so interested in the psychologist, whom he had never met before, but he's now a sociable seven-year-old who loves his friends and family, even when there are no toys at stake.

Dr Luke Beardon, writing a piece for this book, explains his views on a diagnosis: 'My belief is that being autistic is, simply, being autistic. It is not a curse, blessing, miracle, personality decider, predictor of the future, disability, impairment, disorder, nor indicator of savant ability. It can be an extremely powerful and important identification in terms of understanding of self, others' understanding of the autistic person, and a huge help in explaining what various support mechanisms might be useful (and which are not).'

If I were in a position to advise paediatricians on what to say when it comes to telling parents their kids are autistic, I would suggest they tell them that a diagnosis doesn't mean you won't be close to your child; if anything, it probably means you will be extra-close. It doesn't mean they won't have friends. It doesn't mean they won't have a job and live a fulfilling life. It doesn't mean they won't be happy.

Not all of these things will happen organically, which is where you come in – the parents, grandparents, family, friends and carers who love the little person lining up toys in neat colour-coded rows. There will be challenges, naturally, but most will have less to do with your autistic child than with the structures, society and world around them.

The beginning

Make an appointment with your GP. Ask for a referral to the local autism team and, if there are delays in communication, a referral to the speech and language therapy (SALT) department.

Keep a diary of your child's behaviour. Make a note of what triggers melt-downs, what makes them happy and situations they find difficult. Gathering as much information as possible is a good idea before appointments, and over a longer period you may also spot things you haven't noticed day to day.

While there are some extremely on-the-ball professionals out there, there are also some health visitors, GPs and even paediatricians who have received little training on autism. I spoke to parents who were told by their GPs that if their child talked or liked soft play they couldn't be autistic.

'GPs, health visitors or childcare workers, who might not be very skilled in child development, can say unhelpful things like, "All children develop at their own pace", which is not true when it comes to social milestones. Copying, for example, starts at birth,' says Rina Picciotto, a retired portage services manager in Hackney, London, a service that provides support for parents of children who have delayed development.

If a GP is unwilling to refer and you think they should, seek the opinion of another GP or go to your health visitor. In some regions you can refer yourself to a diagnostic service. The National Autistic Society (NAS) has a helpline that can provide more advice.

'Different parts of the country do things in different ways,' says Tim Nicholls, policy director at the NAS. 'In some areas, the diagnosis might be led by CAMHS (Child and Adolescent Mental Health Services), in others by the community paediatric team or specialist multidisciplinary team. It can be helpful to find out what the process is for diagnosis – also known as the "path-way" – in your local area. Each area should have an autism diagnostic service. Some will have a pre-assessment phase. This can allow them to diagnose more simple cases quickly. It can also help them to refer to other services the children they think aren't likely to be autistic and may have a mental health con-dition, for example.'

From what age can a child be diagnosed?

'Few professionals will diagnose a child under two, but faced with a child show-ing symptoms at 18 months to two and a half years, a decent one will at least use words like "we need to keep an eye on his social communication",' says Picciotto.

Some parents I've met are under the impression that a child can't get diag-nosed until the age of five or even later. This usually isn't the case. While it's common for some children's differences to be picked up when they start school – because they haven't been spotted by nursery staff, for example – it is a good idea if your child is likely to need support at school to start as early as possible. Dr Julie Maxwell, a community paediatrician from North Hampshire Hospital, points out that for some children it can take a while to detangle whether they have a language disorder or autism, and in these cases it is appropriate to wait.

How long until you get an answer?

Guidelines set by NICE – the National Institute for Health and Care Excellence – state that the process should begin within three months of the referral, but unfortunately they don't state when the assessment process should end. The three-month figure suggests an efficient, quick process, yet at the time of writing, the average waiting time from first going to a professional to receiving a diagnosis is three and a half years, according to research carried out by Goldsmiths, University of London.

While some of this time will be spent observing your child, the reality for many families is that it takes far too long. One family had to wait nine years, at which point the experts concluded their child was indeed autistic.

I read blog posts by parents who say they have been told by paediatricians that they can't give a diagnosis until the start of the new budgetary year, which suggests doctors are working to a set quota. In 2017, one London mental health trust, faced with demand for assessments almost double its current annual capacity of 750, was reported to be considering restricting autism diagnoses only to those children with additional mental health conditions, and/or attention deficit hyperactivity disorder (ADHD). It backtracked after complaints but there is suspicion other trusts are operating just such a policy, albeit not openly. Some trusts have suspended their waiting lists because they have got too long, meaning they are not accepting new children for assessment, hopefully only temporarily, while they try to cope with current demand.

It's appalling and it will only get worse unless more funding is provided. It leaves children struggling at nursery or school without the understanding or support they need.

For all these reasons, you need to have your wits about you. I'm not saying don't listen to the people assessing your child, but don't listen to them *exclusively*. Inform yourself. Follow your instinct. Access help under your own steam if necessary. Have a healthy scepticism about the system you're involved in.

While you wait . . .

Considering that the assessment process largely moves at the speed of a snail on a tea break, it may be best to get cracking with some form of intervention while you wait. Call the Speech and Language Therapy (SALT) department and ask to speak to its autism specialist (make sure it's the specialist – I have been amazed at the lack of autism knowledge among general SALTs). If your child is of preschool age, see if your borough has a portage service (see page 92 for more on this) or an Opportunity Group playgroup, where children who may be developing differently can play while you get advice from the staff there. There are some health trusts and local authorities offering support for families who don't yet have a diagnosis, so explore what is available. Be persistent!

Judith Gould, lead consultant at the Lorna Wing Centre for autism on what to do in the meantime:

'If you think your child has autism and you are on a long waiting list, then put your time to good use by focusing on structure, routine and understanding what autism is. What you can do while you wait is read, read, read. Understanding what autism is will help you work with your child. You will discover your child finds it easier to present things visually. Explore their sensory issues. Check to see if their environment is overwhelming. If they are exhibiting behavioural problems, look at the triggers.'

Who carries out the assessment?

The NHS diagnosis process is a multidisciplinary one, meaning more than one professional is involved. The assessment will typically be carried out by an autism team consisting of a:

* Paediatrician and/or child and adolescent psychiatrist
* Speech and language therapist
* Educational and/or clinical psychologist

What is the autism team looking for in order to identify autism?

What tools/manuals do the professionals use?

The main manual used by clinicians in the UK is the International Statistical Classification of Diseases and Related Health Problems (ICD-10), published by the World Health Organization. Some clinicians use the DSM-5 instead (the fifth edition of the Diagnostic and Statistical Manual of Mental Disorders), produced by the American Psychiatric Association (APA). A revised edition of the ICD, ICD-11, is expected to be published in 2018.

Other methods include the DISCO assessment tool (Diagnostic Interview for Social and Communication Disorders), devised by Lorna Wing and Judith Gould and used in diagnostic centres run by the National Autistic Society. Some professionals or services also use ADOS – the Autism Diagnostic Observation Schedule – while some will use a mixture of methods.

Autism is diagnosed according to 'impairments' in the two areas shown in the below table, according to the DSM-5.

Impairment	Indicators
Social interaction and social communication	Difficulty with non-verbal communication, such as eye contact; not developing relationships or showing emotional reciprocity. Delay in language development; difficulty initiating and sustaining conversations. Lack of make-believe play.
Restricted patterns of behaviour, interests and activities	Repetitive behaviour getting in the way of functioning; a resistance to interruption or being redirected from their fixated interest by others.

On the day

The goal is to be as precise as you can about your child's development, so bring along any behaviour diary you've been keeping and a list of things you or your child's teacher have observed. My husband and I took a list of things that we noticed our son was good at and some things he found difficult and gave a copy to the paediatrician together with a list of questions so we didn't forget to ask anything. Other people take videos of their children to show the professionals.

It is likely that one member of the diagnostic team will ask you questions about your child and jot down notes, while another plays with your child and observes how they interact with you, with them and with the array of toys they'll have ready for this purpose. The professionals will be looking to see how your child plays – are they keen to involve an adult or do they want a toy to themselves? Are they playing with it 'appropriately'?

After they've made their assessment, the team may confer in private. They will either give you a diagnosis immediately or will ask you to come back in for further assessment. From speaking to the NHS professionals involved, we were fairly certain our son was going to receive a diagnosis – in order to speed up the process, I was advised to tell the paediatrician that we were ready for a diagnosis, and received it in that first meeting.

Autism is identified using clinical judgement and can be a hard thing to confirm at a young age. Inevitably, some clinicians get it wrong. If you feel this has happened, you can write to the autism team at your local authority and explain why you think your child should be assessed again. Either that or wait six months and try again. That way you may be able to include more information on what is going on at nursery or school.

Going privately

Considering the stresses and delays involved in getting an assessment through the NHS, it's not surprising that at least one in ten of us are now opting to go private, according to NAS figures. A private assessment costs anything from £650 to £800-plus and should include a detailed report that you can take back to the NHS autism team to support your case. You will still need to get a diagnosis from the NHS if you want to access its therapists and local authority professionals, as well as to get the support for your child at nursery or school. The NHS usually won't accept a private diagnosis, but it is possible that the private one will accelerate the NHS diagnosis. It's a good idea to use a private doctor who also has an NHS practice. Be aware that while some health insurance companies pay for assessments, most don't. Anecdotally, some parents have reported that if they ask for their children to have a mental health check rather than an autism assessment they can get the cost covered by the insurer.

What is a learning difficulty and learning disability?

A learning disability crudely refers to intellectual ability and generally means an IQ below a certain level (usually 70). 'People with a learning disability tend to take longer to learn and may need support to develop new skills, understand complicated information and interact with other people,' according to Mencap. 'The level of support someone needs depends on the individual. For example, someone with a mild learning disability may only need support with things like getting a job. However, someone with a severe or profound learning disability may need full-time care and support in every aspect of their life; they may also have physical disabilities.'

A learning difficulty is not related to intellectual ability but to learning – that is, how knowledge is gained and processed. Learning difficulties are common in autistic children and the label can be applied when there is a discrepancy between achievement and intellectual ability.

The diagnosis

You've waited a long time – years, most likely – and finally receive a diagnosis. A diagnosis report written by the paediatrician usually follows a few weeks later. It should be detailed, stating your concerns, giving a history of your child's development, the clinician's observations, a diagnostic conclusion and recommendations for what future support your child is likely to need. It should also include which methods were used to reach the diagnosis. Before my son's report was circulated more widely, his paediatrician sent it to us so we could check everything relevant was included and that it was all accurate.

The report may include medical jargon that you don't understand, in which case you can email the paediatrician to clarify. Raise any points you don't agree with or areas you feel are missing. Several pages about your child's difficulties can be a tough read, but these points need to be in there in order to access the right support. You can take this information then file it away as a one-sided view of your child's differences that is far from the whole picture.

It's important that you receive a report with a clearly stated diagnosis. Make sure any 'co-morbid' condition – one that's present at the same time – such as hypermobility, Ehlers-Danlos syndrome or Obsessive Compulsive Disorder (OCD) – are also stated. Phrases such as 'autistic tendencies' are unhelpful; the clinician needs to be specific, otherwise the local authority won't accept the diagnosis.

'What I tend to say to parents [who have received a diagnosis] is I'm not downplaying the difficulty or challenges, but life is challenging for everyone, whether you are autistic or not,' says Dr Catriona Stewart, co-facilitator of the Scottish Women's Autism Network. 'The diagnosis just gives you a heads-up of what those challenges might be.'

Different diagnoses you might receive

Asperger syndrome or autism?
Asperger syndrome (AS) or Asperger disorder is a diagnosis that can be given to autistic children who have communication and social difficulties but no learning or language delay. They often have average or above-average levels of intelligence.

The rate of people receiving an AS diagnosis has decreased since 2013, when it was subsumed into the broader autism spectrum disorder category in the DSM-5. The criteria were dropped because research had shown that most people diagnosed with Asperger syndrome also met the criteria for autism. It begs the question, though: what has happened to those Aspies who did not meet the criteria for autism?

While the UK's most commonly used diagnostic manual, the ICD-10, still includes AS as a possible diagnosis, that decision nevertheless had an impact here. Clinicians are now more likely to diagnose an AS child with autism spectrum disorder 'of the Asperger type'. This may change once more in 2018, when the WHO is expected to publish its updated ICD-11, which is intended to come more into line with the DSM-5. This means it is likely to drop Asperger syndrome too. As with the DSM-5, people formerly diagnosed with Asperger syndrome will be given the diagnosis of autism spectrum disorder.

Pathological demand avoidance (PDA)

PDA was first identified by the late developmental psychologist Professor Elizabeth Newson and applies to autistic children who persistently find even simple demands and requests intolerable. If pressed to comply, they may fly into a rage or have a meltdown. Some are adept at using distraction or provocative behaviour to divert attention away from a demand. Children with PDA often need to be in charge and can have difficulty judging how to respond in social situations.

Some other features are:

* Appearing sociable but without real understanding
* Sudden and excessive mood swings, together with impulsivity
* Comfortable in role play and pretend, sometimes to an extreme extent
* Initial language delay but a child may catch up quickly
* Obsessive behaviour, often focused on people

It is important to find out if your child has PDA, because, while it is found within the autism spectrum, autism-friendly strategies can either be ineffective or harmful for the PDA child. An approach based on negotiation, collaboration and flexibility will work better than setting clear boundaries and offering rewards, for example.

PDA currently isn't recognised by the DSM or ICD and there isn't a standardised test for it. Some clinicians aren't aware of the condition, others diagnose autism with a 'demand-avoidant' profile, or misdiagnose it as 'attachment difficulties'. The Elizabeth Newson Centre, in Nottingham, is the country's leading centre for diagnosing PDA.

More information on the diagnostic criteria for PDA:
www.autismeastmidlands.org.uk/wp-content/uploads/2016/10/
Defining-criteria-for-Pathelogical-Demand-Avoidance-Syndrome-with-a-
comparison-to-autism.pdf
More information on the Elizabeth Newson Centre, which diagnoses PDA:
www.autismeastmidlands.org.uk/family-child-services/
diagnosis-assessment
Good information can also be found from www.pdasociety.org.uk

Does my child have autism or ADHD – or both?

The DSM-5, published in 2013, for the first time allowed a dual diagnosis of autism and attention deficit hyperactivity disorder (ADHD).

A report written by Mike Connor and published in February 2013, entitled 'Differentiating Autism Spectrum Disorder and Attention Deficit Disorder', concluded that ADHD accompanies autism in an estimated 30 to 80 per cent of cases. Autism, meanwhile, accompanies an ADHD diagnosis less frequently, in 20 to 50 per cent of cases. Connor believes the presence of ADHD symptoms in autistic children might actually lead to more social interaction, as a result of increased talkativeness.

'As the child becomes older, similarities between the two conditions will separate out,' he says. 'Children with ADHD, on the other hand, are unlikely to become calmer with age unless they receive medication or high-quality therapeutic interventions. They still develop social and communication skills and are unlikely to have the anxiety levels of a child with autism.'

The main symptoms of ADHD are inattentiveness, hyperactivity and impulsiveness.

Symptoms of inattentiveness include:

* A short attention span and tendency to become easily distracted
* Difficulty organising and sticking with tasks
* An inability to follow instructions
* A lack of attention to detail, leading to mistakes in schoolwork
* Frequently losing or forgetting things

Symptoms of hyperactivity and impulsivity include:

* Excessive talking
* Interrupting others when they are talking
* Difficulty with turn-taking and standing in line
* Constant fidgeting and an inability to sit still
* Acting without thinking
* A reduced or absent sense of danger

As with autism, the diagnosis relies on the judgement of a paediatrician, clinical psychologist or psychiatrist.

Going forward

Hopefully this chapter will silence some of the people who, based on no experience whatsoever, say that autism is being overdiagnosed. That somehow local health authorities who are close to bankruptcy are choosing freely to hand out diagnoses that come with massive cost implications.

Paediatricians are still nervous about diagnosing early – I assume they are worried about making the wrong judgement call when children are little (fair enough), and I suspect they are under subtle or overt pressure from the local authority not to diagnose too many children. All this wouldn't be such a problem if families were receiving good-quality support during the process, but often they aren't.

FAQs

Why should we get a diagnosis?

Because, quite simply, it's the key that will unlock the support your child probably needs. Although, in the current climate, even with a diagnosis, it can be difficult enough getting help for them at nursery or school. It can also help a parent to understand their child better, and for the child to understand themselves.

Author Sarah Hendrickx received her own diagnosis in her early forties. When people ask what a difference it can make at her age, she responds: 'All the difference in the world.

'Confirmation means that we weren't wrong, stupid or rude. It means that all these decades of being frowned at because you said something "weird", being missed off invitations, wanting to talk about permaculture when everyone else wants to talk about *EastEnders* and hitting the deck with your hands over your ears at the sound of a passing police car are all explainable.

'And the explanation isn't – as you had suspected – that you are crap at life, it is because you process information differently. You see things that others don't; you miss things that others see. Intricate detail and social signals are given different priorities in the autistic brain.

'Diagnosis means you can find your tribe: people who nod with empathic recognition at your tales of faux pas.'

What does it feel like as a parent when your child receives a diagnosis?

You may be a parent who has felt all along that your child is autistic, only to be 'reassured' that they aren't. You might equally be someone who has spent the past few months or years rowing with your husband, wife or significant other, trying to convince them of what you know: that it's important to start the assessment process. Relationships can come under intense pressure in pre-assessment limbo, when the question being asked of the autism team becomes horribly bound up with one that is all-too-familiar to many couples: who's right?

For these reasons, and many others, confirmation of the diagnosis can actually bring relief. Other parents are unfazed by the diagnosis, of course, not least those who are autistic themselves. For others, particularly neurotypicals with no experience of autism, it can be tough. What all of us want is a happy child – which to us neurotypicals usually means a popular, sociable child – and this fantasy is being challenged early on. Society presses us to compare our children with some intangible norm, and as parents we are fearful when our son or daughter doesn't fit the mould.

It also signifies a massive shift in your life. You are thrown into the world of SEN – special educational needs – with an almighty splash. Before diagnosis I was a young(ish!) mother, any stress I experienced was largely of my own making. Then I found that I was having to learn a new vocabulary; how to navigate the NHS; how to sometimes challenge professionals working with us but also to maintain those relationships; to learn the horrendously complex legal system that is the gateway to gaining support for my child at school, and how to deal with the nursery and school in a constructive yet assertive way. On a practical level, there are a lot of things that need doing, all while you're trying to come to terms with everything.

'I can understand why parents would grieve,' the author Steve Silberman told me. 'It's part of being human, and when something happens that presents challenges it's understandable. Until we develop social structures so parents don't have to stay up all night worrying that, if they die, their children won't get adequate help, it's appropriate to grieve. But you can also grieve for a society that doesn't meet your child's needs. After a certain point, if you are still grieving for the child you thought you would have rather than accepting the child you have, it's a good idea to stop.

'One of the things my parents said made them sad when I came out [as gay] to them was the thought I wouldn't get married. Forty years later they were at my wedding.'

It is important to add that for the parents of a child who is having frequent meltdowns and has difficulty communicating, as well as health problems, like epilepsy, this version of acceptance may seem a privileged view that parents of children with lower support needs are able to hold.

When my son was diagnosed, I remember quite a long period afterwards of wanting to talk about it non-stop. I would weave it into the conversation on the flimsiest pretext. It was on my mind the whole time; I wanted company while I obsessively mulled it over.

How useful are 'low-functioning' and 'high-functioning' labels?

'Low- and high-functioning labels don't help because I don't believe anyone is *always* low-functioning or high-functioning,' says one female autistic academic. 'It sets functioning in very neurotypical terms: people who don't do a very good impression of being non-autistic are labelled low-functioning. On a practical level I'd be labelled as high-functioning, because I've done a PhD, but I can have extreme anxiety that might not be experienced by someone who is "low-functioning", and sometimes I can't function at all. I can't get out of bed, I spin, rock, don't understand basic questions or basic language.

'I think low-functioning is a dreadful label – it puts a ceiling of expectation on people. One of my cousins has a classical presentation of autism – when young he didn't do joint attention and he didn't respond to people; he went to a special school. But he has a degree and worked as a concert pianist. His writing is superb but his verbal speech is fast and monotone. I don't know if he will live independently. How do you easily classify him?'

What causes autism?

No one knows, but the race to find out is clearly on: new studies claiming to have made a breakthrough in pinpointing the origins of autism are published almost every week. With so much simultaneous and often contradictory speculation around, I can't help but feel anything other than weary indifference, and wish they would put their efforts into figuring out better ways to support autistic people instead.

Doctors will tell you that it's likely to be part-genetic, part-environmental. However, a study published in March 2015 suggests it's almost entirely genetic in origin, with between 74 and 98 per cent of cases down to biological make-up. The research, conducted by the Medical Research Council, looked at 516 identical and non-identical twins raised in the same household and found that rates of autism were higher in identical twins who shared the same DNA.

Meanwhile, the psychologist and psychiatrist Professor Simon Baron-Cohen, of Cambridge University, has posited the 'extreme male brain' theory, suggesting that exposure to high levels of testosterone in the womb can cause the brain to focus on systematic knowledge and patterns more than on empathy.

Is autism a disability/disorder?

Dr Luke Beardon, senior lecturer in autism at Sheffield Hallam University, describes his concept of a 'theory of disadvantage', preferring it to the deficit-based term 'disorder'. He writes for this book:

'I think using "disorder" in day-to-day narratives can impact very negatively on an individual, and/or parents, as well as have implications for wider society. Imagine what that must be like for the autistic child, to be referred to constantly as someone who is "disordered"? At the very least it's pretty unpleasant, but it could also impact in a very real sense on a person's self-esteem, confidence and wellbeing.

'From a parental view, too, being told your child is disordered – is this fair? Or even accurate? Of course, there are many individuals (very often with co-morbidities such as ADHD or an intellectual disability) who *would* regard themselves as disabled. But the fact that there are also very clear examples of autistic individuals who in no way consider themselves as disordered, who might be deemed highly successful individuals, means that ascribing the term "disorder" to the entire population is somewhat of a nonsense.'

Should I be worried about vaccines?

No. This debate has raged since the gastroenterologist Andrew Wakefield's compromised, discredited and yet widely publicised study, published in *The Lancet* in 1998, suggested a link between the MMR vaccine and autism. Major studies around the world involving huge sample numbers have found no link between childhood vaccines and autism.

A recent American study, meanwhile, has addressed a lingering concern of parents who already have one autistic child and are worried about immunising a younger sibling: what if vaccinations cause autism in those predisposed to developing the condition? Even in these cases it is not the vaccine that increases the risk, according to research published in the *Journal of the American Medical Association* in April 2015. The study, based on insurance-claim data on 95,727 children, followed them from birth to age five between 2001 and 2012, and data on their older siblings. It established that 2 per cent of children had an older sibling with autism, and this 2 per cent were just as likely to develop autism whether vaccinated or not.

Parents' experiences

Lucia Santi, head teacher of an autism school and mum of an autistic daughter:

'When we received the diagnosis, I dithered over how to tell my daughter. I wanted to explain the idea of a spectrum that would make sense to her. Everyone in our family wears glasses, so I put eyesight on the scale. One end was 20/20 vision, the other end was blind.

'So I went into her room with my visual representation of the scale and she just threw the duvet over her head and said everyone was stupid and she wanted to slap them all. Luckily I had asked the team who diagnosed my daughter to write to her and include child-friendly information about her diagnosis that would make sense to her. I knew she would take time and that she would process it when she was ready.

'One day I came home and her sister yelled out that they were just going through the notes.

'My daughter doesn't believe the diagnosis, she doesn't want it to be true. She doesn't want people to know – she's embarrassed and has that sense that she's different.

'I wanted to tell her because it's her, but I want to make sure it doesn't define her. She's still the same person, she just has problems with social communication, predictability. It's very subtle but manifests in real anxiety.

'She asked me if we should tell her friends and I said: "Look, if you had broken your leg and you couldn't walk, then your friends would put an arm around you and help you walk. If you're feeling broken, you have to let friends help you." She got that and we've told two friends.'

Arabella Carter-Johnson is a photographer and mum of Iris, now seven. Aged three Iris started painting. Now her artwork is bought by galleries and collectors all over the world, including Angelina Jolie.

> 'Iris was two years old when she was diagnosed. I felt angry that the doctor couldn't see all the qualities that I saw in her – his outlook was depressing and his predictions frightening. For me the diagnosis was empowering: I now had a path to follow. The next stage of figuring out how I could help her was challenging. The vast array of therapies to try and the confusion of information between professionals can be exhausting to deal with so I kept on coming back to the same conclusions: I needed to follow Iris, her interests, her passions. Observe her, understand her in a way I hadn't done before so I could reach her.'

* * *

4

WHAT IS IT LIKE TO BE AUTISTIC?

⁎　⁎　⁎

*'Nowhere am I so desperately needed as among
a shipload of illogical humans.'*
Star Trek's Mr Spock

The first autistic adult I met – or at least the first adult whom I knew to be autistic – was the television presenter Alan Gardner, star of the Channel 4 series *The Autistic Gardener*. I was asked by my editor at *The Times* to interview him, a prospect I was excited by but then, as I left my flat to meet him, I became aware of a different emotion. Nervousness? Fear?

I'm embarrassed to admit that I felt this way. I had spent time with a lot of autistic kids but never adults. It felt absurd and wrong – why was I feeling nervous about meeting an autistic adult when I have an autistic son? The fear left as soon as I met Alan. He was easy company and a dream interviewee: totally honest, he didn't dodge any questions. It was a very different experience to my previous encounters with media-trained celebrities – so much so that the Channel 4 PR looked occasionally horrified, coughing nervously a couple of times to try to move him back onto topic.

I loved hearing the juicy stories no other celebrity would have told me, but most of all I loved hearing about his autism. He described his sensory difficulties as feeling like he was 'drowning in my brainwaves'. In one short sentence he'd been able to help me understand what it must be like better than any book I'd read on the subject.

My experience with Alan emboldened me to seek out other autistic adults. I tweeted Laura James – author of *Odd Girl Out*, a book I loved reading, about her diagnosis as an adult and her childhood. We spoke on the phone and she was immediately supportive and generous with her contacts, giving me names of people I should speak to for my book and agreeing to write the piece for this chapter. She hasn't stopped helping me since.

Laura suggested I contact other autistic adults on Twitter, so I started following these people and we tweeted, or talked over the phone or in person. They gave up their time to talk to me, for no payment, because they want the world to understand autism better. I spoke with young men and women in their early twenties; with older men and women, some unable to work or keep on top of cooking, day-to-day organisation and housework; others in highly successful jobs, often working in computing and academia (many were self-employed – offices were too noisy and socially demanding). One articulate, bright woman told me she had a learning disability, which instantly made me re-evaluate what little I knew about the subject.

I was similarly blown away during a phone conversation when Dinah Murray, an intimidatingly clever person, told me she had failed her O-levels. How was it possible that the woman who helped develop the theory of monotropism could fail any exam? It makes you realise the extent to which autistic people were and still are being horribly failed at school.

Having these conversations changed my book, and my whole outlook. I started to understand why autistic people are so frustrated when non-autistic people speak for them in the media. It's not just that it's annoying, it's that the information we are being given about autism is wrong.

It's the details that get lost. For example, I would research a topic – say, eating – and speak to a (neurotypical) clinical psychologist, who would give me advice that I felt I already knew. Then I would speak to an autistic adult, who would explain that eating is difficult because of the sensory aspect; that a lump in their mashed potato could literally make them gag; that as soon as something unpredictable happened, they couldn't eat.

I also understood for the first time the true width of the autistic spectrum. I met warm, funny, highly self-aware, empathetic, married autistic people, the type we rarely hear about. It could be easy to conclude that their lives were easy, as on a surface level they have achieved all the goals expected by neurotypical society – they are working, have kids, are in meaningful relationships – but learning more about their challenges gave me a more accurate picture.

One woman, a very confident public speaker, described lying in bed for an hour every morning going over any possible outcome of the day in a bid to mitigate her anxiety. An academic who works in autism research told me that her anxiety can leave her in something close to a catatonic state.

Speaking to these adults made me more precisely aware of the challenges – particularly how debilitating anxiety is. Yet even though I could see the difficulties clearer than before, it also lessened my fear. Some of the conversations were so interesting and funny I would race home to tell my husband about them. Getting to know these people, who wouldn't want their child to be like them?

Laura James told me during one conversation that she believes the key to non-autistic parents understanding their child's autism is to speak to autistic adults. I now totally agree. If we all take to Twitter or Facebook to ask autistic adults for advice and learn about our differences in a respectful way, our kids will benefit.

I think if we are honest, fear is the thing that stops non-autistic parents like me from making that connection with the autism community. I don't think it's necessarily a fear of autism itself, though we have all absorbed some terrible ideas through popular culture over the years portraying autistic people as being weird or scary. For my part, before meeting Alan Gardner, I think I was worried I wouldn't know the right language to use, or how to be with him.

But most of all, I think I was scared about the possibility of meeting an autistic adult who wasn't happy, which would have sent me spiralling into panic over my son's future. Meeting Alan, who is married with three kids, and has an amazing job and whom I liked very much, had the exact opposite result.

This chapter is for autistic people to tell us what their life is like, what their childhood and school experiences are or were like. I asked a range of autistic people – one 11-year-old, two men and three women – and they either wrote about their experience, or were interviewed. One piece is written by someone who is non-verbal and painstakingly typed her piece using one finger. This is a way of starting off the dialogue between autistic people and neurotypical parents that you may wish to continue after reading this book.

Laura James is a journalist, author and mother of four children. She is the author of *Odd Girl Out*, a book published in 2017 about what it's like to be an autistic woman in a neurotypical world:

'I was diagnosed with autism when I was 45. By the time I found out, I had married twice, raised four children to adulthood and had forged a career as a writer. The diagnosis changed my life. It allowed me to see myself as successful for the first time. Up until then I had always felt as if I were failing, as if there was something that everyone else inherently knew and I was somehow missing the point.

'Had my autism been spotted earlier, I suspect my life would have been much easier. I would have been taught useful coping mechanisms and I would have received support in education, something I failed miserably at, leaving school at 15 and a half with no exams to my name.

'I don't think I would want to be neurotypical (NT), though. I would, quite literally, be a different person and the idea of it makes me feel dizzy. I think life as an NT would be too confusing and emotionally led for me. I like things to be neat and logical and struggle to cope when people operate from an emotional standpoint.

'If there were a pill I could swallow that would remove my autism, I might have taken it as a child. During later childhood and the early teen years it can be hard to be different from one's peers and the lack of control one has when growing up – with adults making all the decisions – can be hard for any child, but almost physically painful for one with autism.

'I hated primary school. It was noisy, the food was disgusting, the rules impenetrable and seemingly silly. I was never really seen as bad, I was written off early as hopeless. My teachers didn't try to understand why I struggled, choosing instead to believe I was failing deliberately. It shattered my self-esteem as I genuinely tried very hard.

'I think it would have helped had my parents known about autism. I came from the generation where children had to conform and I was often made to do things I felt uncomfortable with. Food was a massive problem for me as a child and it took me many years to develop a halfway healthy attitude to it.

'Sensory issues played a big part in my early life, too. My mother tells a story about my having two coats that were identical, except that one was blue and the other yellow. I would happily wear the yellow one, but screamed at the sight of the other. The blue one hurt, the seams down the arms were scratchy and less well finished and the pain felt unbearable to me. It was the same with some socks and anything that put pressure on my throat, such as a high-necked blouse. I can see why my mother thought I was being "difficult", but had I been able to explain how I felt I am sure she wouldn't have put me through that discomfort.

'By any standard, my adult life is a good one. I have a lot of control over my environment, working from home as a freelancer. I can wear what I want, eat when and what I want. I am lucky enough to be able to say no to most things I don't want to do. I have gorgeous, funny, quirky children and we all enjoy spending time together.

'I do get stressed about things many people would find easy, such as filling in forms or planning journeys, but am lucky that I have a supportive husband who is always happy to help. Autism as an adult is far from plain sailing and I do have awful days as well as good ones.

'Although my work is quite social and I do have some friends, I find socialising tiring. I can find other people's emotions overwhelming, whether they are happy or sad ones. Empathy is often raised in the context of autism and I, and many other autistic adults, feel that it is almost as if we experience it too much rather than too little. It is this feeling of drowning in sorrow for someone else that makes us unable to react in a way that is deemed appropriate and empathetic.

'There are things I love about my autism, such as my ability to hyperfocus, my intense special interests, which bring me much joy, and my ability to think quickly and differently. I am quite self-contained, love my own company and genuinely don't understand how it feels to be bored, envious, or myriad other negative emotions. My mindset is quite childlike and I definitely don't think like someone in their mid-forties. It means I have a great understanding and closeness with my children and also am able to keep on top of trends and technology, which in our fast-paced world feels important.

'Less lovely are my sensory issues. A crying baby can send my heart racing; lights that are too bright and smells that are too strong can instantly induce a migraine. I also dislike my fear of the unknown. Having to negotiate something new brings about the kind of fear most neurotypical people would only experience in a major event, such as a car accident. It makes any new experience stressful, strips the joy from it and, unless I am vigilant, it can make my world quite narrow.

'I have a lot of hope, though, for future generations of autistic people. I am hopeful that the more autistic voices we hear, the easier it will become for children with autism and their families to gain acceptance, understanding and a meaningful place in the world.'   .

Alex Marshall is a 12-year-old boy who lives with his parents and brother Sam, who is ten, in Halifax, West Yorkshire. He wrote the piece below when he was 11 and in primary school:

'School can perhaps be described as a mixed bag of good and bad. 90 per cent of school is just dull. I think most people can relate to this. This isn't a fault of the school so much as a fact of life.

'I'm not the biggest fan of schoolwork. I can sink my teeth into a good maths lesson, but there's just so many problems and faults in the curriculum. And don't get me started on the horrendous way English lessons have to be taught . . .

'Homework is just so stupid and I don't like playtime. All everyone does is play football, and I loathe sport. Why run about when you could be doing something useful? And then I get to experience the absolute joy of standing around awkwardly.

'I regulate my life with a set of rules. I can't have any doors open around me. Our curtains have to be adequately neat. I probably sound like a fussy housewife, but it's just how I live. I enjoy writing as a hobby. I don't like crowds or sudden noises. I'm OK with a slight change in routine, but many autistic people aren't. Loud noises don't bother me, nor do bright lights, but smells seriously do.

'I don't think I'll end up getting an "ordinary" job, or end up going to university. There's just so many better things to be doing – I have plans to start several companies before leaving primary school in five weeks' time, invent my own currency, become a YouTuber, or an author. Anything other than mundane, boring, regulated and repetitive work.

'When I grow up, I think I'll prefer my own company, relying on online communities for most of my socialisation needs. That's not to say I don't think I'll have any real-world relationships, more to convey where exactly I'll be spending a lot of my "hanging out" time. I love computers and social media already, so it's not too far of a leap.'

Ian Adam Bellamy, 29, was diagnosed with autism as a child. He works for the charity Ambitious about Autism:

'When I was young, I was averse to noise. I didn't enjoy interacting with other children and, when I did, I wasn't comfortable with or "good" at it. I also presented challenging behaviour: frequent explosions of temper, without any clear or consistent cause, which seemed to last an unusually long time and carried on well beyond my early years. I can now see that this was how my autism manifested itself, although this wasn't known at the time, and wouldn't be until I was ten years old.

'The frequency and severity of my behaviour at home – in contrast to the fact that I was a quiet and socially marginalised child at school – led my parents to seek a referral to a clinical child psychologist. This is where I was diagnosed with autism. The term meant absolutely nothing to me at the time. It was a label that seemed more relevant to my parents than to myself. I was engrossed with my interests: bike riding, buses, Grand Prix racing. It only took on more importance as I got older, gained a greater sense of self-awareness and moved into adulthood.

'In my pre-teen years I was academically able with limited social skills. This was a combination that didn't stand me in very good stead to attend a selective school at which the staff and pupils alike believed in their own self-importance. Spending time in that environment only made me feel stressed. Ultimately, this came to a head and I ended up out of school, self-teaching my first qualifications prior to entering further education at the local sixth-form college.

'I cannot overstate the importance of my parents believing in me at this stage of my life: having aspirations for me, maintaining these and support-ing me to meet my potential. It allowed me to grow and to lead the life I have today. That isn't to say this was easy for them or for me. We often had heated conversations and felt despondent on numerous occasions.

'Getting back into education was the key to social enrichment for me. I made some of my best friends at university. I've found that our relationships work because we have qualities that complement one another. We bring out our best sides and we've opened ourselves to new experiences (though a little patience certainly helped!). It's just taken me longer to get there than it has for others.

'While autism is more widely known about than it was when I was a child, it's not necessarily better understood. I think that the efforts we make to engage with young people who have autism, from offering our encourage-ment and support as family members or friends through to providing opportunities as working professionals, will determine how many have a positive experience of adult life.'

Isobel Pierce is a non-verbal 23-year-old autistic woman with dyspraxia. She lives in Barnet, in north London, with her mum. She typed her piece using Grid 3 software – a computer program that helps people communicate – on a touchscreen tablet, using one finger. Her mum, Clare Pierce, explains: 'She will only type around certain people she feels safe with and sometimes needs some physical support to type, usually a hand on her leg. She has good receptive language but is greatly affected by her autism':

'I have autism. I can remember when I was young, I was in a magical world. It's a safe place for me and I feel relaxed there. I find that the world is based on ideas I find different. Slipping into my world is relaxing for me. I am often confused by the way people are with each other. I have autism but I think I have a higher understanding of things such as nature and emotion because I experience them purely. I can see how people feel; however, I find it hard to help them as my experience is not the same. People rarely understand me.'

Below is a transcript of a Skype conversation between me and Jamie Knight, a 28-year-old programmer working for the BBC. He is a senior accessibility specialist; previously he worked as a senior developer on iPlayer Radio. He lives on his own with Lion – a four-foot soft toy that goes everywhere with him. NB: The spoon theory of energy mentioned below was first written about by Christine Miserandino in a piece explaining what it's like to have a long-term sickness.

JK: I rode a bus today by myself [happy bounce]:

JH: How did it go?

JK: It went OK, about two spoons which is pretty good.

JH: What does two spoons means?

JK: Spoons are a measure of energy; it's a way of basically budgeting it so you can focus the energy you have on what's most important to you. For example, if I sleep well, I start the day with ten spoons. Everything I do takes spoons, and if I run out of spoons, I get very spaced out or, if in a bad environment, [I] melt down. You can use spoons to build up routines and budgets. For example, I know my evening routine takes three spoons. So as long as my evening routine is stable and I leave myself three spoons for my evening, I will be fine. I am on four to five spoons now. I can probably do the trip back without a problem, but I might be spoon-limited tonight. It's kinda important to know how much energy things take rather than how much I wish it took. I am very able, but depending on spoons, I may not be capable.

JH: When were you diagnosed?

JK: I had a working DX [diagnosis] as a kid, got another diagnosis as a teenager, and got the complete set a couple of years ago against DSM-5 criteria.

JH: Did you get good support at school and at home?

JK: Not as such. I ended up in care. Back in the 90s the system was pretty different. I had a few diagnoses (ADHD, Autie [autism], etc.) but not a huge amount of suitable support. I eventually did my GCSEs in Oxfordshire with support from a unit. Even though I couldn't speak I still managed to make friends and got web design and development work. Then eventually I re-entered education and supported housing, etc.

JH: *Did your speech come and go as you grew up?*

JK: *The environment around me and structure changes, therefore my ability to communicate changes. I don't think my actual speech changes – just the ability to use it on demand. For example, I am sat in a cafe I don't know very well right now. I haven't any speech; I used pointing to order my food and gave a thumbs-up. I don't think I've had working speech in a cafe for about two or more years. But I can communicate fine with my AAC apps [communication apps that help an autistic person communicate via their iPhone or iPad/tablet. The apps help a person create sentences and visuals to express what they want to say]. My friend popped in for lunch and I had speech then. Generally speaking (ha, irony), I find that speech isn't as important as many people assume it is. Communication is important (as the ability to express decisions is fundamental to autonomy!) but speech is one of many ways to communicate. Sometimes people call it the 'gold standard' but I generally don't experience that. For example, if I can communicate what I want and it takes half a spoon to use speech (and I sound terrible, and it's slow and frustrating) but only 0.1 spoons to use my app, I may as well use the app and save the spoons for something which actually matters, like working. My speech is better when there's no pressure to use it.*

JH: *What things would have made life easier when you were younger?*

JK: *Respect for being who I was would have helped. I was taught that I was ill or in some way broken. I wasn't, I was just different. We medicalise autism and, by gosh, that messes up so many things. As a kid I probably spent more energy trying to pretend to be 'normal' than anything else. It didn't work. We tend to prioritise the wrong things with autistic people. Rather than helping people learn how their body works and adjusting the environment so it doesn't disable them we tend to try and change the person.*

JH: *Could you explain more about learning how the body works?*

JK: *I work like an electric car: I can do LOTS but I run out of energy quickly and need to recharge. By modelling my day in terms of spoons I can account for the energy I have. As a kid I wasn't taught anything about how energy works. I think it's something most NTs [neurotypicals] don't need to consider.*

JH: *Tell me about elephants and anxiety.*

JK: Ooo, yes! Anxiety feels like an elephant is stood on my chest. As a kid I was taught to 'cope' or 'mask' anxiety, e.g. how to pretend all was well when it wasn't. I was basically taught to always ignore my body and how I feel. Thus my body got stronger and stronger at telling me something was not fine! That just leads to burnout. A good coping mechanism is not the same as having a healthy solution! For elephants I had to stop fighting them and start listening to them. Recognise the emotions as valid and then change the environment around me to reduce them. Once I started approaching it that way, engineering my spoons and elephants to achieve what I want to achieve, I understood how to 'drive' my body. I need more structure than most people. Add the structure, and the elephants go away. Add routines (which allow pacing and easy spoon prediction) and everything works pretty damn well.

JH: How are you so happy/positive when you've had some very challenging experiences growing up?

JK: I am not my past, I am my present. My present is pretty darn good. I have a job I love and great friends, I have an environment which meets my needs and I basically get to help people for a job. Sometimes I am helping people to understand autism (or at least, how I approach it), other times I am helping people by making things more accessible. My job is extremely varied but it always comes back to helping people some way. I help people, people help me. It works pretty darn well.

Alis Rowe is founder of the Curly Hair Project (thegirlwiththecurly-hair.co.uk), a social enterprise supporting autistic people. Below is an email interview between her and my colleague Eve McGowan:

What sort of things did you struggle with at school?

I really struggled to 'fit in'. I did not have friends and I was bullied for being quiet. Even teachers used to comment that I was 'too quiet'. At the time I did not realise that the major feeling I had was intense anxiety. I absolutely dreaded group work and lessons that involved working with others, such as PE and drama. I felt completely overwhelmed by the sensory aspect of school.

What might have helped you cope better?

I wish my parents and my teachers had educated me more about anxiety and I wish that I had been home-schooled. Having somebody say 'It's OK to be quiet' would have helped a lot.

Did you adopt coping strategies of your own?

I used to avoid doing anything outside of school hours and would take myself away and go on my computer to escape from the stresses of life. The thing that kept me going was my home life and ability to be genuinely happy at home.

What was secondary school like?

I did not cope well with the transition and having to deal with a completely new environment, a very large building and a large number of unfamiliar people. It was very frightening. This increased my anxiety, which led to mutism and an inability to build friendships. I wonder if going to a smaller secondary school with a higher proportion of the same children who went to my primary school would have helped.

What prompted your diagnosis at 22?

I got tired of making 'excuses' to people about why I was the way I was, e.g. 'I can't come out tomorrow, I'm too tired/I've got a headache.' People always used to try to make me be someone I was not and it is a great relief to have an authentic reason for my behaviour which people seem to take more seriously. I have a lot of jobs now and my managers have been able to make 'reasonable adjustments' for me, which have made my life much less stressful.

Have things been easier since getting a diagnosis?

I am kinder on myself. I don't push myself to do things that I used to think I 'should' be doing. Nobody should have to do things that do not feel intrinsically right for them.

What did your parents do to make your home life so happy?

They never judged, did not push, encouraged me to be myself most of the time. They naturally provided a lot of structure, rules and routines, which worked for me. My mum and I used to communicate a lot in writing, pictures and visuals. Plans were important to us and my mum always let us know what we were going to be doing on any given day. When we went on holiday, we would usually go to the same place every single year. If we went anywhere new, we'd look at lots of pictures and find information about it. My parents have always openly been very proud of me and have helped and encouraged me a lot throughout my education.

*   *   *

5

SENSORY DIFFERENCES

* * *

'My hearing is like having a hearing aid with the volume control stuck on super loud.'
Temple Grandin

A child with sensory difficulties may experience sound and light, among other senses, differently compared with a non-autistic child. The more I learn about autism, I realise this has to be the first sensible area for parents to explore. It's insane expecting an autistic child to learn anything in a noisy, busy environment such as school without looking into this first. It would be like non-autistic people being asked to learn another language while riding a rollercoaster.

My son is sensory-seeking so he looks for movement to feel more secure. Sound affects him, but not consistently – a large village hall or a small flat with low ceilings and lots of people can leave him trying to escape by squeezing himself under the sofa.

I don't think he's always aware when he's hungry, thirsty, tired, hot or cold. When he was young he didn't register pain consistently. Once my husband was making him squeal with laughter pulling him across the floor of our lounge; it was only later we realised, to my husband's horror, that he had a huge carpet burn on his back.

He is often trying to top up his proprioceptive input – he loves to be squashed/squeezed. He wakes at night and seems jittery. He comes into our bed and pushes his legs against mine for more input. He talks about the 'fizzies' and sometimes I think I know what that sensation must be like – my body feels uneasy, almost like it's fizzing, and I have to move to get comfortable, which works for a second or two, then the feeling returns.

Something interesting has happened as I have been learning about sensory differences: I've become far more aware of noise. Before I might not have registered when an environment was particularly loud, but now I find those situations hard to cope with. Hectic crowds exhaust me in a way they didn't before.

What puzzles me most is how inconsistent my son's response to sound can be: sometimes he's very bothered; other times he can walk past a brass band and be fine. Speaking to Professor Liz Pellicano, the former professor of autism education and director of the Centre for Research in Autism and Education, who now lives in Australia, I found out that the difficulty with sound is as much to do with predictability as with the sound itself.

Sensory processing is highly complex – one reason why we are really only scratching the surface in terms of our knowledge. The other reason is we haven't tried hard enough to find out more. It's been over 70 years since Leo Kanner first described it and, yet, it's remained off the radar. Our neurotypical obsession with social skills has blinded us to what is causing autistic people the most difficulty.

Sensory Processing Disorder FAQs

What is sensory processing disorder?

The term sensory integrative disorder – now known as sensory processing disorder (SPD) – was coined in the 1960s by the American occupational therapist Dr Anna Jean Ayres, who observed children struggling with a hidden disability linked to the way their brains received and responded to information delivered by their senses.

'Sensory integration is the organisation of sensation,' she explained. 'Our senses give us information about the physical conditions of our body and the environment around us. Sensations flow into the brain like streams flowing into a lake. Countless bits of sensory information enter our brain at every moment, not only from our eyes and ears but also from every place in our bodies. We have a special sense that detects the pull of gravity and the movements of our body in relation to the earth.

'The brain must organise all of these sensations if a person is to move and learn and behave normally. The brain locates, sorts and orders sensations – somewhat like a traffic policeman directs moving cars. When sensations flow in a well-organised or integrated manner, the brain can use those sensations to form perceptions, behaviours and learning. When the flow of sensations is disorganised, life can be like a rush-hour traffic jam.'

SPD may affect one sense, like hearing, touch or taste, or many at the same time. It can mean being too sensitive to some stimuli (hypersensitive) and not sensitive enough to others (hyposensitive).

As many as 90 per cent of autistic people are said to have SPD and 5 per cent of the general population. Features of SPD may include:

* Finding sounds painful and/or overwhelming.
* An inability to filter out background noise. While a non-autistic person's brain (usually) relegates noises it doesn't need to the background, for many autistic people this doesn't happen and a supermarket trip can result in a cacophony of sounds. My son was distracted in nursery by police or ambulance sirens that were miles away.
* Clothes feeling harsh or uncomfortable against the skin. Soft tracksuit trousers will be far easier to wear compared with jeans.
* A lack of coordination; floppiness.
* A tendency to touch things a lot – or, conversely, a dislike of being touched.
* Poor proprioception. They may not know where their body is in space and, if they close their eyes, they may be unaware where their limbs start and end. They may seek out things that reassure the body where it is: hugs, to be squeezed or squashed, and crash into things.
* Difficulty coping with visual information, which can appear fragmented and consequently hard to make sense of.
* Finding smells overwhelming.
* For some children, praise and emotional warmth can launch a wave of pain known as emotional overload.

SPD is also a spectrum, meaning people experience different triggers and it affects their lives in different ways. At its worst it can leave kids and adults locked in a daily struggle as they try to cope with a hostile sensory world in which they are barely able to function. Frequently SPD reduces the ability to engage with others. People may also struggle to process more than one thing at a time. Talking to someone *and* looking at them? It can just be too much.

Awareness of SPD

In 2013, the American Psychiatric Association updated its handbook for clinicians, adding one sentence on sensory processing. The DSM-5 says:

Hyper or hyporeactivity to sensory input or unusual interest in sensory aspects of the environment (e.g. apparent indifference to pain/temperature, adverse response to specific sounds or textures, excessive smelling or touching of objects, visual fascination with lights or movement).

This was a big moment. It was the first time any diagnostic manual had referred to SPD, and it is only recently that we started thinking about the sensory difficulties that underpin behavioural 'challenges', i.e. signs of distress.

As the author Steve Silberman told me, even scientists didn't know about sensory sensitivity until Temple Grandin started talking about it. 'Sensory processing is not very well known and not very well studied. It has gone totally ignored while millions and millions of dollars have been spent searching for causes [of autism].'

Not all sensory input is unpleasant

'What I find particularly interesting about sensory issues is not all of them are debilitating,' says Liz Pellicano. 'Sensory-seeking behaviours such as watching a fan, a washing machine or light flickering through trees can be really pleasurable for people. People with other developmental conditions may also be hypersensitive to sound and things they see, but hyposensitivity – or sensory-seeking behaviour – might well be unique to autism.'

How many senses do we have?

At the moment it is thought we have eight. They are:

1. Visual

2. Auditory

3. Olfactory (smell)

4. Gustatory (taste)

5. Tactile (touch)

6. Vestibular (sense of head movement in space)

7. Proprioceptive (sensations from muscles and joints of the body)

8. Interoceptive (sensations related to internal organs)

What is it like to have SPD?

It's easiest to watch simulations rather than try to understand by reading. YouTuber WeirdGirlCyndi, who describes herself as 'an autistic adult who is sick of so-called "experts" trying to explain what they think an autistic person is going through', has made a short film (www.youtube.com/watch?v=BPD-TEuotHeo). As she explains, her brain cannot process information as quickly as other people's – she compares it to a dial-up modem versus a cable modem: too much information and it crashes. To illustrate how SPD affects her she takes a clip from the 1986 animated film *The Transformers: The Movie* (clearly a favourite of hers) and mixes it with an unrelated sound clip. It's loud, confusing, overwhelming – and very illuminating.

The National Autistic Society launched its 'Too Much Information' campaign with a short film offering an insight into the world of 12-year-old Alex Marshall, showing from his perspective what it's like to visit a shopping centre. (Alex has written a piece for the 'What is it like to be autistic?' chapter.) It's a hard but essential watch. You can see it here – www.autism.org.uk/get-involved/tmi/about.aspx – or try the 360-degree experience here – www.autism.org.uk/get-involved/tmi/about/vr.aspx

I found the interviews on the Caldwell Autism Foundation website between its founder Phoebe Caldwell and Janet Gurney, training director of Us in a Bus, a Surrey charity that helps children with learning disabilities, really helpful (www.thecaldwellautismfoundation.org.uk/index.php/responsive-communication-the-films). Caldwell has been working with autistic children for more than 40 years. She's compassionate and dedicated to the children she works with, and mildly grumpy with people who don't share her tremendous knowledge.

SPD and anxiety

'There is a significant correlation between sensory issues and anxiety but we don't know what the causal direction is – which triggers which,' says Liz Pellicano. 'My prediction would be that difficulties dealing with uncertainty – which I believe underpins sensory differences in autism – could make people more anxious. But it is possible that the causal direction goes the other way, such that the more anxious you are, the more hypervigilant you are within your environment, which could make you more likely to notice and respond to aversive sensory stimuli.'

The more anxious or tired a person with SPD feels, the worse their sensory processing difficulties. They may be able to tolerate a certain level of noise when calm, but not if they are feeling stressed.

Nick Walker, an autistic aikido teacher explains the relationship between sensory difficulties and social difficulties on his blog neurocosmopolitanism.com:

'An autistic child's sensory experience of the world is more intense and chaotic than that of a non-autistic child . . . [and] thus occupies more of the autistic child's attention and energy. This means the autistic child has less attention and energy available to focus on the subtleties of social interaction. Difficulty meeting the social expectations of non-autistics often results in social rejection, which further compounds social difficulties and impedes social development. For this reason, autism has been frequently misconstrued as being essentially a set of "social and communication deficits" by those who are unaware that the social challenges faced by autistic individuals are just by-products of the intense and chaotic nature of autistic sensory and cognitive experience.'

How is SPD treated?

An occupational therapist (OT) will carry out an assessment, pinpoint where the difficulties lie and suggest strategies to help. They will also work on basic age-appropriate skills, such as getting dressed and pencil grip (handwriting is often an issue) – as well as looking at gross- and fine- motor skills and core strength.

A good OT will ideally be experienced in autism (this is not a given). They are likely to compile a 'sensory diet' – physical activities that can be added to your child's daily routine to give them the sensory feedback they need to feel more regulated and focused. These can include lifting something heavy, being squashed between cushions, throwing beanbags into hoops, crunching on ice cubes or rolling on a gym ball. The activities may well need to be repeated, sometimes several times a day. We were first given a sensory diet when my son was two and a half. We taped it to a kitchen cupboard door so he could point out which activity he wanted to do. In truth, I didn't really take the SPD side of things nearly seriously enough, as I didn't know how important it was.

Why hasn't it been better researched?

Liz Pellicano explains that when she was an undergraduate student, theory of mind was the big thing in autism research, and the vast majority of the focus was on autism being a 'disorder of social information processing'. Over the years, her focus has changed. Although the social aspects can be significant for people, she now feels that the 'sensory aspects, special interests and repetitive behaviours are more central to people's lives than the social difficulties'.

She remembers attending an event at which Temple Grandin was given an award and delivered her thanks by video message. In it, Grandin said that all the research was on recognising facial expressions and learning about emotions. 'But,' she said, 'I don't care about that.' What was more important to her was that she could hear everything, and much more intensely. That had much more of an impact on her life than her social difficulties.

'Topics of research into autism go in fads,' Pellicano adds. 'The theory of mind-related research has been the thing for so long that research into sensory processing has not got much of a look-in. And yet all the children I've seen have some sensory differences at some point in their lives.'

One of the difficulties in addressing sensory differences is that they are hard to pinpoint, and children don't exhibit them all the time.

'If you go to observe a child in class, you might not see any sensory behaviours – because there are no adverse stimuli to trigger any such behaviours or because the people supporting the child have put necessary accommodations in place. But they are extremely important to understand – in classrooms but also for families. Parents often talk about not being able to go out, for example, to the supermarket or shopping centres, as there's just too much going on for their autistic child, so the families then don't go out at all.'

What is happening in the brain?

Part of the problem is that of connectivity: areas of the brain that are over- or under-connected, so that messages get delivered to the wrong place, are not delivered at all, or too many messages are being delivered at the same time.

Liz Pellicano believes it isn't that autistic children's sensory receptors – nerve endings that gather information for the brain – aren't working properly. Instead, she thinks SPD has more to do with the brain's inability to check that information against what has gone before.

The neurotypical brain makes sense of the world using an internal working model built of experiences. You know what birdsong is, for example, because you've heard it so often; the brain doesn't need to digest it in its entirety every time you hear it.

She believes autistic people have a fundamentally different way of experiencing the world, however, and that this learning process – the way knowledge is acquired, ordered and filed away – is different for them. They aren't necessarily using past experience in the same way.

'Your brain usually relies on past experience to make sense of sensory information. For instance, my two-year-old gets scared of the vacuum cleaner – she is oversensitive to it – but developmentally that will dissipate. We don't tend to see that with autistic people. They rely more on the incoming sensory information in the moment, which can get all too much for them, causing "sensory overload".'

Stimming

Stimming – also known as self-stimulating behaviour – is something almost everyone does. My stims are nail-biting and speaking to myself to calm myself down when I'm anxious.

Autistic people stim more than neurotypical people in order to increase the level of sensory feedback they are getting, topping it up to a comfortable level. It is a way of regulating yourself if you are too full of emotion or pent-up energy, in the same way as bleeding a radiator. Stimming can allow an autistic child or adult to better focus on the task or conversation at hand.

Two of the most common types include hand-flapping and echolalia. From the Greek words *ekho* (echo or repeat) and *lalia* (speech or talk), this means repeating a phrase over and over again, not in order to impart information but simply because it's enjoyable saying the words. My son enjoys this a lot. Other children may rock, wiggle their fingers, spin objects. Young children often turn around in a circle, transforming the world into a gyre of blurred lights and shapes. Sometimes they flick their eyes up, down or to the side in order to increase the sensory impact.

STIMMING ISN'T BAD Stimming can be vital for self-regulation – it can give a child a sense of control and a way to feel safe, so it shouldn't be stopped. If a child can't stim, they may have a meltdown or turn to hitting themselves or another person. Many autistic people will separate their stimming into two categories: public and private, luxuriating in their favourite but less socially acceptable stims only at home.

'I do enjoy a good [hand-] flap,' says Robyn Steward, an autistic woman. 'When I went to Russia I met a lady on the spectrum and we flapped at each other and it was really fun. We did it spontaneously – it was nice to connect with someone on that level without words.'

For children who have little communication, stimming is part of their language and you may look at their stims as a language to work out how to connect with them. What is that person 'saying' to themselves?

Stimming can be difficult for parents. It's not so much that my son's stims drive me mad, rather that he becomes non-responsive when he's stimming and suddenly even the easiest tasks are hard work. His main stim is singing, and I start off coping as I know there's a need for him to do it. Then after half a day of feeling ignored and finding it difficult to get him to do anything, I get frustrated. These periods used to last for a week or longer, now it's not so long. When he re-engages with the world, I resolve next time to be more relaxed and not take it so personally, but every time I lose perspective.

If the stimming stops your child from functioning – perhaps it stops them interacting with others or getting dressed – then it's reasonable to address it. It's about finding out what the meaning or function of their stim is and trying to replace it with something that does the same job but less obviously or harmfully.

Meltdowns

Autistic children rarely talk about their sensory difficulties. They may lack the communication skills and how would they know that not everyone experiences the world as they do? They must wonder how on earth other people cope so well – and why can't they?

Meltdowns occur because our children don't have a way to ease these difficulties or an outlet to express their frustration and distress. They can scream, lash out, hurt themselves or others – basically lose control. These experiences can be painful and intensely frightening: the late Donna Williams, an autistic writer, described a meltdown as a 'near-death experience'.

Phoebe Caldwell believes that meltdowns are *always* the outcome of sensory overload and distress.

'It's we who are triggering the behaviour – by our activities, what we are wearing, our emotional pressure, the sounds and our demands for socially acceptable behaviour,' she says.

'Children with SPD are often described as "challenging",' adds Corinna Laurie, a specialist OT who works with the National Autistic Society. 'Rather than challenging, we should remember that they are anxious, overwhelmed and exhausted. This can manifest itself in many ways. While some children may have meltdowns, others may withdraw and some will become unwell.'

What to do when your child has a meltdown

KEEP YOUR CHILD SAFE 'If my daughter is having a meltdown in public, I know, first, that she doesn't have the skills to handle the situation she is in, and second, that losing control in front of other people is her worst nightmare,' says Ruth Moyse, an autistic academic. 'My response is therefore to do whatever I can to protect her dignity and keep her safe.'

DON'T TALK TOO MUCH There's no point telling a child who is having a meltdown to calm down. If you see the signs they are going to blow, putting in speech overwhelms the child even more.

AVOID CERTAIN SITUATIONS If your child is too young or can't explain the trigger, be aware of what happened just before the meltdown. Were there too many social demands? Too much visual information? Not putting a child in these situations is the main thing.

RECOGNISE THE WARNING SIGNS 'It may be a look in the eye, a movement, a phrase that signals the child is about to lose it emotionally,' says Professor Tony Attwood, a psychologist who specialises in working with children with Asperger syndrome. 'It's important parents share those signals with those who care for their child. If you are able to spot the signs before the meltdown occurs, you might be able to use a distraction or take the kid away from the situation. Or it can be reassurance, such as, "Mummy's here to help, you're going to be OK." The despair can be externalised and manifest itself with kicking, punching, breaking and destroying things.'

STAY CALM 'Your agitation will only add fuel to the fire. Be like a GPS in a car, which in a calm voice tells you what to do next, rather than criticising you for what you did wrong,' advises Attwood. 'At this stage you want them to move out of it, not look back.'

STAY THERE 'Tell them it will go and as soon as it's over you'll do something fun together,' he adds. 'Affirm the emotion: "You're feeling really upset, I get it." Afterwards, make sure you do what you promised you'd do, whether it's letting them watch a TV programme, going for a walk or having peanut butter on toast.'

Meltdowns are extremely tough for the child, but they are also hard on parents and siblings. It can wear you out, leaving you exhausted and emotionally drained, fragile and stressed. If your child is having frequent meltdowns, it is important to take time away for yourself if you can. It may feel counterintuitive but you need to keep your strength up too, for their sake as well as yours.

Exit strategies

When things are getting too much for a child they will tend to engage in certain 'exit strategies', according to Caldwell, as the body's self-defence mechanism kicks in, trying to head off a painful meltdown. These are some of the signs that may indicate your child needs help:

Avoidance: eyes are shut, a hand is over the face, or the child runs away.

Shutdown: brain stops. The child may not be able to move. They are frozen and stop whatever they are doing.

Aggression: the child thinks: 'You are the source of my processing difficulties. I'm going to hit you or myself.'

Try to find a practical solution that will lower their stress levels and give them more head space to process other things. Pay attention to the messages they are sending, both verbal and through their body language. If a child is shouting 'Shut up!' then shut up! Take them out of that noisy environment and sit them somewhere quiet. My son used to have a pop-up tent in his room to retreat to, with his teddies, earphones and books in there.

N, who has a five-year-old non-verbal son and lives in Australia:

'Sometimes he blocks his ears at the slightest noise, yet walks past a noisy worksite. He stares up at the wind blowing in the trees, fascinated by this. He eats such unusual things: orange peel instead of the orange, banana skin instead of the banana. He likes things to be crunchy and tough, never mushy – he is very narrow in what he will eat and this makes meal times challenging.

'My little boy is like no one I have ever known. Although I am the person who knows him best in the whole world, I still marvel every day at how different he is to me and how much I still struggle to make sense of the things he does. He feels like he is made so differently at his core, like he breathes, sees and touches the world in such a different way. It really feels as if he's come from another world, and no matter how much I try I still can't quite seem to understand his language or his customs – but of course I know in my heart that I will never stop trying.'

Common sensory issues explained in more detail

Visual difficulties

If your child is having problems with bright lights, balance, hates loud patterns and can't tolerate your favourite acid-yellow top, then it may be a good idea to get them tested for Irlen syndrome, also known as Scotopic Sensitivity Syndrome. It is a problem with the brain's ability to process visual information and so won't be picked up by an optician.

For an assessment, visit the Irlen East website (www.irleneast.com), which also features a checklist that allows you to judge whether your child may be affected.

Irlen syndrome can be helped by coloured lenses that slow down the speed of information that the eye is receiving, allowing everything to make sense visually. Some people report also being more able to listen – it is not that their hearing has improved, but that the sense of sight is taking less energy so they can concentrate better on what they are hearing.

Caldwell reports observing a young autistic man in a residential home who was desperately trying to take off his carer's T-shirt. Staff were on the verge of sending for the police – until she suggested the carer replace his striped garment with a plain-coloured top. The stripes had been creating a painful visual disturbance for the young man. In a similar way, some children may find heavily decorated or visually distracting walls in schools difficult to process.

Some autistic children's moods can be strongly affected by lighting. Harsh or flickering lighting can be distracting or painful. Dimming the lights and using colours can help a child control the visual stimuli better.

Caldwell also uses optimum colour-changing light bulbs, which, she says, are very useful to find out which colour a child is having difficulty with, or a colour that is calming. She worked with a child who was tearing round the house, then became completely calm when she turned the light to blue.

Some children like and dislike particular colours, so, for example, will want to wear a cap of a particular colour, or hit someone wearing another colour. Others won't eat because a plate is in a colour that causes them processing stress.

Auditory difficulties

'It's not just loud noises that are difficult, but certain frequencies, overlapping speech and unpredictable sounds,' explains Caldwell. 'It can feel like a pain in their head – a real pain, not discomfort. Even rain against windows can be too much.'

For children struggling to cope with noise, noise-cancelling earphones can be transformative. She recommends the Bose QuietComfort 15 or 25, which cut out 80 per cent of background noise. At just under £300 they are expensive but more effective than standard ear defenders, which block out all noise and can leave children feeling isolated. Some children who use headphones in school take them off when they don't need them; just having them on the desk can be a form of stress reduction.

Through her research, Liz Pellicano has found that it's often not just any noise that causes distress, but those external to the child – i.e. noises they have no control over. This is because autistic people have poor prediction skills. 'If they ring the school bell, that's fine. If the bell is rung by someone else and they don't anticipate it, however, that is when it can be distressing.'

Touch and proprioception

Many autistic people are oversensitive to touch and undersensitive to the 'pressure messages' that help them locate their bodies in space, meaning they have poor proprioception. When non-autistic people sit down, a pressure message is sent from our backside to our brain, which whips out the proprioceptive map and is able quickly to tell us, 'You are sitting down.' For autistic people, the messages often don't come through. As a result they seek other ways to establish where they are. If your child is constantly rocking, running, climbing, jumping, fidgeting, scratching their hands or standing on tiptoes, then they are trying to give themselves pressure messages and you'll know they are low on proprioception.

To improve their proprioception, get them to jump on a trampoline – we bought a small green trampoline off Amazon for my son's room; roll them up in a duvet or yoga mat. They could also try a pressure vest – a lightweight body-warmer-type thing filled with air pockets that the wearer can inflate by squeezing a rubber bulb, like taking a blood pressure reading. These cost £200 from www.squeasewear.com, though the company will let you rent one for a fortnight for £50 to try it out first.

Research shows that if you want to make a difference you have to top up on proprioception three or four times a day. 'Put them on the trampoline for ten minutes at the beginning of the day and at points throughout, in school and at home. It's the jerk that gives them the feedback,' says Phoebe Caldwell. 'If you get a movement break, you get the sensory experience of the jerk long after it has happened. The brain continues to send messages. Then it fades. It's like topping up an Oyster card. You can front-load a child with enough proprioceptive information to get them through the next bit of the day, but then you need to do it again.'

Some children have difficulties with boundaries as they have no idea where their body ends and another begins, so they feel invaded by people coming close. Putting up an artificial boundary can help – like a sheet of plastic between the child and person they are talking to.

'A friend of mine who has autism tells me she very often doesn't know where she is and other people are,' writes Caldwell in her book *The Anger Box*. 'She feels like she merges into other people.'

Interoception

This is the least-known sense. Interoception refers to our awareness of what's going on in our bodies; it is the sense that regulates our feelings of hunger, thirst, sickness, pain, having to go to the toilet, tiredness and itchiness, among others.

Hypersensitive children may be distracted by their internal stimuli, say their heartbeat; hyposensitive children aren't getting enough information and may not realise they are tired, cold, hot or need to go to the toilet, meaning they wet themselves or get constipated, or may not feel full after eating or know how to interpret pain signals. Claire Heffron, a paediatric occupational therapist in the US, writes about the sense and its role in emotional wellbeing for a blog post for her website www.theinspiredtreehouse.com.

'So when we see kids who seem to fly off the handle without warning, who can't get the hang of potty training, or who never seem hungry or thirsty . . . it's possible that they are struggling with interoceptive processing,' adds Heffron.

For more information, read Jeanette Purkis's blog at www.jeanettepurkis. wordpress.com. Also, Dr Emma Goodwell has written about experiences that can help in this very useful document: www.web.seru.sa.edu.au/pdfs/Introception.pdf

The sensory hangover

If you go somewhere busy, noisy, bright and chaotic, and the next day your child is all over the place then they could be suffering from a sensory hangover. These can happen after something fun as well as something that was over-whelming – a post-Legoland comedown, if you like. It may be wise to factor in a few days of relaxing in a calm place after a day of sensory demands, perhaps including a few walks in the park – something that involves minimal sensory arousal – while the child regroups.

✳   ✳   ✳

6

INTERVENTIONS

* * *

'What would happen if the autism gene was eliminated from the gene pool? You would have a bunch of people standing around in a cave, chatting and socialising and not getting anything done.'
Dr Temple Grandin

The word 'intervention' sounds very technical but for the purposes of this book I'm going to use the definition given by the charity Research Autism: an intervention is anything you do for an autistic person that is designed to help. Listening can be an intervention; so can a weekly 30-hour intensive behavioural programme.

What defines a successful intervention is a more complex question. It depends on the child and how you measure success. It also raises ethical questions, particularly if a child is young and not able to tell you what they want help with. What would they consider a helpful intervention if they were able to tell you?

Virginia Bovell is one of the founder parents of the charity Ambitious about Autism and a member of a group that established the Centre for Research in Autism and Education. She has also been a member of various government working parties in relation to autism. If anyone can explain what a successful intervention looks like, it's her.

'Success might be in promoting two-way communication, mutual understanding or mutual adaptation,' she tells me. 'It could be in allowing coexistence, which means reasonable adjustments are made – for if autistic people have to change their behaviour, it means neurotypical people should change theirs too. While neurotypicality is the majority, it doesn't mean that neurotypicals should have the dominant perspective on everything. Therefore success in therapy doesn't mean getting someone to behave as if they weren't autistic.'

That makes perfect sense to me: intervention should be a two-way process. You will have to make changes too, adapting your parenting style to accommodate your child, rather than insisting they do all the hard work. Meeting in the middle means both of you have less far to travel.

The next question is: how do you know the right way to intervene? This is particularly hard for non-autistic parents. A certain type of behaviour might be linked to anxiety, for example. Some interventions might focus on minimising that behaviour, when really what is needed is a reduction of what makes that child anxious.

Knowing when to intervene and when to just let your autistic child be is an extreme version of a problem all parents grapple with, according to Bovell. 'How far do you push your child, whether in getting them to do their homework, learn a musical instrument or tidy their room? Some parents operate tough love, being cruel to be kind. Others don't rush or push their children. There's a similar variety of views – but magnified – across the autism spectrum.'

What further complicates things is that views change. At first you may consider autism to be a terrible, frightening life sentence, only later coming to see autism as a difference, but not one that makes your child any less of a person. As a result, what you consider in your child's best interests will change.

I've seen completely well-intentioned parents roar into action when their child gets a diagnosis, subjecting them to very intense programmes of intervention that make me feel uncomfortable. There are also parents who don't intervene at all, even as their child struggles.

These are extremes, of course. There is a middle way, which is to be more relaxed and, as long as you have a happy child who is more than coping at nursery and school, perhaps focus on interventions within the family.

Interventions can be wonderful. Others – in particular the ones that attempt to train an autistic child to be non-autistic – can be harmful. Some can also be a bit crap and ineffective. And if the ineffective intervention has cost you, it may mean you don't have money to spend on one that might have been helpful.

My own experience suggests that, rather than opting for a type of intervention, you should work with someone you trust. My son currently goes to a social communications group with other autistic kids run by Dr Debora Elijah, someone who knows him better and can talk about him more precisely than any other professional I've encountered. The emphasis isn't just on the social: she works on executive function and promoting his abilities. She cares for him and I like that her centre provides him with a community of autistic people who accept him. I'm not sure the perfect intervention exists, but this is the closest I can find.

What is the best intervention?

According to Bernard Fleming, the information manager at Research Autism, the single most important intervention is to listen to the person in front of you and hear what they are saying – that includes those who are non-verbal. Find out about them, because then you will have a better idea of how to give support. 'Non-autistic people always assume they have to do all the fixing, which can exclude autistic children from the discussion,' he says.

What is early intervention?

It usually means one begun before the child reaches the age of five. The idea is that it is important to start early when the brain is more elastic and rapidly developing synaptic connections – the links that allow messenger molecules called neurotransmitters to pass between neural cells, or neurons. Forming these connections can help a child more easily process social information, among other things. Some have claimed that children who receive early intervention also show improvements in IQ (though IQ only measures a certain type of intelligence).

One particular form of early intervention that has been shown to have a long-term impact is improved communication between parents and children. That was borne out by research carried out as part of the Preschool Autism Communication Trial (more information on this below), which saw parents receive training to better help their kids. Six years after the trial, the research team continued to record improvements in the children's communication, behaviour and ability to self-regulate.

While this is one reason it can be a good idea to crack on with an intervention as soon as possible – even before a diagnosis, if you feel one is on the cards – effective help can be given at any age. Parents of older children who have only just received a diagnosis shouldn't despair. While 'early intervention' can be two of the most panic-inducing words in the English language to autism parents, decisions made while parents are feeling fear or panic can lead to them spending a lot of money pursuing questionable therapies they might not have chosen if they had taken more time to reach a decision.

'The history of autism suggests a growth curve that is very different to that of neurotypical children,' says Steve Silberman. 'Temple Grandin, for example, couldn't speak when she was two and a half and she was very disruptive and self-injurious at that point. I have had parents coming up to me asking why their young children aren't like Temple Grandin and I reply, "Temple Grandin wasn't Temple Grandin when she was your child's age." Autistic adults, including Temple Grandin, have told me that they had experienced a huge acquisition of social skills when in middle age.'

How to choose the right intervention for your child

Steve Silberman summed it up very neatly. 'The history of autism is a history of interventions that have been complete bollocks,' he told me during a phone interview. While he definitely has a point – a lot of them have been bollocks – there are some effective and helpful interventions. Research Autism has independently evaluated more than 1,000 interventions and published the results on its website, which should help you to sort the cowboys from the professionals. It gives the evidence for the effectiveness of each intervention, highlighting the ones that are harmful.

'We would say a good intervention is essentially about improving the quality of life for child and parents,' says Bernard Fleming, who has co-written a book, *Choosing Autism Interventions: A Research-Based Guide*, with Elisabeth Hurley, the research director at Autism West Midlands, and the Goth, also known as James Mason, an autistic man who edits the National Autistic Society's *Asperger United* magazine. The book lists 70 interventions.

'One of the biggest difficulties for parents is knowing what is out there. The interventions we look at are very much not about trying to cure someone of autism. We take the view that it's about looking at practical problems – anxiety, having difficulties communicating with other people, for example – and finding what are the best solutions to those problems. It's about asking: where is the evidence base and what do people like NICE [the National Institute for Health and Care Excellence] say about it? It is about making decisions based on evidence and not based on what Google says.

'If someone is having a meltdown, you have to look at what's behind the behaviour. And equally you can't just write people off, saying, "They're autistic, they can't change this." As a parent, you will always want what is best for your child; you will want to equip them to face the world.'

Research Autism has come up with 12 key principles to bear in mind when choosing an intervention. If you go with one that covers most if not all of these, you can't go far wrong.

1. The intervention is based on a good understanding of autism.
2. The people who deliver the intervention know the person well and respect their feelings and views.
3. The person's capacity for consent is taken into account.
4. The intervention is adapted to the needs of the person receiving it.
5. It is based on a logical and scientifically feasible theory.
6. Research evidence shows the intervention can work for autistic people.
7. The intervention works in the real world, not just in a research laboratory.
8. It is delivered by, or supported by, appropriately qualified and experienced professionals.
9. The people delivering the intervention follow established guidance.
10. The intervention is carefully monitored and reviewed on a regular basis.
11. It provides significant benefits.
12. It does not cause physical or emotional harm.

Damian Milton, an autistic academic:
'When autistic behaviour is labelled as the autistic person's deficit, and interventions employ remedial measures that train people to be less autistic, then people get damaged. To me, interventions should be about building understanding and connection.'

High expectations

The advice parents used to be given on discovering their children were autistic was bleak. Researching his book *Neurotribes*, Steve Silberman came upon the words delivered by a psychologist at the Johns Hopkins Hospital in Baltimore in 1980 (1980!), speaking to the parents of a child newly diagnosed with autism. 'I'm very sorry,' he told them. 'This is the worst thing that can happen to a parent. I can't think of anything worse than this. And you must learn to manage.'

'Yes, it's true that some profoundly disabled autistic people will require high levels of support for the rest of their lives, but even profoundly disabled autistic people can learn,' said Silberman. 'And even those people may be capable of surprising you with what they can do, and by that I mean being able to have a happy life on their own terms.'

The author David Mitchell, who has an autistic son, on why we should have high ambitions for children who have limited language skills:

'We neurotypicals are suckers for equating communicative proficiency with cognitive ability. If someone is pre- or non-verbal, our estimation of what they can or can't do, what they are or are not capable of, drops. We don't even notice ourselves doing it.

'I would like to see the overdue retirement of the assumption that children who have little or no language also have little or no awareness of themselves, others or the world around them. I would like to see the adoption of the opposite assumption: that behind speechless there may well be a person as intellectually, imaginatively and emotionally engaged as a person who can speak. What have we got to lose?

'At worst, the assumption of full sentience is wrong. So, what? The outcome is that a person who is usually deprived of his or her fair share of respect is no longer deprived, even if that person isn't cognisant of the increase in respect given. Surely, that's still a net gain? At best, however, the assumption of sentience behind speechless is accurate, and the person on the receiving end gets treated like a full, card-carrying human being for perhaps the first time in his or her life. Very often, the truth will be somewhere between these two poles – but everyone is still quids in.

'You don't need to be a qualified psychiatrist, or the parent of a child with autism, to understand how respect can kick-start a virtuous circle. The person with autism will sense the new respect; its lack of condescension or indifference; and sense the raised expectations; and will act accordingly. I've seen this in my own son. After a few, even trifling, victories the child's self-esteem is bolstered, and a little self-esteem goes a long way for people with special needs, for kids who can often feel like dead-losses or nuisances. John Milton observes in Paradise Lost: "Oft-times nothing profits more / Than self-esteem, grounded on just and right / Well-managed." John Milton is damn right.'

Building your team

As your journey progresses, you will gather a team of people to help your child and you – everyone from family members and teachers to therapists and professionals (NHS, private or accessed through charities) and people you trust to look after your kids while you take some time for yourself. Our son's team, not counting me and my husband, are my mum Jean, my mother-in-law Ann, my sister Abby and her wife Jessica, all of whom have dropped everything to help out more times than I can remember. On the professional side there is the wonderful Debora Elijah, who runs the social skills class that my son goes to; Kay, his NHS speech and language therapist; his teaching assistant (TA) at school, Sally; the knowledgeable school SENCO, Nicola; and the inclusion manager, Adelle – all of them brilliant – and Dorota, the most amazing family friend, who I pay to help on Saturdays from 4 p.m. to 7 p.m. (my husband works weekends) when I'm about to start screaming at the kids. Without the team we'd be sunk.

It can take a long time to work out who should be in your team, for the simple reason that it takes a long time to get your head around what your child needs help with; which interventions you're comfortable with and what is the best use of your money, energy and time. One thing that makes the journey more difficult is the number of professionals working in the field, both NHS and private, who either aren't trained to a very high standard or aren't very knowledgeable about autism, despite claiming the opposite. It is important to be engaged both with any intervention your child is receiving and the therapists. Ask questions, observe the intervention and ask for a second opinion if you feel uncomfortable with anything.

Below is a list of some interventions and professionals you may encounter along the way. These are either interventions of which I have had personal experience, or whose efficacy is supported by good evidence, or which have been highlighted as helpful by autistic adults. There are lots more out there, so this is just a starting point.

The Interventions

Improving executive function

Professor Liz Pellicano, director of the Centre for Research in Autism and Education, told me that we can get overly caught up with trying to improve children's social skills, and should instead be working to help improve executive function.

One of her studies found the executive function of autistic children, measured at the age of four, to be the most accurate predictor of the life skills they will exhibit in later years.

'This suggests that early executive function is really important in children's later development and is exactly the kind of thing we should be focusing on,' she says. 'Some of the young adults in my study are clever, articulate people who should be able to do whatever they want. But they feel significantly hampered by their difficulties with planning, organisation and transitioning from one thing to the next. These difficulties with executive function can see people dropping out of college or university because they can't cope with the demands of independent living.'

At the moment there is very little research on how to improve executive function in autistic children, but Adele Diamond, a professor of developmental cognitive neuroscience in Canada, is involved in studying its importance in education and ways to improve it among the general population. Pellicano is hoping to replicate some of Diamond's research with autistic children.

The skills a person needs to be successful, according to Diamond, are creativity, flexibility, self-control and discipline. 'Central to all these are executive functions, including mentally playing with ideas, giving a considered rather than an impulsive response and staying focused,' she wrote in her paper on the subject in 2001. In terms of improving executive function, the strongest evidence favoured computer programs, such as the Cogmed working memory training program, and traditional martial arts. Weaker evidence, though still reasonably strong, exists for aerobics, yoga and mindfulness.

Here is a paper Diamond wrote on ways to improve executive functioning in children: www.devcogneuro.com/Publications/Activities_and_Programs_That_Improve_Childrens_Executive_Functions.pdf

EarlyBird

This is a course for parents of children with a diagnosis, or pre-diagnosis, run by local authorities across the country, under licence from the National Autistic Society. It is divided into EarlyBird (for preschoolers) and EarlyBird Plus (for ages four to eight). Some local authorities offer this for free; others ask for a contribution of £25 or £30. No family should be excluded because of the cost, so if you can't afford to pay this, you don't have to.

I didn't do EarlyBird, as annoyingly it was offered to us two years after our son's diagnosis. When I *really* needed EarlyBird was in the year before my son received a diagnosis. It's just at this point that I was contemplating some crazy interventions, including homeopathy, until my husband put his foot down. EarlyBird, I'm sure, would have set me straight.

Speaking to parents who have been, it is practical and useful for meeting other families in the area at a similar stage of the journey to you – a bit like an autism NCT. You also get to meet some of the local authority professionals you might be working with; having a word in person and explaining what is going on can get their attention in a way an email doesn't.

The groups are usually six families. Two adults per family are allowed to go on the EarlyBird course and three adults on the EarlyBird Plus course; one of these will ideally be a TA or someone from the school, though some schools are less than cooperative when it comes to letting TAs attend EarlyBird Plus, unfortunately. There are eight sessions lasting two and a half hours led by trainers who include educational psychologists, specialist teachers, speech and language therapists and portage workers (we explain what all these people do below). They focus on a different element of autism each week.

'The course increased my understanding of my child and taught me the importance of structure, planning ahead and keeping language simple and positive, even with highly verbal children,' says one mum who went on the course.

One downside, she adds – if it is appropriate to criticise something that is clearly A Good Thing – is that it is held during working hours. My experience of this type of course is also that some parents can hog the conversation, particularly those still coming to terms with everything, which, if inevitable, can waste time.

Social skills classes

Autistic children almost always struggle with neurotypical social skills – things like showing an interest in something that isn't immediately interesting to them, listening to someone else talk, or waiting their turn to speak. Social skills classes are becoming more popular as a means of support in this area. Some schools run social skills classes, while some private speech and language therapists offer group social skills classes outside of schools.

When they're done right, these classes can be a good place for your child to learn social skills in a 'live' situation, rather than an abstract exercise, as part of a group. Done wrong they can be ineffective and formulaic – i.e. not customised for the individual child.

Some signs of a good-quality social skills class:

1. It is based on an approach that is backed by evidence and where progress is tracked.
2. Parents are involved, meaning skills used in the class can also be practised at home, so they are reinforced.
3. It is small and the other kids are appropriate peers for your child.
4. The person running the group doesn't look at just the use of language but explains all the invisible information and non-verbal signals being given off too.
5. The person running it understands autism and your child.
6. Your child skips into the class (mostly) and regards it as fun.

The American cognitive psychologist Scott Barry Kaufman has an interesting take on these classes. He believes that the most recent evidence indicates that autistic children, rather than being socially impaired, merely have an unconventional social style. It's an important distinction, he argues in a piece for the magazine *Behavioral Scientist*, entitled 'Rethinking Autism: From Social Awkwardness to Social Creativity'. The tendency to process social information more slowly, avoid eye contact and difficulty understanding social cues can give the impression of social disinterest, whereas most autistic children do crave connection and friends, he says.

Most well-meaning social skills interventions, he argues, try to teach autistic children the 'correct' ways of responding to situations but this often doesn't work because 'the social world is so much more complex and dynamic than learning a social script for every interaction' (if that were even possible). Drawing on the thinking and research of Matthew Lerner at Stony Brook University, Kaufman reframes the argument that autistic people aren't socially awkward; instead he prefers to think of them as 'socially creative': 'They may not do things the *right* way, but they do things *their* way.'

Kaufman references some interventions, including ones based on drama, that are promoting social creativity. 'Rather than teaching social skills as rote knowledge, it uses improvisation to teach ways to respond to unexpected social scenarios. The idea is that if individuals with ASD can get comfortable with the exaggerated and ridiculous . . . then answering the question, "Hi, how are you?" will be a breeze.'

'It is important to be aware that many autistic adults say they found socialising as children exhausting – and they still do,' says Robyn Steward. 'Some people do not want friends and are content to be on their own, but they still need to learn to work in groups and compromise: these are things everyone has to do.'

Social Stories

An example of a basic Social Story for a child that is hitting is this: 'Everyone gets angry. Sometimes I have to wait for something when I don't want to wait, or I may have to do something I don't want to do. This makes me angry. When I'm angry it's good to tell someone I'm angry, but it's not OK to hit. That hurts someone, etc.' Social Stories ideally include pictures as well as words.

'A Social Story shares missing social information,' says Dr Siobhan Timmins, who runs training workshops for writing them. 'It patiently and respectfully provides this information by describing the relevant clues in life, clarifying the context of a situation and providing a comforting sense of predictability. It may share other people's thoughts, feelings and experiences too, linking these to others' reactions and expectations, thus explaining behaviour. It does so in language that is always positive, literally accurate and pitched at the exact cognitive level of the child and therefore comfortable and accessible for them. It works hard to engage the child by considering their choice of interests and may include illustrations which highlight the content of the text. The result is a uniquely individual, meaningful, patient, non-judgemental, respectful and reassuring description of life.'

She adds that the best way to write a Social Story is to first abandon all assumptions, opinions or judgements of the child's unexpected or unusual response and work hard to understand the situation from the child's perspective. 'His/her perspective will lead to the correct missing information required which can then be shared with him using the criteria to guide you.'

What you can do to help your child's communication at home

Sue Moon, a speech and language therapist whose company Moon Therapy is based in central England, suggests families get in the habit of describing out loud what they are feeling. This helps a child to match up the emotions their parent is telling them they are experiencing with the facial expressions they are seeing. She also suggests modelling good problem-solving strategies and proportionate reactions to problems. For example, if you lose your purse, you could say out loud, 'Oh no, I've lost my purse, but I'm going to stay calm because when I'm calm, I'm smart, and I'll be able to think where it is.'

She also works with autistic children on perspective-taking, by drawing cartoons populated by stick figures with speech and thought bubbles – a technique called Comic Strip Conversations, developed by Carol Gray, who has developed the use of Social Stories. 'The more visual and fun you can make these strategies, the better.

'It's not just a question of a child learning social skills, it's about generating a deeper understanding of what happens in social situations – how people feel and the impact what you say has on people. A lot of these social processes don't happen at a conscious level, so teaching these things is difficult. You have to think about what it is you are doing socially and teach it to your child.'

Attention Autism

Attention Autism is a way of building attention and working on communication and joint attention for children who are younger or who have limited speech and a learning disability as well as autism.

Gina Davies is a veteran speech and language therapist who creates what she describes as 'irresistible invitations to learn' – games that are attention-grabbing enough for a child to concentrate on them and, hopefully, comment on. The child is only allowed to observe what is being done – at least in the early stages – rather than take control of the activity. This encourages them to follow someone else's lead and to share the experience. Pictures are used to show what will be happening, to lower anxiety, add structure and make it easy for the child to take the risk to join in. She also talks about the importance of autistic children laughing and having fun.

One of Davies' techniques is the 'attention bucket', basically a bucket full of toys that light up, spin or make noises. The adult with the attention bucket demonstrates one toy at a time in front of the children – winding up a toy snake, for example, then watching it move and using a single word, 'snake', for the child to learn. If a child gets up out of their seat, they are gently, non-verbally guided back. This is to encourage attention and listening skills.

I went on an Attention Autism course for two days. On the morning of the first day, Davies arrived on stage with a singing doll. We all stopped nattering and started listening to the doll. This is her approach: she grabbed our interest and we did what she wanted us to do – which was to shush – without her making a demand on us.

Some local authorities have adopted Davies' method in nurseries and preschools, and there are private speech and language therapists who use it too. There are also videos on YouTube demonstrating her methods.

Virginia Bovell on her son Danny Hornby, 23:
'For me it's totally normal that Danny doesn't speak, but he's quite eloquent in terms of sounds, facial expressions and gestures. He takes me by the hand and shows me what he wants, and he has his communication book. I get caught short when I hear other parents tell me what their kids have told them – things Danny and I will never talk about. That's something we can't share.

'On the other hand, Danny's communication is incredibly rewarding

in other ways. He'll eat meals and he'll gaze into my eyes and he'll hold my arm. We sit and gaze at each other with love and I couldn't do that with anyone else.'

The author David Mitchell on his 11-year-old autistic son:
'Our son has a vocabulary of hundreds of words, maybe thousands, in English and in Japanese, and he's interested in language and language apps: which makes him sound verbal. Yet he's never had a conversation of more than three or four short lines in his life: which makes him sound non-verbal. So, what is he? Verbal or not? My best brief answer is, "He's kind of non-verbal", though I feel the need to qualify that by explaining that compared to kids in his unit at school, who have never uttered a single word since birth, he's a chatterbox. Yet compared to kids whose autism has not applied brakes to their speech and language development (sometimes autism hits the accelerator) our son is mute. Autism has a habit of turning apparently simple questions into complex ones.'

The Transporters and the Mind Reading Emotions Library

The Transporters is an animation series developed by the Autism Research Centre at the University of Cambridge, led by Professor Simon Baron-Cohen. It's a bit like *Thomas the Tank Engine*, except the engines have human faces with real emotional expressions.

Baron-Cohen and his team asked parents of autistic children between the ages of five and eight to get their kids to watch the DVD for 15 minutes a day for a month. They recorded their ability to measure emotional expressions at the start and end of that period, comparing their responses with those of a group of autistic children who didn't watch the DVD and a group of non-autistic kids who also didn't watch the DVD. The autistic children who watched the DVDs proved to be better at recognising emotions in other films they watched than before, which meant they were able to generalise and recognise emotions in a different situation and context.

Recognising emotions is vital to cognitive empathy and theory of mind – the ability to imagine what others are feeling (see the chapter entitled 'Is my child autistic?') – which can be more difficult for autistic people, according to Baron-Cohen.

'I think the point of the study is you can improve aspects of empathy just like any other skill,' he says. 'If you don't intervene, a lot of kids will avoid looking at faces, missing out on social experiences and learning how emotions match experiences. If you present things in an autism-friendly format – with repetition and predictability so it's not intimidating – then you are trying to reach the child in their world, rather than asking them to come to us.'

Baron-Cohen has also produced the *Mind Reading Emotions Library*, an electronic encyclopedia that helps older autistic people learn about emotions via their computer. You type in the emotion you are interested in and up pop the faces of different individuals showing that emotion. Using this regularly has shown improved ability to recognise emotion in both faces and voices. 'They could tell when they heard someone saying something whether they were being ironic or sarcastic,' he says. 'Learning this on the computer is a better medium: you are not trying to pick these things up in the rapidly changing social world in the playground. It's all too fast – you can't rewind and study it carefully and slowly.'

Lego therapy

Take three autistic children. Get one to read out the instructions, the other to hand out the Lego pieces and the third to put them together. You not only have three happy kids but one effective and evidence-backed therapy. Research shows that carrying out Lego therapy once a week for 16 weeks leads to improvements in eye contact, communication, turn-taking and many other areas. My son's school runs a Lego therapy group, which he enjoys, and I can see the skills of working with others transferring into other areas of his life. It's a good idea to check that a speech and language therapist, or someone experienced, is training the people taking the classes.

It was pioneered by American clinical neuropsychologist Dan LeGoff and evaluated by Simon Baron-Cohen, who observes: 'Lego is very systematic; you are using a format that might be intrinsically attractive to someone with autism, so you've already won half the battle. We heard lots of anecdotal stories about kids with autism loving Lego but playing it in their bedroom at home alone and not in a social way. This way they are learning collaboration and using material they feel confident with.'

Responsive Communication

Developed by Phoebe Caldwell, who has been working with autistic people for more than 40 years, this is a version of the Intensive Interaction technique, in which parents attempt to engage with their child by 'mirroring' their movements or body language (see the chapter on 'Learning to play'). The difference is that Responsive Communication first looks at the sensory difficulties that might be making life a misery for the child before moving on to find a way of making a meaningful connection.

The technique has three main elements:

* Observing and identifying which sensory inputs cause distress or discomfort and which are neutral or positive;
* Creating an autism-friendly environment by reducing or increasing those sensory inputs;
* Tuning into and responding to the person's body language using Intensive Interaction.

Responsive Communication can be a useful technique for children who may have little or no language and are showing signs of distress. It involves trying to start a conversation with them using their own language, not necessarily spoken – if the child isn't using words, then neither does the parent or the therapist. By tuning into them, it's possible slowly to encourage them to move from their internal world to enjoy a shared activity.

'You are picking up on the sensory language they are using to connect with themselves: what is it about tearing that piece of paper that is so wonderful for that child?' says Janet Gurney, who works with Caldwell and is head of training for the charity Us in a Bus, based in Redhill, Surrey, which helps children with profound disabilities and complex needs. 'What physical feedback are they getting? In order to do that, you have to do it too. Take a piece of paper and tear it yourself.'

'It's about having a conversation as equals,' adds Caldwell. 'When it goes well you can see that it is the first time someone has spoken to a child in a way that has meaning for them. You can see the relief pouring off them.'

Intervention Programme in Social Cognitive in Groups of Pairs (PROSCIG)

This method, devised by Dr Debora Elijah, a cognitive neuropsychologist who runs the Elijah Social Cognitive Therapy Skills Centre in north London, focuses on how the brain processes social information. Its 15 steps are divided into three modules: social solving, social perception and self-regulation.

Elijah works with children who have a range of abilities, running an individualised programme for each child and using group work to help them gain social understanding and develop strategies for coping more positively in social situations. The centre runs games that are highly structured and offers occupational therapy. Targets are set for each child and measured regularly. The centre works on skills that a child is likely to need at school, including cooperation in groups, independent thinking and behaviour, developing cognitive skills, self-confidence and functional spontaneous communication.

My son has been going here for over two years. Since starting, he's grown in happiness and confidence and I have always felt that Dr Elijah, a wise mother of four, knows him better than anyone else (parents aside). At the centre he gets to learn new skills in real life and he has access to a community of autistic children, who accept him for who he is.

'Autism should no longer be seen as a negative label,' she says. 'Autistic people are necessary for the development of our society. To show possibility and the ways we can make a different world with more understanding and opportunities.'

How the Preschool Autism Communication Trial (PACT) proved the benefit of early intervention

PACT was a randomised controlled trial funded by the Medical Research Council (MRC) headed up by Professor Jonathan Green of the University of Manchester, which ran between 2006 and 2010. Green's team of therapists worked with 152 autistic children aged two to four. This social communication intervention focused on helping parents communicate better with their children and established that there was long-term improvement in 'the severity of [their] autism symptoms' – using the words of the researchers – that continued for six years after treatment.

Therapists worked with parents to help them understand and respond to their child's communication style, and to embed those techniques into family life. Families visited a clinic twice a week for six months, where parents were videoed playing with their children beside a box of toys. If the child offered a toy, the parent followed their lead; if the child said a word, the parent repeated it and added something. The practice was repeated at home every day. The therapy continued with the parents for the next six months with less intensity.

More information: www.thelancet.com/journals/lancet/article/
PIIS0140-6736(16)31229-6/fulltext

Parent Infant Centre

While PACT was a trial and isn't, at the time of writing, offered as an intervention, the psychotherapist Dr Stella Acquarone has been running a version of it for the past 30 years at the Parent Infant Clinic, which is based in her north London home. Acquarone is a pioneer of early intervention arguing, at a time when other professionals treated this as a ridiculous suggestion, that it was possible to change the outcomes for autistic children by starting help early.

Her work focuses on family dynamics and the communication held between the autistic child, and their parents and siblings. She also addresses the emotions felt by the child, rather than just looking at changing behaviour caused by each emotion and she works from the point of view that the autistic child is highly sensitive to emotion and, most likely, in a state of fear. From this, she teaches parents how to connect with the child.

Acquarone runs a ReStart programme, designed for babies and children up to the age of four, not all of whom will have a diagnosis. This is an intensive treatment that lasts from two to four weeks, depending on the age of the child. It is a whole-family approach that involves spending each weekday at the clinic, so expect to take time off work and school. The charity wing of the organisation, ipAn, arranges fundraising for families who do not have funds.

We went there for three weeks when my son was two-and-a-half. The rooms in her residential-style clinic are set up with video cameras so the therapists can see how you interact with your child, and vice versa. The children get music therapy and the parents get individual and couple's psychotherapy. This gives parents a chance to address any issues they have and therefore be in a better place to support their child.

My son went into the clinic disengaged with few words, and came out with more language and a greater awareness of the world around him and other people. I felt we understood him better and we were happier as a family. We came out with a plan.

Music

Adam Ockelford, professor of music at the University of Roehampton in London, has worked with hundreds of autistic students, most notably Derek Paravicini, the blind autistic musical savant christened 'the human iPod' by the media for his ability to play any song on the piano after hearing it only once.

'Music could have been designed with autistic children in mind,' says Ockelford: it is simpler than language for the brain to process, highly structured and reassuringly predictable. So if your child has musical ability – 10 per cent of autistic people have perfect pitch, like Derek Paravicini – then get them lessons as soon as possible.

'That person [teaching] should adopt a child-centred approach,' he adds, meaning they go with the flow and relish teaching through playful imitation. As the trust grows, it may be possible to guide the child more and more, underlining Ockelford's belief that music has potential far beyond simply learning to play an instrument.

How music can help your child

Improved communication: children with little language may be able to sing a phrase like 'No thank you' or 'Yes please' easier than they can say it; others with no language may be able to tap or hum the phrase.

Signalling change: you can use a piece of music to indicate an activity is about to end (a 'finished' song) or to help sequence activities (a 'First we do this, then we do that' song).

Turn-taking: 'songs with rules have turn-taking built in; practising patterns of give and take, listening and responding, can be a way to help support social interaction' says Ockleford.

Helping make friends: sharing musical interests with others is a great way to make friends, particularly in the teenage years, when relationships can be tricky to find and sustain.

Extending concentration: music is a predictable structure that can last for as long as you want.

Assisting emotional regulation: 'The children I work with respond powerfully to certain styles of music,' says Ockelford. 'Young children may need help to choose music that calms them down, for example, but being able to select tracks as they get older could be an important strategy in helping them manage their feelings and behaviour.'

MUSIC THERAPY Music therapy has been practised informally for centuries, but it was Paul Nordoff, a gifted pianist and composer, and Clive Robbins, a special needs teacher, who are arguably its best-known proponents. They collaborated for more than 17 years in the 1950s and 1960s to devise the Nordoff Robbins method. Much of their work centred on autistic children and they successfully proved they could establish a means of communication and relationships with children written off by other professionals.

Sessions usually involve the child being encouraged to explore instruments, then the therapists will either help them improvise a song based on a child's interest, or play a song the child enjoys. Some examples of how music therapy can improve a child's social interaction include passing and sharing instruments; playing music and movement games; learning to listen; and singing greetings and stories. One-to-one improvisation is claimed to be effective at increasing joint attention, and can help a child express themselves emotionally. For more information, go to the websites of the British Association of Music Therapy (www.bamt.org) or Nordoff Robbins (www.nordoff-robbins.org.uk).

Autism trainer Robyn Steward on her love of music:

'When secondary school was tough, playing the trumpet gave me a way of dealing with that and expressing it emotionally. My main problem was having to read music. When I realised I was a jazz musician, it fitted my learning style. I had always noodled around on the keyboard. I went to a workshop and I learned how to improvise on the trumpet: the teacher played something and I came up with my response. You're having a conversation musically. It's a social thing. A lot of improvisation is about using your ears – it's not about thinking. Once I'd learned how to do it, I was away. This resulted in me being able to access more social opportunities where people would value my skills and be more likely to forgive any social skills issues I may have.'

Yoga

While taking a child to a yoga class can seem a bit too like something Gwyneth Paltrow would do, there is now evidence that this ancient practice can help counteract anxiety in autistic children under ten, as well as help improve executive function. The physical aspect can help your child improve their coordination, balance, muscle strength and flexibility; the meditation and relaxation aspects help decrease stress and promote a stillness of mind, which helps with increasing attention span and managing anxiety. Breathing exercises can improve emotional self-regulation – meaning finding another coping strategy other than freaking out. Yoga teachers are also, as we know, uber-calm and their serenity can rub off on your child. To see my son lying still and chilling out to some hippy music makes me want to cry every time.

Generalising skills

Generalising skills is the ability to learn a new skill in one setting then use it in another. It's something autistic children can have trouble with. For example, a child may show wonderful social skills in a SALT session but not be able to apply them in the playground. Autistic children don't always struggle to generalise every skill – they may be fine with self-care skills, for example, but not social skills. Tips to help generalising skills include practising the same skills in a variety of locations, with a variety of people, and making small alterations in day-to-day living if they don't cause distress (using a different cup, for example). Also speak to the professionals working with your child and ask them how they are working with them on generalising.

People you might work with

Speech and language therapists

Speech and language therapists, or SALTs, assess and treat difficulties with speech, language and communication. An autistic child who has social communication difficulties – one of the 'impairments' a clinician needs to observe before making a diagnosis – is likely to need support in one or more of these areas.

Some definitions that will come in handy when dealing with SALTs:

Speech is talking, the actual sound of spoken language.

Language refers to the use of words, gestures and body language to communicate meaning.

Communication is how people share information, including thoughts and feelings.

Receptive language is what a child understands.

Expressive language is the child's thoughts put into words and sentences.

Pragmatic language is essentially social skills. A child with difficulties in this area knows the words but struggles to use them communicatively. It may be hard for them to:

* Follow conversational rules (they may veer off topic or not wait their turn to speak)
* Change language according to the situation
* Understand jokes, sarcasm, idioms – they may be very literal
* Understand non-verbal communication
* Read comprehension
* Infer meaning
* Say appropriate things

If you think your child has difficulties in the areas above, you can refer them to your local authority's SALT department. Nurseries or schools can also refer.

WORKING WITH SALTS They vary hugely in quality. The NHS SALT who visited my son in school for two years was appalling. She didn't take the time to get to understand him, talked to him as if he were an idiot and demanded he listened, rather than taking an approach that was fun and that he could willingly engage with. I wish I could go back in time and take him out of those sessions.

The measure of a good SALT is that they assess your child during unstructured times of the day, such as break or lunchtime at school, as well as structured ones, such as lessons. They will then be able to pinpoint what they need help with. They will then come up with an individual programme that contains targets, and strategies to achieve them, communicating it to you and the nursery or school, so you can use these methods at home and elsewhere. Consistency is important; ideally the same strategies should be used at home, at grandparents' houses and in nursery or school.

The SALT programme will usually be administered by a TA, who the SALT will have trained up. If your child doesn't have a TA, find out from the school who will be responsible for delivering the programme. Some schools send children to these sessions on their own. This is not OK. It isn't the session itself that will result in the most change, it is the bits that are taken from the session and applied on a day-to-day basis.

SALTs will also measure progress before setting new targets. They will be open to talking to you and won't view themselves as the only expert who should have input.

If these things are there, it's looking good. If not and your SALT works within the NHS, speak to the head of the department and ask for a new therapist. You may be viewed as the parent from hell, but hey, you will be the parent from hell with a child who communicates effectively.

Increasingly, SALTs working for local authorities don't have time to help children with social communication or pragmatic language difficulties because of cuts to budgets, arguing that these children should be supported by their school, which often doesn't have the money to do this either. If your child needs the help, try to get the SALT's input by emailing the department your evidence and observations.

Portage

Portage is a child development training technique that hails from the city of Portage in Wisconsin. Originally a means of helping parents on isolated farms understand how best to play with their preschool children, on this side of the pond it has become a local authority-run system of home visits targeting the parents of babies and preschoolers who have begun to miss their developmental milestones.

'Portage focuses on what the child can do and is interested in and builds up from there, concentrating on all areas, from play and cognitive learning to communication, self-care and even motor skills,' says Rina Picciotto, a retired portage manager who was based in Hackney, east London, and helped my family immensely in the early days. 'In essence, it is about joining the portage worker's knowledge of and ability to promote child development with a parent's knowledge of their child.'

While at one stage more than half of all local authorities offered portage services, cost-cutting has meant that fewer LAs now do.

The best portage workers act as a family's key worker, introducing benefit information and advice on how to fill in an EHCP (the document stating what support a child gets at school), joining up services and providing support.

Educational psychologists (EPs)

The main role of the educational psychologist is to help children make progress at school. They should identify any barriers to learning, whether they are environmental, physical, mental, emotional or social, and suggest strategies to remove them.

EPs are central to the EHCP assessment process – by law they must be involved in the assessment. Usually, the EP will come to school, discuss your child with you and their teachers, and observe them in class and perhaps at play. They will also look at classwork, chat to your child and give them some tests to check on skills and intellectual development.

They will then write a report giving an overview of your child's strengths and weaknesses. This can also give recommendations for teaching strategies or additional materials to be used with your child, or advice on suitable school types for your child.

Most EPs will be used only in the EHCP assessment and in the initial setting up of support, or they may be called in if a child is struggling. They are likely to recommend what support they know the LA is realistically going to be able to afford; it might be very different to what support a child ideally needs.

Clinical psychologists

Clinical psychologists work with children to reduce emotional or psychological stress at home. If a child is showing their distress by frequent meltdowns, a clinical psychologist can help.

They often work in a team and are based in health premises (for example, with CAMHS – Child and Adolescent Mental Health Services) and rarely visit a child in his or her educational environment. They are usually a member of the multidisciplinary team which identifies autism.

Occupational therapists (OTs)

Occupational therapists identify sensory processing difficulties and come up with practical strategies to help a child manage these difficulties. In many boroughs OT can be extremely difficult to access, viewed as a luxury rather than the necessity it is. Often this department is the most frazzled and least responsive of all, and that's saying something in the context of local authority-run services.

This means the therapy children receive is often piecemeal; those who are able to afford it often end up paying for private practitioners to supplement what little they get. When a child sees an OT, it is important the OT understands autism. The National Autistic Society book *Sensory Strategies: Practical Ways to Help Children and Young People with Autism Learn and Achieve*, by Corinna Laurie, is excellent. Buy or borrow two copies – one for yourself and one for your child's nursery or school. (Also, see the chapter on 'Sensory differences.')

Physiotherapists

OTs commonly refer children to physiotherapists if they have problems with their gross- or fine- motor coordination – gross is catching a ball; fine is holding a pen. Physios will also look at core strength and stability. Often kids on the spectrum have hypermobility, low muscle tone, poor balance and stability. They may also lack the core strength to sit in a stable way on a chair.

'A child with ASD may avoid playground equipment because of the noise of other children and therefore won't practise those skills,' says children's physio Wiz Chilton, of Chelsea Children's Therapy.

By the age of four and a half a child should be able to walk up and down steps without using the handrail. A physio usually offers advice to parents, demonstrating exercises for them to do with their child at home and for a TA to do at school.

* * *

7

CREATING AN
AUTISM-FRIENDLY HOME

* * *

'Autism + Environment = Outcome'
Dr Luke Beardon

What Dr Luke Beardon is saying in this equation is that environment is key when it comes to happy autistic children and adults. If you drop them into a noisy room full of screaming people, an unstructured environment where things are changing constantly, they may very well cease to function entirely. But put that same person in a quieter, calmer, more predictable and structured environment and the same child or adult may function brilliantly.

In the past I've paid too much attention to what my son is or isn't doing, and haven't looked enough at his environment. Now I'm all about changing the environment. We have a predictable routine: he has swimming after school on Monday; Nutella on toast for breakfast on Saturdays and Sundays; he gets the iPad in the morning from 6 a.m. to 7 a.m. every day (a shameless bribe, since otherwise he's up at 5 a.m. on the dot); he can wear ear defenders at dinner if the noise of knives scraping on plates bothers him, or in the car when his baby brother screams; he takes melatonin to help him sleep and gets to move one place up the reward chart for getting dressed on his own.

We don't go to my mum's place for big family gatherings as much as we used to – the acoustics in her new-build flat are difficult for him – and when we do have big get-togethers he knows he can escape to a room on his own with an iPad if it all gets too much for him.

We have tackled individual problems as they come up and found practical solutions where possible, but it's taken us years to get to this point, to have nailed down strategies to make life more secure, predictable and manageable for him.

Just as I was starting to feel smug, however, a new dilemma cropped up.

What I am now struggling with is knowing when he genuinely can't cope with something related to his autism, and when he's just being a kid who doesn't want to do something.

Only this morning he was extremely upset and angry (distressed? I wasn't sure) at the thought of going to his social skills club on a Wednesday. It means he misses an hour of school at the end of the day, which he hates. It could be that he has stopped liking his club or something has happened there that he's not telling me. I just don't know, and my questioning him about it annoys him more.

I often find myself wondering if some things are too difficult for him, or whether I need to build his resilience; questioning whether he's reacting to something because it's overwhelming him or trying it on because he'd rather not. If he gets to stay home from his social skills club, am I helping change something that's been causing him distress, or just . . . giving in? And if I've allowed him to have his own way because he's kicked off, will he get used to doing that, rather than learning to deal with his frustration?

This is one thing I can't come up with a neat strategy for, I'm afraid. I've spoken to autistic adults and professionals and they agree it's a hard one to judge – I have been told I have to trust my instinct. This stresses me out, as I'd rather be told by someone else what to do. Just like my son.

Social model vs medical model of autism

In the 1970s, disability rights campaigners put forward the social model of disability – a reaction to the medical model that had been the dominant viewpoint up until then. They were sick of being told they lacked whatever it took to navigate the world, when society and the environment played such a key role. If a wheelchair user cannot access a building, they argued, that has less to do with their disability than with the flight of steps leading up to the entrance.

This works for autism too. Instead of 'fixing' the autistic person, we should instead fix their environment.

Jamie Knight, the 28-year-old programmer working for the BBC whom I interviewed in the 'What is it like to be autistic?' chapter, expands on this on his excellent blog www.spacedoutandsmiling.com, in a post entitled 'Developing an Autistic Identity'.

'The social model can be summarised as "the environment disables people because the environment is badly designed". In other words, in most scenarios, the challenges I face are not actually due to some defect with me, but due to defects in the environment around me. This change of perspective . . . helped me move my focus away from trying to "defeat" the autism. Fixing the environment has worked MUCH better.'

Below is a brilliant example of how to fix the environment courtesy of Knight. In a post entitled 'How to Make Bath Time Awesome', he describes what he used to find difficult about having a bath, including the sensory overload and concerns about doing things in the right order. He also covers the strategies his babysitter, Carrie, whom he pays to help him live independently and who sounds pretty awesome herself, came up with to overcome these obstacles. Carrie, who works at a special school close to Jamie, is literally his babysitter: unable to find a suitable carer, he went on findababysitter.com and found her.

1. **Routine + Timer**

   In the bathroom she placed a whiteboard with a routine [written on it giving step-by-step instructions for what to do].

   She also covered the whole process, including 'change into PJs' and 'return to bedroom and hug Lion [Jamie's soft toy]'.

   She also put a timer in the bathroom so I could set a countdown. I also bath for a prime number of minutes – 23 or 29 normally.

   The routine and time provide structure. If I am uncomfortable, being able to watch a countdown helps me to complete the task.

2. **Lighting**

   She brought over a snowglobe, which changes colour, and some LED lights. She puts the lights in coloured pots and puts the snowglobe on the loo to light the room. She also hangs a torch above the bath, pointing away.

3. **Toys**

   At first we didn't focus on 'washing'. Instead I just 'played' in the bath. Simply getting wet was a start.

   The babysitter brought all sorts of different toys. The toys which work for me are functional. For example, I have a wall-mounted toy with water wheels and funnels. I also have coloured blocks of acrylic I can hold up to the light and mix colours.

   These toys help me fill the time. They are distracting and fun. I always thought toys were 'naughty' as I was too old. However, the babysitter's view is that if they help, it does not matter. She says 'autie not naughty'.

The most recent addition was a bag of ball-pit balls. Poured on top of the [water], they float and are extremely relaxing to play with.

4. **The future**
After the bath I am clean and generally relaxed, ready for bed. So it has helped with my sleeping.

Washing has gone from a chore to a joy, something I look forward to rather than [being] put off [by]. This technique is simple but has been life-changing.

How to make your home more autism-friendly

Structure

Structure is not a preference for an autistic child, it's essential. Some autistic people find uncertainty physically painful. 'The reason schedules and routines help is that they provide a concrete, static, visual map in a moving, abstract world,' says Sarah Hendrickx, an author and autism consultant. 'They are an anchor in a sea of confusion.'

Structuring things means there's a beginning and an end. When it comes to play, it's the difference between a board game – which has a clear set of rules and parameters – and a dressing-up box.

Conversation can be structured too. For example, an autistic child is more likely to answer a direct, focused question than an open-ended one, which requires them to fish around for the 'correct' response in a sea of bewildering possibilities. For example, 'Tell me five things about Holland' is specific and closed. 'What do you know about Holland?' is more problematic.

Number lines

Dr Debora Elijah, a cognitive neuropsychologist, suggests creating a number line to help your child get dressed. The night before, lay out their clothes in five piles, write the numbers 1–5 on different Post-it notes and stick a number on each item of clothing. So, for example, maybe 1 for pants, 2 for trousers, and so on, with the last one a reward, perhaps five minutes playing on the iPad or bouncing on the trampoline. We tried this and it worked like a dream for about a month. I suspect all such things have a motivational shelf life, so to speak, but this one lasted longer than most.

You could also use a number line for getting out of the house in the morning – stick a number 1 Post-it on their clothes, a 2 on their breakfast cereal, a 3 on their toothbrush, a 4 on their coat, a 5 on their shoes and you're out the door.

For kids who can cope with a bit of choice (see below), try making breakfast times more visual: draw or print out a picture of three choices and stick them onto the table for them to point at – maybe 1 for eggs, 2 for cereal and 3 for toast. As I am terrible at drawing and always short on time, I came up with a shortcut: grab the egg carton, box of Shreddies and a loaf of bread and line them up on the kitchen table. Bingo: no tough negotiations. Breakfast means breakfast.

Visual timetables or day planners

A visual timetable can help bring a sense of order to the world, allowing your child to see what's going to happen now and next, and to check off what they've already done. I'm an inveterate list-maker; it helps me calm down when I've got a lot on my plate. I imagine that's what role visual timetables play too.

It's a good idea to have a visual timetable at home as well as school. Write down times, days and activities, adding pictures or photographs of what they'll be doing and with whom. These timetables are a good idea even for chatterbox children who seem to have fewer support needs. As Robyn Steward says: 'Despite being what some may label high-functioning I feel more relaxed when there are symbols rather than written words in my environment – including my own home. Just because someone is bright doesn't mean they can't benefit from symbols and pictures.'

Here are a few tips on putting together a visual timetable, whether you make it with your own fair hand or download it from the internet.

* You can buy ready-made visual timetable kits from websites such as asdvisualaids.com

* If you decide to make your own, Pinterest has plenty of examples to copy, while images of anything, anywhere and anyone can be printed from the web, using Google Images, for example.

* Apps such as First-Then Visual Schedule (iOS, £9.99) allow you to create a visual timetable on your smartphone or iPad for when you're out and about. They will either come with ready-made images or you can use those on your phone or from Google Images.

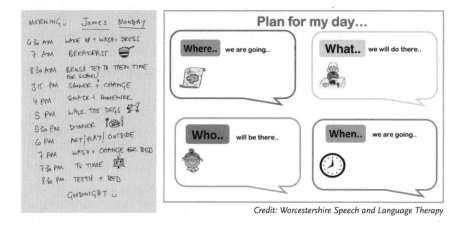

Credit: Worcestershire Speech and Language Therapy

Preparing for change

Changes in routine can cause real distress. If you get advance warning, talk your child through it, if they have language, or use your visual timetable and cross out the bit that is changing – if the swimming lesson has been cancelled, for example. My son always finds the beginning of term very difficult, with so many small and big changes happening in one go. This term it's taken five weeks for him to seem OK again.

Some strategies to make things easier:

* For the children with no language who find change extremely distressing show them why there has been a change in plan. If swimming has been cancelled, you may have to take them to the pool and show them the locked gate.

* When we visit friends for the first time, I ask them to email pictures of themselves and their home so we can look at them together. Or we go on Facebook and look at the photos on there. Now my son often asks to see someone's picture before meeting them. You could create a visual timeline for the day and agree beforehand with your friend when you will be leaving, so you can let your child know.

* One parent, before a family outing, would do a dummy run of the day, taking pictures on their iPad of the route and what they were going to do, which helped their non-verbal child immeasurably. It did make it harder to tolerate a change of plan, however – seeing the pictures had set up a firm expectation. Still, brilliant.

＊ If my son goes to see a film, we usually watch the trailer online first. For many autistic people, there is no such thing as a good surprise, so don't worry about spoiling the plot. If you are going to a museum or a hospital, have a look online together for footage on their websites or on YouTube.

Transitions

The sky can also feel like it's falling for a monotropic autistic child who is asked to move from one all-consuming task to something else. (For more on monotropism – the ability of a person to focus only on a single task or interest – see the chapter 'Is my child autistic?'.) Giving them advance warning can become second nature: dinner is in five minutes; we're turning the TV off in ten minutes, I'll need you to brush your teeth next. The next level of 'pre-warning' is to add images or a prop – perhaps using an egg timer or the timer on the oven to signal when the activity is over. Timers are good, as it's not you ending the activity; you can apportion blame elsewhere. Naughty timer!

Sleep

For many autism parents, this is the hardest nut to crack – it's the brazil nut of problems, in fact. The depressing reality seems to be that some autistic children don't appear to need that much sleep. There are many theories as to why this is: anxiety; irregular production of melatonin, the hormone that helps regulate sleep; a light sleep pattern due to sensory processing difficulties. Theories aren't much help to the poor knackered parent whose child is wide awake at 3 a.m., however.

I used to fill my son's days with after-school activities and exercise, hoping he would be so dog-tired by 7 p.m. that even he couldn't fight sleep. And he was dog-tired, but still there he was, calling from his room, hopping in and out of bed right up to the moment I crawled into mine – and often beyond. Years of trying to deal with this left me most nights wanting to throw open the window and howl at the moon. Then I discovered melatonin tablets – and we haven't looked back.

Many studies have established a link between autism, poor sleep patterns and an irregular production of melatonin, which is secreted by the pea-sized pituitary gland at the base of the brain. It isn't that autistic children don't produce it, just that they don't produce it at the right time – i.e. when they (and you) need to get to sleep. Melatonin in tablet or drop form, prescribed by your GP, can help children who struggle to fall asleep do so quickly. Studies suggest it can stop working after a while – a prospect I cannot bring myself even to consider. In addition, the long-term effect of taking melatonin has not been established.

Pre-melatonin, there was no time off from being a parent. The moment I realised we had to do something about it came as I angrily tucked my son back into bed for the nth time and saw how sad he looked. For the first time I thought about what it must be like for him to be in a room on his own for hours, powerless to do the thing his parents were angrily insisting he do: sleep. The first time we gave it to our son, within half an hour he was yawning and rubbing his eyes. Minutes later he was asleep. My husband and I were stunned. Up until now, we realised, he had never yawned before going to bed. Never. If anything, he would get increasingly revved up.

Melatonin is not a drug, it's a hormone produced naturally by the body. I don't buy into the nobility of maternal sacrifice: disturbed sleep impacts on a child's brain function and behaviour – recent studies are revealing just how great that impact can be. It also turned me into a moody cow, and no one needs that.

Knowing about the impact poor sleep has on brain development, of course, is only going to stress out a parent who is desperate to get their child sleeping well and has tried everything. One parent told me the years she spent battling to get her two autistic sons to sleep were far more stressful than when she gave up and accepted that they weren't going to sleep well.

For younger children, cutting out naps at an earlier stage than you other-wise might will probably help them settle quicker at night – with my son we stopped just after the age of two.

Gro-Clocks, which you can set to light up at specific times with a blue 'star' face at night and a yellow 'sun' face in the morning, can help provide structure and a visual reminder for sleeping and waking up, but they aren't a magic bul-let. Our son may now sleep well at night but he's still up super-early in the morning. He gets the iPad if he stays in bed until 6 a.m., though. It might not win me a parent of the year award, but needs must.

Some more tips on getting your child to sleep can be found here: www.autism.org.uk/about/health/sleep.aspx

L from Staffordshire, mum of a teenage autistic boy:

'My son is frightened of darkness and scared of being on his own. The TV in my son's room is on all night with his favourite DVD on constant repeat and the landing light on outside his bedroom. He still does not sleep much, but if he does and then wakes in the night, as soon as he opens his eyes he can see and also watch his DVD, which is obviously comforting and reassuring, and entirely predictable. He also remains in his room and does not demand I sit with him all the time. What works for us is the exact opposite of what any professional has told us to do.'

Eating

Mealtimes can be fraught. You want your child to eat nutritious meals, have a broad palate and ideally to stay at the table for the duration of dinner. Good luck with that.

My son's dinner repertoire is limited but he eats four or so different vegetables and the same number of different fruits. As that's enough to avoid scurvy, it's the one area where I've drawn the line in terms of stressing. His paediatrician referred him to an NHS nutritionist, who recommended sitting down to eat as a family more, keeping offering him what everyone else is having and getting the school to give him his food unmixed, so he eats more (for example, if they are making a fish pie, they could give him the fish, cheese sauce, potato and peas separately) – and that we should do the same at home.

Rather than force the issue, resulting in a traumatised family and walls redecorated a beautiful shade of spaghetti bolognese, Sarah Hendrickx advises going with the flow, both in terms of what your kids eat and when. You won't be making them any more rigid in their thinking by serving them food they like, she says.

'Let them eat whatever weird combinations give them nutrition in as stress-free a way as possible and repeat the same meals as often as they like. Mealtimes are easier if everyone is relaxed. I routinely eat exactly the same meal six or more times a week, because I like it and see no reason for variety. Don't make food a battle.'

While wariness of new foods, textures and things touching each other on the plate is common in all younger children, Sam Perkins, a registered nutri-tionist and former NHS dietician, says it's a stage that autistic children often find it difficult to come out of.

'Kids usually start to become more open to trying new foods at around the time they go to school, but I find with autistic children this tends to happen later, say at the age of nine, ten, even 12. If your child is restricting their diet to a hand-ful of things, then you have to seek help early. The first port of call should be a paediatric dietician, who will check if your child's diet is adequate nutritionally.'

She argues that the best way to help a child with a limited diet is to create positive experiences around food. Don't bribe or pile pressure on them. Since autistic children commonly want to eat plain food that is kept separate on the plate, with nothing mixed together, give them crunchy, dry food rather than wet food. Choose fruits and vegetables that have a firm, consistent texture rather than tomatoes, for example, which have seeds and sloppy bits.

Perkins also cautions against any diets that claim to be able to 'treat' autism, such as those that cut out gluten and casein, which can lead to children who eat only a limited range of foods losing access to even more.

'There's some really dodgy advice being given to parents of autistic children. Some are putting their children on very restrictive diets, often with limited evi-dence to back it up. If they do see an improvement in behaviour, it could be be-cause sugar has been cut out of the diet, for example, or they're eating less junk food. It's also likely they will be doing other therapies at the same time. Parents want control and this is something they can control, but it can be damaging.'

Top five tips for eating – Sam Perkins, registered nutritionist and former NHS dietician (www.happyeaters.co.uk):

* Instead of mixing food up, separate it out and work towards eating a meal in small steps. For spaghetti bolognese, start with penne pasta with cheese, then move to spaghetti. The rest of the family can eat spaghetti bolognese so it's familiar to the child. Always ask if they want to try some, but without any pressure to do so.

* Let children know what to expect. Tell them at breakfast what they are going to have for dinner, for example.

* Let children have some control. Let them choose a vegetable or decide what music is on at dinner.

- ✴ Don't get bogged down with demanding a child uses cutlery but do encourage self-feeding – i.e. kids using their fingers. It's about going with the constraints of their ability, to encourage independence and motivation to eat.

- ✴ Finally, if you are going to seek out advice, seek it from a registered paediatric dietician – they are the only people who should be advising you. If your child is seeing a paediatrician, they can refer you.

Sitting still for dinner

I now have two kids who don't sit at the table for dinner. I tell them dinner's ready, they come to the table, have a few mouthfuls then pop down from their chairs, run about, my husband or I persuade them back (many times), then we lose all energy and suddenly we're on our own at the dinner table. I've accepted it mostly, but sometimes when I go to other people's houses and see their perfectly behaved children staying put, I wonder if I should be firmer about it.

Mealtimes are fluid, noisy occasions. Everybody talks, sometimes over each other; people get up from the table for more food; glasses chink; knives grate on plates; toddlers throw cutlery on the floor. Small wonder autistic kids can find it difficult to stay put amid all this commotion. Hokki stools can help, as they allow a child to carry on moving while sitting on them; they're available online for about £80.

Lucia Santi recommends using a timer or stopwatch to keep young escapees in place. 'Start with two minutes, then three, then four, then five,' she says. 'It might be they need to go running and jumping before dinner to bring them down. Get them to do 200 bounces on the trampoline before they eat.'

Special interests

In the past, a rather patronising view has been taken of special interests, subjects that can be all-consuming for your child, anything from train timetables and space travel to dinosaurs. They were seen as obsessions of little value, to be discouraged – but opinion is changing. Being an expert in something can build a child's confidence, they may get a job out of it when they are older, and special interests can be a way to motivate a child to do or learn something new.

Laura James adds that special interests can be a form of mindfulness for autistic people – a way of focusing on one thing to calm the body.

When Robyn Steward was younger, her special interest was computers. 'I was in a special needs class at school; I can't do punctuation very well, can't spell. I need a lot of support, but I was good at learning how to use a computer. I started teaching other kids how to use other computers. Computers got me out of trouble. I learned to program and to build websites, all sorts of practical skills.'

Your child's special interest may very well be good for them, but sometimes you feel that if you're forced to listen to one more word about a particular little blue tank engine, then Thomas and friends will be fast-tracked through the nearest window. It's natural, then, to worry about how their classmates and other children at school, who aren't genetically obliged to be as patient, are putting up with it. What to do?

'Allow your child to talk about their special interest in a controlled way for a set amount of time or at a certain time of day – for example, for ten minutes, or at 7 p.m.,' advises Alis Rowe, an autistic woman. 'Think about other ways of expressing this whereby the child is independent, such as writing it down, reading, drawing. Reading about it sometimes can be as good as talking about it. Or you can find someone who may have the same intense interests as your child, someone who won't mind listening to them and talking about it.'

Aggressive behaviour

Some apparently 'violent' behaviour can actually be sensory-seeking: a child may bite, push or pinch others because of the sensory feedback they get from the action, which provides a sort of release. But it may also be triggered by the child feeling completely overwhelmed. Thirty years ago, if an autistic child bit someone, it was simply viewed as an attack; now we're increasingly realising there's often more to it.

Some things to try:

* There is usually a ten-second delay between a child beginning to think about lashing out and the lashing out. Stop talking if you see the early signs, as your words will be just another thing the child has to process. (See 'Meltdowns' in the 'Sensory differences' chapter.) Remove them from that situation.

* Redirect the child to another source of sensory input. A child who bites might benefit from the use of a chewy toy, for example.

* A child who pinches might benefit from regular opportunities to play with Play-Doh or Theraputty. A child who likes to push and shove will probably benefit from rough-and-tumble play on crash mats, being rolled up in stretchy fabric like Lycra or gently squashed under the cushions of your sofa, deep-pressure hugs and squeezes, a weighted bed cover or a deep-pressure vest.

* Your child may also be acting out because they don't have the words to explain how they're feeling. If they are verbal, teach them stock phrases such as 'Stop it, I don't like it'.

Toileting trouble

For children who are avoiding doing a poo, the best advice is a visit to the GP, who will most likely prescribe them a laxative, such as sachets of paediatric Movicol, either flavoured or unflavoured, which you dissolve in water, maybe adding a bit of squash. A good paediatrician can really help if this is an ongoing problem: they may oversee a course of Movicol high enough that your child's poos are never hard and so they lose their fear of going to the toilet. They can also refer your child to a dietician if their diet is restricted. Some children stay on Movicol until they are teenagers. Not addressing it can lead to horrendous pain for the child and stress for the parent, so don't ignore it – not that you'll be able to!

Dr Eve Fleming, a community paediatrician and co-author of *Toilet Training and the Autism Spectrum: A Guide for Professionals*, offers some more advice:

* Children with autism can find the bathroom a frightening place to go to and will need more support to encourage them to go.

* For children with delays in language and understanding, use pictures, signs and objects to help them understand and communicate. Sense Toys sell toilet-time cards and flip-over books with velcro pictures that can be selected for the stage the child is at.

* Don't leave toilet training too late, or children learn that wee and poo goes in a nappy.

* 'Some autistic children don't have good proprioception (a sense of where they should position themselves) or have poor coordination, so

may have difficulty getting into the right position and feeling secure on the toilet,' she says. A Squatty Potty toilet stool (squattypotty.co.uk) can get them into a good position and can be useful if a child is constipated.

* 'It's very common for autistic children who have been toilet-trained to regress sometimes. It could be triggered by anxiety over changes in their lives – a change in school or class, for instance, or bullying, or a frightening experience in a toilet; a smelly toilet can, for some hypersensitive children, be really distressing. A toilet that doesn't lock or other children peering under the toilet door might be upsetting or distressing and lead to anxiety.'

Smearing

Smearing is – deep breath – when a child wipes their poo onto walls, floors, carpets, anywhere you least want it smeared (which is everywhere), and the best way to solve the problem is to analyse why it's happening.

'It may be a sensory thing – they may simply enjoy the feeling of doing it,' says Fleming. 'Parents may need to offer their child a substitute tactile experience. A really sticky dough – made of flour, oil and salt – will give the same squishy and malleable sensation. Some children like the smell, so try offering them a smelly alternative, like scratch-and-sniff cards.'

It may also be that they are stressed, however, in which case see what can be done to reduce their anxiety levels, she counsels. 'Focus on that rather than on the smearing. Social Stories around using the toilet can be helpful too. Rewards for using the toilet appropriately might also help.'

Emotional highs and lows

A down-to-earth psychotherapist once told me that parenting is basically dealing with all your child's emotional shit and making it bearable for them. Well, you can times that by 100 when you're parenting a sensitive, anxious autistic child who is navigating a world not designed with them in mind. They often struggle to recognise or label their own feelings – for this reason it's really important to suggest what emotions they might be feeling: you look worried; that must make you feel frustrated, etc. They may not realise strong emotions are building up until they burst out in the form of a meltdown.

To deal with this issue, the Autism Education Trust (AET) has developed the visual system reproduced below. You can talk it through with your child and encourage them to state what number they are at when calm; then after a meltdown you can point out that they were at number 5. It also gives tips on what the child can do to self-regulate. The mum of one family who used this scale would say to her child, 'Right, now you're at a 3 because you're a bit over-excited. Do you think you could try to calm down a bit, please?' The child would become more aware of how they were behaving and try to regulate their emotions.

Andrew Carpenter, who is 45, was diagnosed as autistic at the age of 40. He describes living with alexithymia, a difficulty or inability to identify and describe emotions, which is very common in autistic people.

'You are feeling stuff, your body is reacting to something, but you don't always recognise how you are feeling. And by the time you are recognising what you are feeling you are already close to the top of the scale, risking a meltdown.

'If you struggle a bit with theory of mind, you imagine everything is wrong because of you. Mummy looks stressed or angry – it must be my fault.

'I also have problems with social imagination – or visualising the future in a concrete way. If you can't visualise the options on the table, then you get anxious, and it's embarrassing because you are struggling and can't always recognise the nature of your struggle because of your alexithymia and you also have the pain. It can be very difficult indeed.'

How do I feel?

5 LOST IT!

4 I am angry. I want to shout or scream, to make a noise.

3 I am starting to feel cross – I don't like what is happening.

2 I feel a bit upset and sad. I am unsure what to do - puzzled

1 I feel calm. Everything is ok.

5 I need you to help me now

4 Leave what you are doing: listen to some music. Tell an adult what is wrong

3 Walk away. Find an adult to talk to. Do something you know helps you feel better. Tell someone how you feel.

2 Take time to calm a little – read a book, ask for help, think about something you like

1 Keep doing what you are doing

Credit: Reference for the AET tools for teachers: Erbes, V. (2012). AET tools for teachers. London, AET. Revised and updated in 2016 by O'Brien, A.

Getting ready for school

This is about dealing with lots of transitions, with the added delight of these happening under a time constraint. Bear in mind that despite knowing the sensible points below, at least once a week the rush to get out of the flat leaves me so stressed I feel I could cry. Sometimes I actually cry. I try to bribe my children to do things quicker and it works: my son has to have his breakfast, get dressed and clean his teeth, wash his face and brush his hair, then he gets to move up his reward chart. I often give him a countdown to get to the bathroom to clean his teeth – I start at five and he has to get there at zero. Turning dressing into a race between him and his brother, or me, or against himself (timing him and seeing if he can be quicker than the previous day) works too. A rigid routine also helps. Factor in extra time to get ready for nursery or school, if you can, so your child can arrive with as little stress absorbed from home as possible.

Some children find the sensory feelings from brushing their teeth hard to cope with – this might be helped by a double-headed toothbrush or a Collis-Curve toothbrush (three rows of bristles so you only need a single brushing action), which allow you to get to the swilling and spitting-out part in half the time. We bought a Minions talking toothbrush from Superdrug that my son loves – it tells him which bits to brush, when two minutes are up and congratulates him on a job well done. Those little yellow critters have managed to get my son to brush his teeth far better than I ever did by providing structure.

But it's also important to remember, if you're late, you're late. Accept that it's more important to keep your child's mood on an even keel than it is to arrive on time.

Other things that will help

SLOW DOWN YOUR SPEECH AND LIVES With younger people with autism, it can be appropriate to slow down everything, including your speech. Give them time to process what you are saying and think of a reply; be aware of your own pitch and whether you are speaking too loudly. This is not to be confused with patronising a child by barking one or two words at them as if they are a bit of an idiot.

BE PRECISE WITH YOUR WORDS Keep language specific to avoid confusion: for example, 'Tom, don't tell people they are fat' is much more straightforward than 'Tom, try not to be so rude to people'. Similarly, don't ask your autistic child 'When are you going to set the table?' Give it to them straight: 'Set the table.'

LIMIT CHOICE One of the reasons free playtimes at nursery and school can be so anxiety-provoking is because of the choice of things to do. Choice can cause huge anxiety. Now my son is a bit older, he's better able to articulate this, often telling me: 'You choose!' He never took to colouring-in when he was younger and one day, while writing this book, it hit me why – all the choices were up to him. It was overwhelming. To test this, I used his felt-tip pens to put spots of different colours into the different sections of the haunted castle in his colour- ing book. It meant the decisions were made for him. He loved it. (I've now discovered copy colour books, which do this for me.)

'It's a paradox of choice,' says Andrew Carpenter. 'On my 41st birthday, my parents asked me, "Where do you want to go for dinner?" I spent the day in bed unable to make the decision. Similarly, if someone sends me an email with multi- ple attachments, it overwhelms me and I cannot even start to look at it properly. It's just all too much in one go and I don't know how to deal with it, how to break it down into smaller chunks, which order would be best, and so on.'

COMPROMISING I assume all children pick up this skill by seeing adults com- promise with them. 'Going head-to-head in an argument with an autistic child doesn't tend to work, just as it doesn't tend to work with any human being with a strong viewpoint,' says Sarah Hendrickx. 'So bring the child in on the solution. Ask them, "What will make you feel better? How can we help you cope better next time?"'

If you want a child to do something they feel is difficult, be straight with them, advises Dr Emily Lovegrove, an autistic adult and psychologist. 'Say you know it's difficult and ask them: "Are you able to do it, or is it beyond you? If you can do it, and I know it will cost you, how can we make it nice before and after?"'

BOUNDARIES 'For me, this is where parents need to start,' says Dr Isabel Jimenez Acquarone, deputy head of the Parent Infant Centre, in London. 'To regulate their child by putting down consistent boundaries, limits, being able to say "no" and not feeling bad. "No" with an explanation, but sticking to it. If there are two parents both being consistent, even when you disagree it helps the child feel secure.

'Children feel safe with boundaries. Boundaries show us our caregivers are strong enough to fight for us, bear our rage, help us. But it's also vital for toddlers and infants to regulate themselves [to be able to deal with their emotions and the frustration of not getting their way], which is really important for the next step of logic, focus and learning – they have to be calm enough to focus.'

DON'T DOUBT YOURSELF . . . FOR TOO LONG If your child is autistic or you think they might be, or you have that lingering feeling that something is just different but you can't put your finger on it, don't doubt yourself, you are most probably right. Having said that, it's likely you will doubt yourself – we all do. Even Lucia Santi, who runs an autism school and has an autistic daughter, says she sometimes doubts herself. 'I have moments where I think, "Have I invented Ruby being autistic?" It's fleeting but I do doubt myself. I think it's inevitable because people doubt you all the time.'

TECHNOLOGY The time my son spends with the iPad seems to be when he's truly able to relax – it's his equivalent of my reward to myself after a full-on day writing or looking after the kids: to lie semi-comatose on the sofa, watching a box set, glass of wine in hand. I would react very badly if someone took the TV controller and chardonnay away and gave me a book and a glass of water instead. My point is, if your autistic child needs some downtime – it is essential after nursery or school – give them what they need.

That said, I've been to parent groups peopled by exhausted mums with too much on their plates to limit the time their autistic children spend with their screens and it seems like a slippery slope. One mum told us how her son would wake up in the middle of the night and have a meltdown if he couldn't play a computer game.

Researchers at the University of Edinburgh who surveyed over 200 autism parents found that their autistic children spent on average three hours a day using technology, whether it was a tablet, computer, smartphone, Wii or similar, and in 43 per cent of cases over four hours a day.

Sue Fletcher-Watson, a developmental psychologist at the University of Edinburgh, suggests parents try to enter their child's world by having a go at playing with them on the computer or iPad, and being available to them while they're playing, so they can show you their skills. She says not to belittle your child's achievements because they are 'just video games' and to show appreciation for the skill, concentration and dedication involved. She adds that parents of children with autism shouldn't feel they have to meet a higher standard than other parents. Three cheers to that!

'While watching the same YouTube clip over and over may not have any educational value, it might be helping your child regulate their wellbeing, manage anxiety or just relax,' she says. 'Children with autism, just like any other children, don't constantly have to be learning something new.'

BE PROACTIVE While the local authority isn't going to do enough for your child, or most likely even what it's meant to, and school isn't either, your child has you. I remember hearing this quote from Melanie Sykes on a daytime TV interview, which really helped me in the early days: 'My son is going to be OK, because I'm going to make sure he's going to be OK.'

'What parents lose is hope,' says psychotherapist Dr Stella Acquarone. 'They are paralysed with fear, complaining that the school doesn't do enough, the government doesn't do enough. They are basically waiting for other people to help their child, rather than being proactive. There is a perception that you can't change your child's situation. You can change it – you can change everything. You need to take the diagnosis and get to grips with it, not accepting what you are told your child can't do.

'It's our job to tell the parents that it's going to be a good life for both the parent and the child, that they shouldn't be scared.'

Support

I asked a number of adults what support they wish they'd received at home when they were young and what support they did receive that was helpful. Here is a sample of the answers I received:

What worked

* 'The freedom to be myself but also the reassurance of knowing what was expected of me.'

* 'A very sympathetic warm structure.'

* 'The ability to talk openly about things. When I was rude without meaning to [be], my mum would explain to me why I had upset someone.'

* 'My mum helped me to understand my brain but not be limited by other people's beliefs.'

What could have helped

*   'I do wish my mum, etc., had known about the concept of neurodiversity, mainly so I could have found out about it earlier!'

*   'If instead of, "You have £2 and you buy two oranges – how much change is there?", the question could be customised for me. Maybe, "If you buy a pack of Pokémon cards – insert your special interest here! – for £2, how much change will you have?"'

*   'Someone to play with me at home, whether it was mostly sitting in silence and playing Lego or explaining interactions in movies. Even someone I could tell about my day and help me figure out what went wrong, telling me, "No, you've got this wrong, you are missing information and assuming things."'

*   'Someone who explained executive function and theory of mind so I could learn.'

*　*　*

8

MENTAL HEALTH

✳ ✳ ✳

'You are not broken . . . You are not defective.
You are different.'
From *Odd Girl Out*, by Laura James

I'm aware the subtitle of this book – How to Raise a Happy Autistic Child – is a bold statement, particularly coming from an averagely flawed parent like me. If you want to learn how to have unhappy children, feel free to drop over to my flat after 6 p.m. any evening when I'm trying to wrestle mine into the bath and then bed.

However, I do have views on this subject, which I feel I've earned from years of researching this book. And one thing I've become increasingly aware of is how rarely you see the words 'happy' and 'autistic' in the same sentence. It's almost as if we think autism is so awful there's no point aiming that high for our children. Nick Walker, an autistic aikido teacher and speaker on neurodiversity, puts this down to the 'misery narrative' that surrounds autism – a narrative that began with Leo Kanner over 70 years ago.

And so, I've decided the best way of spending my energy going forward is in helping my son to be happy. To build up his self-esteem. And on the good days I look at my son and think: 'What on earth is there to not be positive about? I've cracked it: my son is happy because of my brilliant positive attitude. The future is bright.'

Then when he's not so good I realise the opposite is true. That my attitude was positive *because* my son was happy. Everything feels less certain and the anxiety returns: have we made the right decisions about his support? Is he in the right school? I feel less sure that autism is nothing to be afraid of, even though logically I know it isn't the problem.

This brings me to my explanation of what I define as happiness – an explanation I should remind myself of from time to time. It isn't smiling 24/7 and never having meltdowns and periods of intense sadness. It is a life that is good the majority of the time, while the rest of the time it is a mixture of normal, a bit crap and sometimes downright awful, all the while most likely featuring quite a lot of anxiety. But overall, thumbs up.

Remaining positive when your child isn't doing so well requires the ability not to fall into a pit of anxiety. Or, if you are like me, the ability to fall into the pit every so often, then climb back up and dust yourself off and continue your journey, determined not to fall into the pit next time, which you will.

It's clear from the research below that something needs to change. What you are about to read are frightening statistics taken from research looking into the strong link between mental health problems and autism. It is a good idea to bear in mind while you read this research that it is based upon young people and adults who, frequently, haven't been understood, accepted or supported. While the relationship between mental health and autism is complex and the problems are not down to one thing, acceptance is something we as parents have control of. Seventy-odd years of the misery narrative has indeed made a lot of autistic people and their parents miserable.

What the research tells us about mental health and autism

* About 70–80 per cent of children and adults on the autism spectrum have experienced mental health problems.
* Autistic people have greater problems with low confidence, feeling unhappy, depressed, worthless, under strain and unable to overcome their difficulties.
* The pressure to act 'normal' in a neurotypical world has a negative impact on wellbeing.
* Most autistic people don't know where to go to get help or feel confident that the right help is out there for them.
* Young autistic people experience high levels of stigma – about autism and mental health – and services are failing to meet their needs.

Source: Research commissioned by Ambitious about Autism looked at young autistic people's experience of mental health as part of their 'Know Your Normal' campaign. The research was carried out of UCL's Centre for Research in Autism and Education.

Anxiety and autism

'Intense catastrophising emotions that have occurred since infancy are often the first thing we pick up on diagnostically in young children,' says the psychologist Professor Tony Attwood. 'They will have a history of intense despair, almost catastrophic meltdowns. Distraction, compassion, consoling and affection from the parents may not work.'

There are lots of reasons why autistic people are more anxious, including difficulties understanding language and tasks that have not been expressed clearly or logically; not knowing what they feel, much less being able to express it; difficulty with guessing what will happen next; perhaps being unable to differentiate fact from fiction (and therefore being frightened by horrific events or things that are unlikely ever to happen); having to do things that aren't intuitive and getting it wrong a lot of the time; social rejection; learning by making lots of mistakes and all the other sensory difficulties autistic people have to deal with. On top of this, there is a growing body of evidence linking autism with irregular levels of the 'stress' hormone cortisol, affecting levels of arousal – i.e. how available we are for engaging with the world and processing new information – and levels of anxiety.

When a child is anxious, they may not be able to articulate their needs or feelings, and this can lead to challenging behaviour, non-compliance and further anxiety.

'Almost half of diagnosed autistic children and young people are thought to also experience clinical levels of anxiety,' says academic Ruth Moyse, an autistic woman who is researching autism and is the mum of an autistic daughter. 'The most important thing you can do as a parent is to take their anxiety seriously, even if to you their fear seems trivial or irrational. Telling your autistic child that everything will be OK is not helpful, and rarely accurate. What your child needs is for you to listen, and find strategies to help them manage their fear.'

How to spot an anxious autistic child

When my son was a toddler, it took me a while to realise when he was anxious. The signs were sometimes subtle; he became disengaged, restless or started stimming in a quiet, easily missed way. Now it's more obvious, but he can still go to lengths to cover it up at school, so much so I don't always spot it. We recently went to look at his new classroom before the start of term and he seemed very happy, only for him to cry and hit me as soon as we left the school gates.

Signs of anxiety generally may be nail-biting, finger-picking, stomach aches, feeling sick, going to the toilet lots, controlling behaviour, looking at the clock frequently, not settling or concentrating, not laughing, looking lost. The child's sensory difficulties might become more intense when they are anxious. They might not realise that what they are feeling is anxiety, so you might have to point out to them that they look worried, encouraging them to label it.

Katie Buckingham, an autistic woman and founder-director of Altruist Enterprises, a social enterprise that helps schools and other organisations to prevent, identify and tackle stress among pupils and employees:

'I had symptoms of anxiety from as young as I can remember, although I didn't realise that what I was experiencing was anxiety until about the age of ten. I remember what it felt like at the age of six: discomfort, feeling scared in the moment and also fearful of the future. I felt anxious about not knowing social cues. I didn't answer the register in school and the teacher would tell me off. I didn't have any friends so I'd walk around the playground on my own. I kept my anxiety secret for a long time. I described it as a pain in my stomach and ended up in hospital being diagnosed with acid reflux disease. Really it was anxiety. I think sometimes if anxiety isn't expressed it comes out in a physical way, like migraines, stomach ache, aches and pains in the legs or tingling in the fingers. I was diagnosed with general anxiety disorder at 15 and OCD at 16. I was diagnosed with autism two weeks before I left secondary school at the age of 16, which was a relief really.'

How does autistic anxiety differ from neurotypical anxiety?

In his book *Autism and Asperger Syndrome in Adults*, Luke Beardon explains that it is the intensity and the duration of the anxiety. He gives the example of an invitation for a social event: for many autistic people, the stress starts from the point they receive the invite. 'This can be the case even if the event itself is several weeks or months away,' he writes. 'The stress can then last for several weeks afterwards, so one single event can cause months of increased anxiety.'

Alis Rowe, an autistic woman who writes about autism and runs training groups as part of her social enterprise, the Curly Hair Project, answered the question of what distinguishes autistic anxiety from neurotypical anxiety over taking an exam.

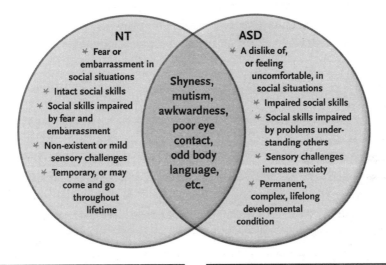

NT
* Fear or embarrassment in social situations
* Intact social skills
* Social skills impaired by fear and embarrassment
* Non-existent or mild sensory challenges
* Temporary, or may come and go throughout lifetime

Shyness, mutism, awkwardness, poor eye contact, odd body language, etc.

ASD
* A dislike of, or feeling uncomfortable, in social situations
* Impaired social skills
* Social skills impaired by problems understanding others
* Sensory challenges increase anxiety
* Permanent, complex, lifelong developmental condition

NT anxiety	ASD anxiety
* The exam questions * Doing well * 'Have I revised enough?'	* Disruption to normal routine * Different venue, different seat, generally a very different educational environment * Socialising before/after the exam * Probably not the exam itself!

Source: This graph is featured in two books by Alis Rowe: Asperger's Syndrome and Anxiety, Vol. 8 *and* Asperger's Syndrome: Social Energy, Vol. 5. *Both published by Createspace Independent Publishing Platform.*

Lessons in anxiety

Rowe recommends teaching children what anxiety is, how it feels, what it looks like. 'Then, help them identify what situations make them feel anxious, and work on reducing anxiety in those situations.'

When children get a bit older, you could explain that it is brought on by your body producing cortisol, a steroid hormone, which can make your heart beat faster and cause you to shake or lose the ability to think about anything else. It may also leave you feeling scared that something terrible is about to happen. Explain that the purpose of the cortisol is to protect you from dangerous situations, but that sometimes your brain makes mistakes and thinks a situation is dangerous when it really isn't. Explain that everyone is anxious at certain times.

Practical solutions for addressing anxiety

There are physical things you can help your child with – going on a run with them, jumping on a trampoline and going for a bike ride. Tony Attwood calls this 'energy management'. 'Regular physical exercise really helps with managing your emotions,' he says. 'Many ASD kids are leading lives that are too sedentary, sitting in front of a screen. They think, "I'm clumsy, uncoordinated, I can't take part in sport." It's really important for their mental health to regularly schedule in physical exercise. Relaxation time should be scheduled in too – things like yoga and meditation. Then you've got social tools, such as quality time together as a family or one-to-one time with a parent.'

TRANSLATING THE WORLD If you go to a playground, you may see an autistic child with his or her head under the merry-go-round, looking to see how it works. For them, explanation is especially important. If there's some logic that can be attached to an event, even better. Knowing what's happening can make a scary and unpredictable world seem less so. If your body is giving you the wrong sensory information and your brain has not equipped you to know some unwritten social rules, then you are not having the same experience as those around you. If it's not annoying for your child, it may help to keep up a running commentary about what your child may be seeing and hearing – if someone is cross in the supermarket, for example, then explain why. If you can decode and translate the world for them, it will hopefully become a far less chaotic place.

How to talk about anxiety

Doing this verbally is not always best. Ruth Moyse has found other ways to talk to her daughter Izzie:

* 'We've used a "Mummy and Izzie" book. We'd keep a notebook on her bed and she'd write to me in it when she was worried about something. She'd then put the book on my bed when I wasn't there. I would read

her message and respond in the book, which I then put back on her bed when she was out of the room. It removed the emotion from the conversation, as we weren't in front of each other, and built in processing time and thinking time. She prefers to use WhatsApp now!'

* 'Going for a drive is good because we're not looking at each other and talking is then easier for her. I have been known to take her for a drive for several hours, to give her the time she needs to organise and share her thoughts and concerns.

* 'We've also used a worry jar, which she kept by her bed. Writing down the worries got them out of her head when she couldn't sleep. We would pull a "worry" out of the jar each day and think about how we could reduce that.'

TALK ABOUT YOUR OWN ANXIETY When you are going through a situation that is causing you anxiety, be honest with your child about it. This shows them it isn't just them who worries or gets things wrong. It also shows them a way of coping with a situation that doesn't overwhelm them.

It's about your child learning 'thinking strategies that include having a calming, easing and reassuring inner voice', says Attwood. If you've lost your car keys and you have an appointment to get to, 'talk out loud about how you manage that anxiety and the child listens in, so that eventually Mum's voice in this situation becomes his voice,' says Attwood. 'You could say things like, "If I stay calmer, I'm more likely to find them." You could put it in perspective – is this a really big problem? Try, "It's OK because there's a spare set of keys or we could get the bus."'

Attwood adds that research is revealing the benefits of yoga and meditation to autistic kids under the age of ten. 'It helps to teach the child that when you're calmer, you're smarter. If you get upset, you may not make good choices or solve the problem. Remember your breathing; get your mind in a state where you can focus on what you need to do. It can prevent racing thoughts too.'

R, from Wigan:
'When my son is angry or worried, I get him to write down on a piece of paper what he is angry about and I think of something that is bothering me too. We read out what we've written then we scrunch up the bits of paper and throw them out of the window. It can help my son let go of the anger.'

The world is going to end!

Autistic people have a tendency to catastrophise – think things are far worse than they really are. If something goes wrong, then everything is wrong. In these situations, it's good to use logic and fact. If the child is worried about a parent dying when they go out, for example, you can talk it through: Mum's only gone to the shop, she's done that hundreds of times before and she's always been all right.

'Thinking about the probability of something happening – like a Third World War or me dying of cancer – works well for my daughter,' says Ruth Moyse. 'The best solution for me is to talk about all the possible happenings or outcomes of a visit or event, because then I'm prepared for any eventuality – almost!'

One example from my own family happened on holiday. The tap in the bathroom of our rented apartment came away from the sink while my son and I were in the room. Water sprayed everywhere. I shouted loudly and started to race off to get the caretaker, who had an office close by, but my husband managed to screw the thing back together. Panic over. But I remember once the situation was resolved seeing the expression on my son's face: absolute terror. We went out and bought an ice cream and he seemed to cheer up, but later that day he started feeling sick. Only months later did he explain that he thought we were all going to drown. This experience also triggered a fear of toilets being flushed – he thinks the water will overflow – which he still has today, over a year later.

'Humanity depression'

Contrary to the damaging stereotype, autistic people can feel emotions more intensely than non-autistic people do. 'I often speak to autistic people who say they feel overwhelmed by the emotions of others, as if they feel empathy far more keenly and this resonates with me,' says Laura James, an autistic woman and author of *Odd Girl Out*. 'I could never cope with my children feeling sad or disappointed and immediately wanted to fix the problem. I sometimes feel overwhelmed with distress at what we humans are capable of doing to each other. I've always thought of this as "humanity depression". It is an inability to cope with the pain of others. It overwhelms me, makes me feel unsure of the world and unsure of my place within it. The unusual way I experience empathy leaves me confused about "human relationships". I find it painful when I cannot second-guess how someone else is feeling or what they are thinking. Humans give out conflicting messages and this blows my autistic brain.'

Dr Stella Acquarone, child psychologist and psychotherapist, founder of the Parent Infant Centre, which runs interventions for autistic children:

> 'To be autistic means to be hypersensitive to emotions and other experiences. I always think that a baby or child with autistic behaviours is frightened, overwhelmed. They can't cope. It is important to reach those emotions that are so strong in them – fear, rage – and give them a way to express themselves, even if it's through drawing or song.
>
> 'Many of the children we see react to tension and it makes them frightened and unable to trust. All our children leave emotionally connected to the family and are better at understanding why emotions happen. How can a child understand someone else's emotions if they don't understand their own?'

Telling your child they are autistic

Psychologist Tony Attwood suggests that between the ages of six and eight, children come to understand difference, so if your little one is starting to notice they aren't exactly like their neurotypical peers or siblings, it may be time to tell them. The autistic adults I spoke to for this book all felt strongly that children should be told that they are autistic.

One woman, who was diagnosed as an adult and has worked with children, says:

> 'People talk about the label but I don't think parents and teachers always grasp that these children have a sense they are different anyway. They know it and other children point it out. You can't get away from it, whether you have the label or not. If the child isn't told about their autism, they will find another way to explain that difference. Some people will feel they are stupid, others that they're weird.
>
> 'At the age of seven or eight, I attributed my social awkwardness to my physical appearance, which tied in with what other people were saying about me. I couldn't fit in because of my size, my hair, my rosy complexion. In primary school, the abuse was very appearance-based. If I had

known about autism, I could have created a different narrative for how I was feeling. It wouldn't have necessarily been easy, but I'd like to hope now that an autistic child in that position would have access to information and an autistic community. The feeling you aren't alone is key to having good autistic wellbeing.

'There is a tendency to think of "coming out" as a one-off conversation, whereas actually it's a series of small conversations. Telling children they are autistic but not that autistic really doesn't help. It means the child will feel they ought to be able to cope and will then blame themselves when they can't.

'It's good to give your child a sentence they can use if people ask them what autism means. I tell people it means I have to learn things other people naturally pick up – learning to have a conversation is like learning a foreign language or how to play a musical instrument – and I explain something about the sensory issues too. It's invaluable to have this sentence, it takes away a lot of stress.'

Depression and autism

How to spot depression

The usual signs of childhood depression include low mood, sadness, tearfulness, irritability, insomnia, behavioural problems and fatigue. On top of these, an autistic child might display aggression, hyperactivity, decreased self-care, self-injury, catatonia, regression of previously learned self-care skills, increased compulsive behaviour and changes in mood in quick succession.

It has been suggested that the very able-seeming child who masks his or her difficulties and who people think cannot be autistic is likely to have more mental health problems than the child with complex needs and little language who needs lots of support. Of course, it could simply be that we're not yet very good at recognising depression in non-verbal autistic children, or those with autism and learning disabilities.

Dr Laura Crane, who carried out the Know Your Normal research on mental health with Professor Liz Pellicano on behalf of Ambitious about Autism:

'It is not acceptable for unhappiness and depression to be seen as the "normal" state for young autistic people. Indicators of the presence of a mental health problem can be subtle – this may make it difficult for the young autistic people (and other people who know them) to identify. This is a particular issue since young autistic people often reported finding it hard to express their needs.'

Practical support for depression

Tony Attwood suggests parents create a 'This Is Me' book. 'Make a list of your child's qualities – covering personality as well as abilities. Under "personality" you could put things like: kind, caring, brave, good at telling jokes. Under "ability" it could be: playing with Lego, learning to ride a bike, maths. Each quality has its own page and you record when your child demonstrates that quality. So there could be a picture of a Lego model he made last week, or his teacher's commendation on his arithmetic test. Under "kindness" you could write: "You asked your brother if he was OK when he fell off his bike."

'This is built up over time as tangible evidence,' Attwood says. '"Look, you learned how to ride your bike when at first you thought your bike was going to kill you." There's a picture of them smiling on their bike. It shows them: "You've faced challenges before and you've overcome them." In this way parents can help their child begin to develop a sense of self as positive.'

The opposite of depression, according to Attwood, can be arrogance – a child's narcissistic view of themselves as superior to others, something that can happen with autistic children too. 'Talk to them about different kinds of intelligence. There's IQ but there's also social and emotional intelligence. Because however good at maths you are, you have to be able to take other people with you and work in a team of mathematicians or scientists. Intelligence includes how to be a good team player and encourage and support other people.'

Helping children with learning disabilities and/or not much or no speech

The reality is we're not very good at spotting depression in children with learning disabilities and little to no language.

The psychiatrists we spoke to for the book said the way to spot depression and anxiety is to watch the behaviour in the same way you do with all children, but this might not help with diagnosing long-term depression or mental health problems, where there is not going to be a change in behaviour.

Janet Gurney, the CEO of Us in a Bus, a charity that helps people with profound learning disabilities and complex needs, has found Intensive Interaction (covered on pages 141–2) helps the young people she works with deal with the physical frustration, discomfort and depression that comes about when you are unable to move your body or communicate.

'It's counselling without words. It's about looking at how I can support that person to express themselves and feel important and feel recognised. To study the emotional language of a person who can't speak.'

Dealing with CAMHS

Child and Adolescent Mental Health Services is the term for all NHS services that assess and treat young people with emotional, behavioural or mental health difficulties. There are local CAMHS across the UK. Find your nearest one using this website: www.nhs.uk/Service-Search/Childrens-Adolescent-Services/LocationSearch/691

Each CAMHS usually has its own dedicated website giving information on who can refer (which means they get in touch with CAMHS and suggest they see your child). Usually a GP refers, but senior teachers – say a head teacher or SENCO – or a social worker can do so too. Parents can sometimes refer, but not always.

In order to get a referral, you may need to be politely assertive with your GP, giving well-thought-out reasons why your child needs help. Like all referrals they frequently get lost in the post/never happen, so you need to phone up your local CAMHS to make sure your child is in the system. As with all things to do with the educational or healthcare system, do not rely on things happening automatically and be prepared to chase.

At the appointment, you and the CAMHS team will need to work out a care plan for your child and what the priorities are, which is signed by a parent and a clinician. If a child needs treatment, cognitive behavioural therapy (CBT) perhaps, they will be put on a treatment waiting list.

Like most NHS services at the moment, CAMHS is cash-strapped and people can wait a very long time for appointments, even in desperate circumstances.

For this reason it's best not to leave things until they are critical. You can ask a clinician to provide advice over the phone while you are waiting for an appointment. It can also help speed things up if a school SENCO calls to explain why an appointment is needed soon. Ideally, CAMHS, the school and the parents should all work together.

Types of treatment

Talking therapy

The consensus among the autistic adults I have spoken to is that talking therapy can be problematic for autistic people. Talking therapy that involves coming up with practical strategies to help specific situations can work better, but on the whole it's too vague and some people will struggle to make sense of it. Professor Emily Simonoff, a child and adolescent psychiatrist at King's College London, says open-ended psychotherapy may be 'positively aversive' for autistic children who find talking difficult.

CBT

There is evidence that cognitive behavioural therapy, or CBT (see glossary for explanation), can be more effective, provided it's carried out by an autism specialist. 'Interventions should use more visual materials – even if the child appears to have highly developed language and communication skills,' says Simonoff.

For younger children, say under eight, it works best through the parents, she says. This means a therapist working with the parents, treating the child through them.

'I have worked with young people using CBT and it can be very successful,' adds Sarah Hendrickx. 'If it's carried out by someone who knows about autism, they will explain the process in much greater detail and accept that what is found to be difficult might not be to a non-autistic person. It's about having that respect, saying, "Whatever you think is tricky, I'm with you."'

CBT is not for everyone, however, and when the therapist is not a specialist in autism it can be a negative experience: they may try to stop a special interest that is a very positive thing for the autistic child, for example.

Katie Buckingham, an autistic adult and mental health campaigner: '*By the time I was 16, I was into my third lot of CBT with somebody who actually understood autism, rather than trying to use CBT to undo things that were just me. One of the previous therapists tried to stop me from being ritualistic in terms of my routine and that wasn't helpful. The final lot of CBT helped me to manage my thoughts and stop compulsive behaviours.*'

Medication

'Sometimes you need to try medication because anxiety or depression is affecting the quality of a child's life and the dynamics of the family,' says Tony Attwood. 'It can be beneficial when used cautiously, but it's one of the tools you use if none of the others is working. For emotion management, medication should be seen as a last resort.

'For anxiety, an ASD child might be prescribed Prozac or other selective serotonin reuptake inhibitors (SSRIs) [a common type of antidepressant]. The way ASD children metabolise medication can be different and they are prone to all the possible side effects, so you need to be very careful in terms of the dosage and monitoring them,' he adds.

'For families of children under ten where psychological interventions are not suitable, or sometimes not sufficient, we might well use medication, either on its own or in addition to psychological treatments,' says Professor Simonoff.

Usually medication will be considered after an assessment through CAMHS and with the involvement of a psychiatrist.

The family should be clear about who's going to administer and prescribe the drugs, for how long and how their efficacy is going to be monitored. While the drugs might initially be prescribed by a psychiatrist, the ongoing monitoring might be done by a nurse-prescriber. They monitor the treatment by checking whether a) the child is actually taking the medication; b) there is an improvement in symptoms; and c) there are any adverse effects.

'How long the medicine is taken for depends on the severity of the difficulties,' adds Simonoff. 'It tends to be taken for between six months and two years, with a gradual withdrawal. Anxiety and depression are conditions that come and go, so while the drugs are being taken, other forms of intervention to help the child cope should also be tried. Typically a child would stay on the medication until they have been symptom-free for some time.

'For children who are autistic and have ADHD over the age of five, medication is still the first line of treatment,' she says. 'With ADHD medication, one continues to take it for as long as it continues to be useful. This tends to continue into adolescence and sometimes into adult life. Most clinicians tend to evaluate it in a periodic way: the child stops medication for a week or two to see if symptoms come back.'

For kids with learning disabilities and no language, assessing the benefit of drugs is problematic. There are huge concerns that drugs are prescribed too quickly without enough thought given to helping a child with sensory processing difficulties.

Unpicking what is really going on is hard and takes a lot of time. For example, is the child with no language slamming their head against a wall doing it because of a deep depression, or because it's helping them deal with a pain they are feeling, or because they can't cope with a sensory difficulty? Which is not to say drugs can't be helpful and totally appropriate, just that more time needs to be given to understanding behaviours before attempting to eliminate them.

Recommendations from the Complex Learning Difficulties and Disabilities Research Project:
'Mental health is the most pervasive and co-occurring need to compound and complicate children's SEND (Special Educational Needs and Disability).'

Building self-esteem

'The happiest children are those who have been allowed to be themselves,' says Sarah Hendrickx. 'That doesn't mean they can do what they like, but that what matters to them is validated. If they want their food in a certain bowl, then the family should respond by showing that, if it matters to them, they'll make sure it happens. That sense of not being wrong all the time is crucial for a child to be able to grow up and say, "It's OK to be me," rather than consistently being frowned on.

'There is a tendency among parents to think it's not good for their kids to become fixated on something. Well, no one is 100 per cent flexible and everyone has things that matter, without which they feel shaken. The last thing you need is someone telling you that you are wrong to feel that way.

'My son is autistic and was born into a quirky family. He likes his mayonnaise precisely on a certain spot on his plate. We've upheld this wish, and others like it. He's grown up to be someone who is assured and very happy with himself. He's never felt wrong on the basis of who he is. Yes, he was naughty, and yes, he's been told off, but his core self was never challenged. We are not saying autistic children should do what they like.'

Another route to self-esteem is to encourage something they are really good at: it could be Lego, swimming or gaming. 'Computer time might not be what you imagined for them, but everyone needs to do what they love,' says Sarah-Jane Critchley, the programme head of the Autism Education Trust. 'Computer time might be their safe place.'

Good books to get out of the library to support your child's mental health

Books about difference and standing up for what you believe in:

Long Walk to Freedom (illustrated children's edition) – Nelson Mandela

Manfish: A Story of Jacques Cousteau – Jennifer Berne and Éric Puybaret

The *I Am* series (a biographical series looking at the lives of Rosa Parks, Albert Einstein, Martin Luther King, Amelia Earhart among others) – Brad Mettzer

The *Little People, Big Dreams* series (looking at the lives of Coco Chanel; Frida Kahlo; Marie Curie; Emmeline Pankhurst) – various authors

Women in Science: 50 Fearless Pioneers Who Changed the World – Rachel Ignotofsky

Stephen Hawking: Cosmologist Who Gets a Big Bang out of the Universe – Mike Venezia

Books on social rules, feelings and emotions:

Why Do I Have To? – Lavrie Leventhal-Belfer

Have You Filled a Bucket Today? (about happiness) – Carol McCloud

The Great Big Book of Feelings – Mary Hoffman

The Huge Bag of Worries – Virginia Ironside

How Are You Feeling Today? – Molly Potter

The Colour Monster pop-up (for toddlers) – Anna Llenas

The Emotionary – Cristina Núñez Pereira and Rafael R. Valcárcel

Iggy Peck, Architect (useful for talking about special interests) – Andrea Beaty

Ruth Moyse, an academic and autistic woman and mother of an autistic daughter, Izzie, 11:

'One of the things we have done is to encourage her to be who she is, rather than change her to conform. An example of this is her honesty, a trait we hold in high regard at home but that is frequently frowned on in complex social rules. Teachers expect pupils to tell the truth and yet may interpret an honest answer they don't like as rude. A teacher might ask: "Did you all enjoy my lesson?" And an autistic child might say: "No." We are teaching her the unspoken social rules of society, but equally we tell her that she does not have to follow them (as long as she does not deliberately and knowingly hurt anyone); it is more important to be true to who she is.'

Katie Buckingham, an autistic adult and mental health campaigner:

'Football helped me regulate my emotions. I used to feel anger and not understand why, and playing football helped me reduce my anger and anxiety. You've also got the buzz afterwards from all the endorphins. It helped me socially too. My best friend is from football. It was my mum's dream to take me to ballet classes, but I'd just wander off on my own. I'd kick a ball around with my brothers and then learned the names of the football stadiums for every single team. I've been playing since I was nine and I now play at a good standard. It just depends on what works for the individual person. For someone else it might be drama or art.'

Promoting resilience

Resilient children are better equipped to overcome adversity. They have the ability to recover quicker when bad things happen. Dr Siobhan Timmins, an expert in resilience, says that some children can naturally cope better, although it is not known why some children can more than others. The good news for those not born with this ability is that it can often be taught.

For children who can read, Social Stories are useful. Dr Timmins has written the book *Developing Resilience in Young People with Autism Using Social Stories.* She says resilient people:

✷ Are noted to be realistic optimists, seeing the positive side to any negative situations while acknowledging the difficulty facing them;

* Are usually flexible to change;

* Have the capability to self-reflect and empathise, as well as the support of a network of friends.

'All of these qualities are compromised for young people with autism, who in contrast may have a tendency to focus and dwell on the negative events in his [or her] life,' says Timmins.

The Social Stories in the book focus on developing an awareness of these key skills she argues you need for effective resilience.

Environment plays a part too. For autistic children of differing support needs, it's important to build resilience around skills and independent living. That could mean walking to the shop for a pint of milk and coming back with the change. 'Teaching them how you behave in certain situations is really important in building resilience,' says Professor Simonoff. 'Autistic children tend to have areas where they are really skilled and talented, so capitalising on those strengths is also really important in building long-term resilience.'

Carrie Grant, on the mental health problems of her 15-year-old daughter, Talia:

'By year 6, Talia was displaying more noticeable anxious behaviour – old or black-and-white pictures would terrify her. She would go on school trips and have to put her hood up when she saw these pictures. It was also the time when girls in her class started doing things that were a bit more grown-up and Talia felt left out, like she couldn't relate. That caused massive anxiety for her socially.

'Things got worse. Talia was asking me how to be happy – then when she was ten she asked me, "Mummy, can you kill me? I don't want to be here. Can you do it?" I said, "I definitely can't do that. Mummies and daddies can't do it, I'm really sorry."

'Secondary school was like throwing her to the wolves. The school don't get it and are absolutely no help. She was getting into trouble for not having her socks at the right level; teachers shouted at her. Getting a detention became a phobia. I was saying to the school, "Can you cut her some slack? I think this is what comes under reasonable adjustments." [Schools are obliged to make 'reasonable adjustments' under the Equality Act 2010.] I pointed out that they would widen a door for a wheelchair user but weren't prepared to make any adjustments for my autistic daughter – but it did no good.

'She started to get bullied and that was really bad. The bullying went onto social media. Two years ago, she did a massive self-harm and we ended up taking her to A&E and she went on suicide watch.

'Talia was in hospital five times. We'd asked many times before this for an appointment with CAMHS but didn't get any reply. I was phoning them begging them to see us. Then Talia ended up on a ward and suddenly they brought out the cavalry. There's no doubt that the NHS is built for critical care, rather than for preventive care. Suddenly we accessed the most amazing people through CAMHS and we've been seeing them ever since. There are now people who come to see us at home too. The services are out there but you have to find them yourself. No one is going to tell you where they are. They are secret. It's not until something really bad happens that they get on board.'

Looking after parents' and carers' mental health

The research shows we all need to be taking far more care of ourselves, reporting high levels of mental health problems for mothers and female carers in particular.

One piece of research carried out in Australia in 2012 by the academics Matthew Molineux, Anneleise Safe and Annette Joosten reported that some mothers described the conflict of accepting their children as they are, but also wanting a 'normal' life for them. Mothers reported a process of grieving, followed by the establishing of different expectations. Most important among their ambitions for their children was their social inclusion, happiness and independence, connectedness with other people, and the chance to contribute to society.

Negative comments about their parenting and people's misunderstanding about autism left some parents socially isolated. They felt friends and some family members didn't understand.

Another theme of the research was that of mothers as therapists – left to work out for themselves how to meet their child's particular needs, often by trial and error because they were not getting enough support to do this elsewhere. As a result, many ended up anxious as to whether they were doing the right thing or simply making things worse.

The experiences above are reflective of NT parents; autistic parents, in a similar way, may find bringing up their autistic child far easier than an NT one.

A lot of parents tell me that the stress is not down to the child, or their autism – it's the lack of understanding and difficulties dealing with schools and local authorities (LAs). I read a funny Twitter exchange between a local authority and an SEN mum. The LA tweeted that it was offering resilience classes to parents of SEN kids; the mum tweeted back that instead of offering resilience classes they could just support children properly in the first place. To which I replied: Yes Yes YES.

Marriage and autism

Anecdotally, it is frequently said that parents of autistic children have a far higher rate of divorce, yet the largest study so far on the topic, carried out in the US in 2012 and using data from 77,911 kids, suggests this isn't the case. It concluded that American children on the spectrum are no more likely to have divorced parents than non-autistic children.

Jasmine El-Doori (www.psychotherapy4you.co.uk) is a therapist based in north London who works with both mums and dads of autistic children. In her experience, most mothers at first diverge into two camps: those in denial about their child's diagnosis and those who go into obsessional mode, giving up work and devoting themselves to the child who needs them – the 'supermum complex', an impossible mission with an additional needs child.

'Mothers can very easily feel bad about themselves: "I want to resign from this job but I can't" and guilt tends to spiral from this ambivalence. There is an increased need for validation from the child, or dependency on the child's moods/progress, which tends to cause women to be more self-critical. I tend not to hear mothers of neurotypical children berating themselves after a long day at work when they haven't been with their child.

'A lot of mums of autistic children disclose a painful disappointment that their child cannot communicate verbally and a longing for them to return home from school talking about their day, like neurotypical children do. They perhaps feel that the relationship lacks intimacy because of this verbal deficit.

'The fact we can't predict the future is particularly hard to bear for some mums who want certainty. Mothers can withdraw from the child because of an overwhelming feeling of inadequacy.

'Some mums withdraw into this little world of them and the child as a

defensive manoeuvre. It can be that the mother's mood is entirely dictated by the emotional state of her child – a volatile emotional rollercoaster for mums. This leaves little space for other relationships as it's hard to navigate being emotionally engaged with a child without taking in or internalising all the emotional turbulence. It's a back-and-forth between these two states: mums need to be available but resilient.

'Some mothers get frustrated or feel patronised when everyone tells them what a marvellous job they are doing, when inside the last thing they feel like is Mary Poppins. They feel like a fraud and they often feel exasperated. I see some mums who were in denial about the potential warning signs of autism in the first years of life, beating themselves up about this as yet another failure.

'I do wonder if the pressure on mums to be constantly helping their child develop, through teaching and challenging them at home, can sabotage that fun playtime between them. There is a lot of self-questioning: "Am I doing enough? Am I pushing my child to be something they are not? Can I love my child for being who he or she is?" One mum said she felt like she was trying to wean her son into a world that was imperfect for an autistic child.

'An important question is: why does the dream of motherhood have to be shattered with an ASD diagnosis?

'In my work with fathers with children who have ASD or additional needs, I have experienced a proneness to depression. For dads, most often the focus of negative thoughts revolves around anxiety about the child's future. Equally, I often experience fathers expressing their suffering as a result of their partner withdrawing; she is totally absorbed in mothering her child and emotionally unavailable to him.

'So, the father's pain seems to be twofold: fears for their child and a loss of intimacy in their relationship. This highlights a real sense of aloneness for fathers, as women are more likely to reach out to their peer group or family. Interestingly, I've found that fathers appear to be more accepting of the quality of provision of services available and less distrustful of professionals, whereas mothers are consistently presenting as trapped in the cycle of "no one is doing enough!" Psychologically speaking, this might suggest a marked disparity between maternal guilt and the attitude of fathers, who appear less self-blaming.'

* * *

9

LEARNING TO PLAY

✳ ✳ ✳

'I don't really understand why it's normal to stare at someone's eyeballs.'
John Elder Robison, a US autistic author

This is my second attempt at an introduction to this chapter. In my initial draft, I wrote about the best way to teach your child to play with you. Months later I had to throw it in the bin and start again.

Because researching this book has made me see things differently. It's not just your autistic child who is having difficulties with play – it's you too. The parent, family member or carer doesn't know how to play with the autistic child any more than the child does with them.

So really this chapter is about teaching parents to play with their autistic child. I struggled to connect with my son when he was little and so I went on a course run by Dr Stella Acquarone, who taught me, counterintuitive as it may sound, how to play. Through the course I learned that I was tuning out while spending time with him. I felt rejected by him when we couldn't play and this hurt me; my response, much like my son's, was to disengage.

Another problem was the amount of energy I would put into trying to play. I made it hard work and therefore not much fun; I would burn out quickly. What I eventually realised was that playing can be a lot easier and calmer; I just needed to look at what my son was interested in and add to it. I'm sure I often annoyed or overwhelmed him by being too in his face trying to play on my terms, too verbal, too needy, too desperate to make a connection. And if I wasn't on top of him, I'd retreated.

I was working hard at covering up how difficult I found it to communicate with my son and was terrified people would see through me. What kind of mother can't instinctively do this? I thought. Every time I left the house – for a playdate, music class or to the park – I observed parents to whom it seemed to come so naturally.

I therefore spent much of the course, and my son's young life, feeling horribly insecure, obsessing about my shortcomings. My focus was on me, rather than on him and working out what made him tick.

Before the course and his diagnosis, I was sensitive enough to know that my son wasn't happy, but I didn't know intuitively what he needed. I was waiting for him to behave in a certain way – 'normally' – and didn't see him as an individual. That seems such an easy thing to do – see your child as an individual – but it's tough to change the (often unconscious but emphatically neurotypical) expectations of what you think a child should be, expectations that have been built up over a lifetime.

So I wanted my son to behave a certain way and I wanted to be the best parent – as we all do, to a certain extent. Well, he couldn't and I wasn't. Parenting is an imperfect art, meaning perfectionists are heading for a fall. But neurotypical perfectionists with an autistic kid – that's me – will fail doubly, for the reasons mentioned above.

If I could travel back in time, I'd love to tell myself that not being able to play with my autistic son didn't make me a terrible parent. Where's the shame? We were born different, though thinking we were both the same, and it took us a while to clear up the confusion. I wish I could tell that me how close my son and I would end up being. It wasn't that he didn't need me – he did, very much – it was just that neither of us could find a way in.

Vocal coach and TV presenter Carrie Grant, who describes in this chapter her method for reaching her autistic daughter. She is clearly an amazing example of a mother who intuitively gets it. As for me, I had to learn these skills.

I suspect communicative neurotypical children, like my youngest son, teach parents with less than perfect play skills how to do it properly, so it never becomes an issue.

Learning to play with your child means forging a closer bond with them, building a connection. And if they come to see that playing with you can be a fun and pleasurable experience, they may well be emboldened to try it out with others.

What does an autistic child at play look like?

* They may be able to amuse themselves for long periods of time on an activity of their choosing.

* Conversely, their attention span may be short for things they haven't chosen – you may struggle to interest them in these in the first place. Play may have a restless quality.

* It may also be less social: while a neurotypical child would be happy to have Mum or Dad play with them 24/7, an autistic child may be more content playing on their own.

* Play can look – to the neurotypical eye – repetitive, obsessive and functional. Toys that can be banged or spun are often popular, and games with flashing lights and buttons that produce sounds are like catnip. It may be difficult to move your child on from games such as these.

* The child may be fascinated by one small part of a toy rather than the whole – fiddling with a screw beneath a plastic fire engine rather than driving it, for example.

* He or she may not enjoy the imaginative play that non-autistic children engage in, such as dressing up or having a teddy bears' tea party.

* There may be a preference to line up their toys or group them according to colour, size or a category of their choice.

What do neurotypical parents trying to play with an autistic child look like?

* They don't know what is going on with their child, or know what interests them.

* They don't recognise the child's anxiety, sensory processing difficulties or notice when the child is trying to engage with them.

✳ They may copy what other parents are doing but find it isn't working. They are trying to do 'normal' things and it's getting them nowhere. They may blame themselves for this, seeing the problem as their parenting, or subconsciously they may blame their child.

✳ The natural rhythm of play you get between a neurotypical adult and neurotypical child – or an autistic adult and autistic child – is interrupted. This can make it hard for a neurotypical adult and an autistic child alike, who don't spark off each other. Communication is hard work.

✳ They might be depressed because their child isn't communicating with them. Their child appears to reject their offers of play and so the parent may back off because the rejection becomes too painful. Other parents may comment, 'I wish mine would sit still for that long', but they would give anything for their child to involve them.

✳ They may not feel close to their child – a particularly painful feeling.

TV presenter Melanie Sykes, mum of Tino:
'Most of the skills I used to help Tino, I learned from the time I spent at a clinic run by Stella Acquarone. We went there for three weeks when Tino was two and a half. Before then I had found it difficult to tap into his needs. When I was playing with him – or at least trying to play – I had a great deal of expectations. Looking back, I realise I was really more focused on what I wanted for the experience: I was expecting him to "perform" the way I wanted him to. I was missing the point completely. At the clinic, I learned to be more of an observer at first, then to talk about what was happening using simple language. The volume of my voice was impacting on him, so I spoke quieter and slowed down. I discovered that giving Tino the space to react was also key. I hadn't been giving him enough time to respond – the silences and long pauses were difficult for me emotionally, so I felt compelled to fill the air. I learned to step back, be patient, and simply to observe my child.

'Playing with my autistic son has meant finding a balance between what he is comfortable with and pushing his boundaries enough to challenge him but not frighten him. Over the years I have tried to get him

to interact with other children by arranging playdates, but the other child always ended up playing with his brother, Roman, because Tino wouldn't engage. He may like the idea of having a friend over, their presence, but it's hard to say. When he started primary school I tried to help him integrate with his peers by accepting invitations to parties, but this more often than not ended in tears. The levels of noise, the games, music, balloons . . . all these things sent him into a panic.

'Eventually I sent a round-robin email to all the parents thanking them for the invites and asking them to continue sending them, even though Tino would probably not be able to attend. I wanted him to know that he was wanted. I hoped they would understand, which of course they did. Tino always says no to going when we get the invites, but he is aware that he is wanted and that is important.'

The importance of persistence – children's mental health charity YoungMinds:

'It is very important for a child to feel attached to their parent or carer. If they are, they are more likely to seek help, which helps with the containment of anxiety, capacity to tolerate uncertainty and trust. The best advice is: connect with your children. Don't give up.'

How can we play with a young child successfully?

You've turned the toy box upside down and nothing seems to work. From Pop-Up Pirate to Play-Doh, nothing seems to elicit a response. It's time for a change of approach.

Back off and explore different ways of communicating. Observe your child – do they turn and look if your voice is different, if you talk or move slower?

'Whisper, sing, slow things down and interact in a softer way,' recommends psychologist Dr Stella Acquarone. 'Sometimes the way parents interact can be too intense and this can feel threatening to the child, especially if they are a young child.

'Parents despair when you say you have to go slower,' says Acquarone. 'They worry this is how it will be forever. But it isn't forever – it's just about making the experience positive for the child so they want to engage more. The child then thinks, "I can understand what Mummy is doing, it makes sense to me." It's also about careful looking: if your child isn't looking at you, then what is attracting their attention? If you work out what this is, you can use it to interact with your child.'

As a means of engaging with a disengaged child, clinical psychologist Judith Gould suggests rough-and-tumble play rather than serving dolly tea or pushing a train around a track. 'It's not social, it's concrete, structured,' she says. 'You are making sure you are interacting but not in a complex way they don't understand. I feel some intrusion into their world is important.'

There is a balance, though. If your child doesn't like too much physical contact, gets upset or pushes you away, then stop. Listen to the intuition that tells you when to back off, Gould advises. 'Don't give up interacting but choose the right things. The child may be aloof, passive, cut off completely, and if you don't go into their world, they are not going to come into yours.'

So observe what your child enjoys and start there; respect their difference – that's the way to build closeness and shared interests, which is what you are hoping to achieve through play.

For children who seem cut off, a technique called Intensive Interaction (II), a form of mirroring behaviour, can be helpful. The technique was started towards the end of the 1980s by the late consultant psychologist Geraint Ephraim. Further developed by Dr Dave Hewett, a former teacher and academic who called it Intensive Interaction, it can be crudely summed up as thoughtful copying. Here's a brief summary of how it works, with more information available at intensiveinteraction.org. We also discuss a form of Intensive Interaction called Responsive Communication in the 'Interventions' chapter.

Intensive Interaction

* The three main II principles are to be really tuned into your child; to make sure you enjoy playing with them; and to be responsive. Turn off your mobile phone, park any worries or mental to-do list you may have, and ditch any personal agenda you have for your play.

* Start by mirroring your child: run up and down the corridor when they do; jump up and down next to them if that's what they're doing. Stop when

they stop, resume when they do. The child will almost always notice when the adult is doing the same thing as they are, and so a bond begins to form.

* Hopefully this will lead to your child wanting to follow *you*. To encourage this, subtly change what you are doing. Surprise them – add a star jump, for example. Even if they don't follow your lead, copying can help form a connection. This can be particularly useful for parents whose children need higher levels of support or have learning disabilities.

* Extend the play. Take two xylophones and two beaters. Mirror exactly what the child does with the xylophone, then start and stop to your own rhythm. More often than not, the child will copy you. When you stop, say 'Stop!' and hold your beater in the air as a visual clue. If they don't see that you have stopped, gently hold back their beater so they can tune into what you are doing.

Carrie Grant, a TV presenter, on playing with her autistic daughter:
'Talia came along and she didn't really talk very much and she stared at people in this profound way. She was completely verbal but didn't like to speak much. Talia would creep into bed in the morning and face the other way.

'In order to include her I began to use my hand as a character. I would say, "I'm just leaving Mr Hand on the pillow," and turn the other way, and she would lavish love on my hand. She was totally different to my hand compared with how she was with me. So my hand would say hello – she'd get closer and closer and suddenly it would land on her face and she would laugh and say "Mr Hand!"

'We could have really good conversations through my hand and I used it as a strategy to access how she was feeling. I would say, "Mr Hand, could you tell me how she's doing?" and she would share. She found it a lot easier than face-to-face contact. Bit by bit, she would do things like snuggle into me while still talking to Mr Hand. We tend to think autistic people aren't affectionate, but just because Talia wasn't showing affection and because her sensory world was getting in the way, it didn't mean she didn't want a hug.'

What to do if your child has atypical eye contact

We are very hostile towards those who don't like looking us in the eye. We associate direct eye contact with honesty and attentiveness; the opposite with shiftiness and deceit. This is harsh on people who simply find staring into someone else's eyes too intense an experience. Not every culture places the same emphasis on eye contact – some Native Americans, for example, would consider it an insult if a younger person met the direct gaze of an elder.

My son when he was younger would make direct eye contact with the people he trusted and felt more comfortable with. Family got the most eye time; preferred teachers next; his peers the least, because they were less predictable and he was not so confident interacting with them. He had very good peripheral vision, though, so no doubt was far more aware of things in those early days than I realised at the time. One mother, on The Art of Autism website, tells a story of her autistic child walking through a museum, not looking directly at any piece of art, yet later being able to draw with uncanny precision the artworks she had passed.

Not all autistic children have poor eye contact, but those who do can broadly be divided into two camps: those who avoid eye contact because it's so stressful or painful for them and those who haven't yet learned how to integrate it with communication – or because it's hard to concentrate if you are speaking and looking at the same time; they can only do one or the other: 'The visual stuff distracts me from the information,' is how one autistic adult puts it. The result, for both camps, is that whoever they are speaking to is unlikely to know it's them being addressed.

Some autistic people also say they just don't get the emphasis on communicating with the eyes. It isn't instinctive for them – it has to be learned, thought about and remembered. And this is just one of many components of communication. You start to realise why 'simple' communication can be anything but.

Most parents will judge how much stress it causes and, if it's too much, will back off. Yet if they are able to make eye contact, gently and lovingly, as part of a natural game, it may become a less threatening experience, less negative for the child, and next time they may be willing to hold the connection for that little bit longer.

Your child may never become entirely comfortable with making eye contact, of course, but you can teach them to fake it. Tell them to focus instead on the eyebrows or forehead of whoever they're talking to.

Robyn Steward, an autistic woman who trains teachers on autism:
'Autistic people do not always make eye contact. For some it can be painful. Until your child is old enough to tell you if it hurts or not, if they don't make eye contact naturally it can be helpful to just encourage them to look in your direction and remember there are parts of the world and cultures that see eye contact as being rude and their children go on to be happy, productive people. A focus on eye contact is not always essential.'

My child is tuned out/disengaged

Tuning out or disengaging is extreme non-listening, when a child seems unaware of parents, friends, teachers . . . anyone and everyone. You can call their name repeatedly: no response. They seem to have escaped to another world, perhaps because they were feeling anxious or overwhelmed. They're floating serenely in space while Mission Control sends messages into the void.

Whether your child is silently or noisily disengaged, the repetition shuts out the world and allows your child to focus on that one thing – a TV catchphrase, a song, spinning in a circle in the middle of the lounge – that helps them cope with anxiety. Tuning out may have a function for that child, particularly if they are battling sensory processing difficulties. Houston, meanwhile, has its own problems, because it's not easy being a parent of a child who is tuned out for long periods of time. Also, if the Eagle isn't landing for long periods, it's likely to impact on their educational and social progress.

There is some debate over how much you should let your child tune out, if that is something that's within your control. It is also important to say that not allowing autistic people to self-regulate can ultimately make matters worse as they gradually get more overwhelmed. Most people conclude a compromise is best: allowing a child time to disengage or stim, especially after school, while adapting the environment so they don't need to tune out so much at other times.

Over the years my son found it easier to make the switch from tuned out to tuned in, and gradually, as the world started to make a little more sense to him, the need to disengage diminished.

Ultimately the best way to keep a child tuned in is to tackle their sensory challenges; offer them a predictable routine; make them feel safe; try to keep their anxiety under control, or at least not perpetually ratcheted up to 11; ensure there is lots of structure to their day, and try to play with them lots, if you are both enjoying it, so they know how important they are to you. This checklist applies to home as much as to nursery or school. Ticking all the boxes is no mean feat, though, and can take years to achieve.

It is also worth noting that neurotypical people zone out quite a bit too – when I'm anxious I sometimes start singing or talking to myself. I retreat into my own head and am not engaging with others. One reason why autistic people tune out more is they have more to be anxious about.

What can cause a child to tune out?

* Negative emotions: anger, anxiety, boredom.

* Sensory processing difficulties (see the chapter on 'Sensory differences').

* Tiredness. Everyday life can be exhausting for autistic children trying to process the world around them, and the effort it takes to socialise can be even more energy-consuming.

* Unpredictability. An example: a boy goes on a school trip by coach. He sits on a particular seat on the way there but boards the coach for the return journey to find another boy sitting in his place. This is difficult for him to cope with, so he tunes out.

Ways to change the environment

* Take your child somewhere less noisy / visually stimulating / distracting.

* Use simple, direct language rather than long sentences. Even highly verbal autistic kids can struggle to take in lots of verbal information.

* Depending on the nature of your child's sensory processing difficulties, deep pressure can provide them with sensory feedback that calms the body and mind. Try hugs or rolling them up tightly in a duvet, for example. My son has always enjoyed being squashed under the sofa cushions.

* Structured games.

Some general advice for playtime with young children

'Some children are completely indifferent and oblivious to social contact and communication,' advises Rina Picciotto. 'Others feel threatened and are made very anxious by it. In both scenarios, children want to keep complete control of their own actions, either to pursue rewarding goals – such as lining up their trains – without being interrupted, or to do anything to keep others, with their threatening intrusions, at bay.'

When you play a game, the way you go about it is as important as the game itself. Picciotto recommends:

* Playing for only a minute or two at first, so it can be tolerated.

* Make it quick and easy if you are taking turns.

* Be as kind as you can be when using your voice.

* Pretend your child has put everything in the bag to 'finish' even if you have done most of the work. Now praise them for it.

* Give them lots of downtime.

The aim is to help your child see that such joint games might be fun; that they lived through it and came out the other end unscathed; that sharing might not be so scary. It also can extend a child's interests beyond the rigid parameters they have set themselves and make them more open to a new game or idea next time. This kind of parental taking control will hopefully eventually result in your child accepting other forms of social contact – though there is no guarantee as to how long this may take – and, ultimately, information, conversations and affection.

Control

Some autistic children want to be in control of as much as they can – it's a natural response to high levels of anxiety and fear. If they aren't encouraged, with love, to go just beyond their comfort zones, then they can end up boxed in, never going out, restricting themselves to one sort of toy, or having meltdowns if they cannot do everything on their terms.

'It helps if you, as a parent, can distinguish what is genuine fear and distress from a strong desire to control everything by force of will, and anger when this doesn't happen,' says Rina Picciotto. 'Often temper is shown by crying but it is usually a different kind of crying from fear or distress. Try to feel the difference. At some point the penny drops: our sweet and lovely little one can also be a control-freak tyrant.'

Parent, who is a SALT, of an autistic boy, three, who lives in Cardiff:
'Toys might not work but bumping down the stairs with them, cooking, tickling or chasing games might. Children with autism have to be rewarded and the reward has to be quick, at least to begin with.

'A good trick is to put the toys in a jar they can't open so the child has to ask you to open it, otherwise they'll walk away with the toy and turn their back on you. You have to use little tricks like this so they begin to think, "This adult means something to me, we can have fun together."

'Using timers can be helpful. My son's tolerance for a task is better if he can see that it is finite. Autistic children often don't think things are ever going to end – if they know a task is going to end, they cope better with going with your agenda for a bit.'

Ditch the music class

If your child is young and constantly cries, stims or hangs about longingly near the door for the duration of the session, stop going. It's too much. I wish someone had said this to me when my son was one. These classes were pure hell for both of us; he was miserable and I felt like crying, watching all the other parents sharing lovely moments with their children. Try to be aware as a parent of the powerful, unconscious pull to do what's 'normal', when going on trips to the zoo, to a museum, to birthday parties. If any environment is hostile for them, don't go. Make a note of the times when your child is comfortable and try to replicate those situations instead.

Parents' experiences

E, from southwest London, mum to J, seven:

'All J was interested in from the age of two was playing with the household appliances. His favourite activity was sitting on the kitchen floor with his face pressed up to the washing machine, watching the fast-spin cycle. His earliest attempt at making conversation with strangers was, "What colour is your washing machine?" I thought it was my fault that he didn't play "properly", and that other parents must be secretly teaching their children how to play appropriately. But whenever I tried to engage him in conventional play it was nigh-on impossible to keep his attention

'With the arrival of his hugely imaginative little sister – who engaged in make-believe play from the moment she could speak, unprompted by anyone – it really hit home how different J's early development had been. His sister has been much better than me at teaching J how to play – she forced her way into his world and wouldn't take no for an answer. From about four and a half, his obsession with the washing machine gradually began to wane . . . I couldn't believe my eyes the first time I saw him pretend to drive a toy car rather than immediately up-ending it to watch the wheels spin.'

L, from Essex, a single mum of seven-year-old twins, J, who is autistic, and L:

'As soon as she was able, L sought social interaction. J, on the other hand, was more placid. As they grew into preschoolers, I found myself having to make the effort to enter J's world: relating to him via his narrow range of interests, which at that time involved looking at shop logos and drawing dozens of houses for him every day. Looking back, I realise L had my attention more because she demanded it more; I had to make sure I included J and made time for him too. It wasn't unusual for L to be sitting with me making pictures or looking at books, while J happily spun round in circles on the other side of the room.'

N, who emigrated to Australia from London and is the mother of a non-verbal five-year-old:

'My little boy has always felt like a mystery to me. Looking back, since the time he was born he did not seek to interact socially like my daughter did. He seemed happy and content, though, and would giggle and play whenever we initiated. As he became older, around 18 months, he began to lose eye contact with us – that's when I became very concerned. His language didn't develop and he seemed to increasingly be in his own world. He didn't seem to have interest in playing with toys but rather would fiddle with small things. I always tried so hard for him to let me in – but I never felt like I could get through. He always seemed so busy and like he was always wanting to do anything else rather than interact with us. Sometimes he cried for what seemed like no reason. He was sitting happily and then his mood changed suddenly; I didn't know why. Sometimes he laughed so loudly and again the reason was a mystery. He seems to have a very private inner world and finds little need to share this with anyone.'

Danielle, from Bristol, mother of a five-and-a-half-year-old boy:

'Play with my son as a baby and toddler was difficult. I felt pushed away, like I was intruding. I felt a defective mother. I was therefore so deliriously happy when he started accepting me that I wanted to keep him happy while playing with me at all costs. I then realised that letting him take control of the game, or not enforcing when he had lost, wasn't doing him any favours.

'So now when I play with him I insist on the same things I imagine another child his age might insist on. I want to go first. I want to have the counter that is his favourite colour. Or I say, "That's not fair, you cheated!" I believe doing this allows him to practise these difficult scenarios at home, rather than encountering them for the first time at school.'

E, from north London, dad of a five-year-old boy:

'When I observed him at nursery, I would watch the other two- and three-year-olds who were constantly expressing their emotions. They would tell each other, "I'm angry!", "Don't do that!" My son, however, said none of these things. Instead, he would tune out. In the end, I would

try to supply him with the words he was lacking. If a child stole his toy in the playground, I would say, "That's not nice! Let's ask that boy to give the toy back"; "Leave me alone" or "Don't do that". It felt odd, particularly as the other parents were watching me; now my son is more likely to stand up for himself and find the right words.'

* * *

10

SIBLINGS

* * *

'The majority of siblings grow up as well-adjusted, caring individuals who may well go into professions where they can make effective use of their experience of growing up with autism.'
Autism West Midlands, a charity

Sibling relationships can be fraught at the best of times. When I was young I always felt a bit suspicious of brothers and sisters who didn't argue and were fully respectful of each other during their childhoods. It's just not normal behaviour. One of the roles of siblings is to teach us that it's possible for someone you love deeply to annoy you so much you wish they were dead, then to forget all about it ten minutes later. It is one of the vital lessons that prepare you for marriage.

In a family where children are a mix of autistic and non-autistic, those relationships tend to fall into two camps: especially close, with the non-autistic sibling feeling protective of and showing unusual degrees of patience towards the autistic sibling; or strained, with the non-autistic sibling commonly feeling irritated with, embarrassed by or envious of their autistic sibling – jealous that all the family's attention, energy and money seems to be being spent on them.

Whichever route they take – had my sister been autistic I would love to think I would have been in the first group, but I'm fairly sure I would have been in the latter – having an autistic sibling can teach you powerful lessons about difference and supporting people.

Yet something is sacrificed to learn these lessons. Watching interviews online of young people talking about their autistic siblings – particularly those with siblings who also have communication difficulties and high support needs – these neurotypical kids do seem oddly mature. Clearly, they've had to grow up faster. And the siblings I've spoken to have expressed the difference they felt growing up among peers who didn't have an autistic sibling. It isolated them. I can understand this to a degree. I remember feeling that way at school in the 1980s, when the point of difference between me and friends was the fact I had divorced parents (weirdly, I was the only one in my class whose parents had overtly gone their separate ways). It doesn't seem like such a big deal these days, but it didn't feel that way to me at the time.

Now my son is seven and his younger brother two, I watch them and wonder how their relationship will develop. So far the dynamic seems to be hero-worship (the two-year-old) meets irritation (the seven-year-old). I like to think that's pretty typical for their ages, but I don't really know how it is for other families. I'm hoping for that weirdly harmonious type of relationship, but preparing myself for the other sort too.

NB: For clarity, in this chapter, we will refer to the non-autistic sibling and the autistic brother or sister.

Things that are not easy for siblings

* Siblings struggle with angry feelings towards the brother or sister who spoils games, destroys possessions, makes noise and a mess, and can cause the family embarrassment out and about. They may also feel guilty about having these emotions. This can result in frustration, possible aggression or withdrawal, and great sadness and regret about having to live with this disability.

* They may not want to bring friends home, have their brother or sister attend the same school as them, or admit to their peer group that their family is different.

* It is very frustrating for siblings to have family outings curtailed, and for parents to refuse to go to events that might cause stress or anxiety for the child with autism when it would be fun for others, e.g. school fete, birthday party.

* This can cause a sense of family fragmentation, as parents try to divide their time between the person with autism and siblings. There may be resentment that they cannot be a 'normal' family and do the things other families take for granted.

* This may also result from a feeling that they are 'second best' because they have to compete for parental time and attention. Often a lot of time and energy is devoted to the child with autism, and a sibling may feel that they are never given priority.

* Equally, they feel they are supposed to be understanding and supportive because their brother or sister has autism. The siblings' own behaviour may deteriorate as an attention-seeking strategy, or they might underachieve at school. Or they may go the other way: they may feel they have to be good at everything to counteract the difficulties caused to their parents by the brother or sister with autism.

* They may worry about parents not coping and the family splitting up, so they may keep their own worries about schoolwork, bullying or friendships to themselves.

* Siblings often find themselves helping parents with the difficulties their brother or sister causes and may find themselves in the role of a young carer. This may provoke resentment.

* Although they may not express their concerns, for fear of causing anxiety for their parents, they often worry about the future. They may be concerned about the likelihood of having an autistic child themselves, or about what will happen when their parents die.

* They may feel a sense of unfairness that certain rules don't seem to apply to their autistic brother or sister.

Source: The Charity Autism West Midlands.

The positives

* Having fun playing with them – enjoying the way they play.

* Feeling caring, protective and proud.

* Developing tolerance and empathy for others.

* Opportunities for learning new skills – communication techniques, parenting skills, advocacy skills.

* Enjoying teaching new skills to their brother or sister.

* Surprise benefits, such as getting to the front of the queue in theme parks.

* Having a caring or sensitive brother or sister that they love in exactly the same way as they would love a non-autistic sibling.

Source: The charity Sibs

The sibling's perspective

'What parents will typically say in our workshops is, "I've explained to my sibling child why his sister has autism and he doesn't seem to get it, or he forgets we can't go swimming because his sister will have a meltdown on the bus,"' says Monica McCaffrey, founder and CEO of Sibs, the UK charity for siblings of disabled children and adults.

Parents understand that allowances have to be made, but siblings don't see it the same way – they only see their sister or brother. The sibling relationship is essentially more equal; it's harder for the sibling to step back and see the condition like a parent can.

'Parents often come to us saying they get a lot of complaints from their sibling children about their autistic brothers and sisters,' says McCaffrey. 'The sibling might feel annoyed about the lack of interaction, the lack of eye contact, the fact their brother or sister is not able to engage in a game or doesn't follow the rules. Siblings can find this very difficult and interpret it as their brother or sister doesn't like them or doesn't love them.'

What parents can do

TALKING AND LISTENING 'For parents, the most valuable interaction to have with their sibling child is to listen to and acknowledge the difficult feelings they have, rather than explaining away the behaviour of the child with autism,' says McCaffrey. 'So rather than saying, "Your brother doesn't understand", say, "Are you feeling fed up that we're not able to go to the park today? It's really hard when that happens, isn't it?" This change of mindset for parents can be really powerful. It does two things: relieves the pressure on them to solve the problem, and helps the sibling feel their parents care about what they feel.'

For more help with listening to feelings and dealing with frustrations, the book *How to Talk so Kids Will Listen and How to Listen so Kids Will Talk* has lots of really good strategies.

What you shouldn't do

If you want your sibling child to feel able to share their feelings with you, the Sibs website suggests you avoid:

BLAMING e.g. 'Why didn't you call me outside when this was happening?'

If the sibling has done something to cause the problem, it is better to talk about helpful strategies at another time – not when they're upset or angry.

SOLVING e.g. 'Don't worry, we can buy you a new one.'

It is best to discuss a solution to the problem at another time. Although the problem may be easy to sort out, your sibling child still needs to have their feelings acknowledged.

EXPLAINING e.g. 'He can't help it because he's got a learning disability.'

Siblings particularly dislike it when parents explain away the problem because of the disability or illness. Most siblings already know why the problem has happened but that does not change the fact that they feel upset or angry.

Interview with Rhiannon Lucy Cosslett, a freelance writer for the *Guardian* and co-founder of The Vagenda blog:

'My brother is 24, severely autistic and non-verbal most of the time. He lives in a unit set up for young adults attached to the residential school he went to seven days a week from the age of 14. My mum clung on to the idea that she could make living at home work, but by 14 his behaviour deteriorated so much that they were essentially house-bound. She couldn't take him out because he became increasingly obsessive, which was a response to his anxiety.

'We came to the realisation that he needed to be in a low-impact environment. That's where he is happiest; he barely tolerates any stuff in his room.

'My brother left home two years after I went to university. I felt horribly guilty for going away. I felt like I was abandoning my mother to a very difficult life, though she was determined I go away and hid from me how difficult things got. By the time I went to university, he had developed epilepsy. There were occasions I would phone and my mother wouldn't answer – it was usually because he had a fit and they were at A&E.

'I felt very different growing up. I had friends and a good social life, but I certainly felt as though the problems that preoccupied my peers were not the things I identified with. You did mature a lot faster: I was essentially a carer from the age of ten.

'I never begrudged my parents for giving my brother attention. I felt, and still feel, very protective of him. It's like he's my child. Our relationship goes beyond the usual sibling one. He's so vulnerable, he needs protecting.

'My parents split up when my brother was 12. I think it's similar to when a child dies and marriages don't last afterwards. People grieve differently. My mum felt she was better off doing it on her own than with someone who was not on the same page.

'My brother was lucky living in a very rural community in north Wales. He was very well liked, loved, in the community; people weren't afraid of him. Well, some were, but most weren't. We got excellent respite care and support. People took him out for a walk off the books, to give my mum a break.

'Growing up I felt I had to be better behaved. I didn't throw tantrums as a teenager, I didn't cause a fuss. My mum had enough on her plate. A therapist I saw suggested I felt I couldn't be angry, but I am not sure I agree. I never felt like I couldn't talk to my mum. If I was in a bad way, I didn't pretend it wasn't happening. It was a fast-track maturing process.

'I think I've always been open with my parents about what was difficult for me. I remember once there was a parents' evening at my school. My parents both came and, as they didn't see each other much, they started discussing stuff that needed to be sorted out with my brother. I remember saying, "As this is my parents' evening, can we talk about me?"

'Our relationship is great. I saw him on Saturday. He lives two hours away on the train. My mum sees him every week. I find it really hard if I don't see him for a month. We FaceTime in between visits and he goes to my dad's for Sunday lunch. His carers have commented on what a close family we are.

'Although I really miss him, there's no way I could look after him – he needs a monk-like existence of living minimally. He's also tall; he's now six foot four.

'Sometimes I think about what is going to happen when my mum and dad are no longer around.

'What I would struggle with is whether my brother would understand where my mother has gone. I worry about that more than the burden on me. I don't know if he understands the concept of death, whether he would be very confused, though he knows he doesn't see his grandad any more.

'Now I know other adults with autistic siblings – they are the only ones who really get it. I find I can joke with them. The only time you can joke about the funny things that happen with disability is with disabled people themselves, or with their siblings or carers. There's a dark humour there. If you use that humour in front of other people, they get uncomfortable.

'I spoke to my therapist about the time my brother did a shit in the bushes outside Tesco. My therapist told me it was inappropriate to find it funny. And I thought: does it have to be this horrible heartbreaking tragedy all the time? Can't you see the humour in it?'

Permission to feel annoyed

It's important to give siblings permission to be annoyed, embarrassed or worried. As is explaining that you, the adult, feel those things too. Perhaps you could share some of the strategies you use to deal with your anger or embarrassment when your autistic child has a meltdown.

The main emotions looked at in more detail:

ANGER Anger is really common, especially in response to being hit. It still hurts, regardless of whether that child can help it. Parents should make sure the non-autistic sibling is given the message that hitting isn't OK. Even if the autistic child can't understand that, the sibling still needs to hear you say it.

For older siblings, it's a matter of helping them understand how their brother or sister thinks, feels or perceives the world differently, says Dr Isabel Jimenez Acquarone, deputy head of the Parent Infant Centre.

'They can feel fury or jealousy at having to put up with their brother or sister getting all the attention. Helping them deal with that, and getting that anger out of their system, means you can then look at how they relate. The non-autistic sibling can become furious and jealous, but both children need to understand that they can take turns, they both have a space, they both are acknowledged, they have different toys. It's not all about the autistic child.'

DEALING WITH AGGRESSION Parents have to protect siblings from getting hurt. If the autistic child is in a lot of distress and lashes out, come up with a plan the sibling understands that will keep them safe, such as going to their bedroom or calling another adult. They also need to know when they should call someone else in the family, or a family friend, for help.

Siblings who experience this kind of violence, or who witness parents being attacked, run the risk of developing anxiety and depression. Siblings who are on the receiving end of aggressive behaviour and who are heavily involved in care are the ones who have the most difficulties long term, says McCaffrey.

It's important not to let the aggressive behaviour escalate, and to seek help from professionals before things get too bad. In some rare cases the violence can get extreme. Parents could call the NAS to see what behavioural support programmes there are locally.

EMBARRASSMENT One of the main emotions your non-autistic child might feel is embarrassment. They might be embarrassed by their brother or sister's hand-flapping, involuntary noises or public meltdowns. The same emotion might mean they never invite friends home. To have their peers see the visual timetables, the special chairs, the obvious signifiers of difference would be unbearable.

Let your sibling child know that embarrassment is a normal feeling and that you know they find certain situations uncomfortable. Talk about the ones that cause embarrassment and find out if there are things he or she would like you to do to make things easier.

Explain to your sibling child that people do stare, and in most cases they are curious rather than being rude or mean. Some families print out cards with information about autism on, which they then hand to people who ask questions or make inappropriate comments. This can be particularly helpful where there is challenging behaviour.

ANXIETY One worry siblings can develop at quite a young age is about the future: who will look after my brother/sister when our parents are gone? Others worry about them getting bullied, or what people will think in the event of a meltdown. They may have raised anxiety levels regardless, for the simple reason that everybody in the family is under stress.

One way to help them deal with anxiety according to the Sibs website is to make a worry box. Find a small box with a lid you can decorate together, covering it with anything from football stickers to glitter and feathers. Put a pen and notepad with easily removable pages inside.

When a worry occurs, write it down, tear off the page and put it back into the box. At the end of the day they can bring them to you to talk about. If it is hard to do this every day, then make a date and mark it on the calendar when you can give it your time and undivided attention. Make sure you are not interrupted when you talk to your sibling child.

Sort out the worries together into things you can't change – for example, the fact that their brother or sister is different – and things you can. Then take action. Start by acknowledging the worries in the first group, trying to give your sibling child more information on why a particular thing can't be changed. When that worry is dealt with to your child's satisfaction, ask them to put it in the bin.

Next acknowledge the worries in the second group and discuss who is the best person to help alleviate them. If not having done homework is a worry, you can send a letter to the school explaining the situation, for example. If the sibling is worried they shouted at their brother or sister, they can say sorry or give them a hug.

Teaching siblings to interact

'Over the years I have struggled with the integration of my two sons,' says the TV presenter Melanie Sykes. 'From the get-go, really, it wasn't easy. Valentino's arrival was a great intrusion for Roman and he would often say to me when I first brought Tino home, "Put him in the flowerbed."

'Roman is now a teenager and struggles to come to terms with his brother's condition for many reasons. Of course he feels the loss of a "normal" brother and what that could have meant. He has friends who have brothers who play video games together and he wants that. It is also the embarrassment of having a brother who makes funny sounds and different movements. Tino also says really direct and funny things, and people genuinely like him, so he does draw attention to us. Roman is a private person and finds this uncomfortable. Roman is 15 and Tino 13, but Tino's behaviour and interests are a few years delayed compared with the average child, so the age gap between the boys feels bigger.

'I have no doubt that Roman would protect Valentino if he had to, and he always lets me know if he sees someone laughing at Tino because it upsets him.

'His condition has been named and discussed as far back as both children can remember. It helps Tino to understand what sets him apart from his peers; that he just reacts and sees things differently to other children and this does not mean he is less of a person. Equally, Roman has understood his brother has autism and what that means for him.

'It's all still a work in progress and developing their relationship is an ongoing mission. All I can say is sibling relationships are important, so keep the lines of communication open and never give up.'

Dr Tom Connor, an educational psychologist, says it is 'not uncommon for sibling relationships to be more fraught where one child is on the spectrum' but it isn't wise for parents to force the relationship too much. Regardless of autism, some siblings are never close.

If you do get a positive interaction between siblings, think about how you can encourage more, he advises. Where did it take place? What were they doing? Was anyone else facilitating the interaction? What had happened just before? The more detail you remember, the more chance you have that the same thing will happen again and more often.

One suggestion for fostering interactions between siblings is to have a list of ideas on the fridge of things they can do together. Whenever they get bored you can suggest one from the list. It could be listening to music, a karaoke session, dancing round the kitchen, tossing beanbags into a bucket, throwing balloons to each other . . . whatever they both enjoy.

Quality time

Try to spend a quarter of an hour a day – more if you can manage it – with your non-autistic child doing something of their choice. 'We find that when parents start giving siblings 15 minutes a day of regular one-to-one time, their relationship is strengthened and the sibling child's mood and behaviour improve,' says Monica McCaffrey. 'That small set amount of time is better than one uncertain hour at the weekend.'

As important as the time spent is the message it sends, however. While kids may know their brother or sister needs more care and attention, that can often translate into the feeling that the love is being dished out unequally. Get your partner to play a game or read a book to your autistic child – or tap into your support network and ask a family member, friend, carer or another parent – while you spend some quality time with their sibling.

Other things you can do for your non-autistic child

∗ Provide opportunities for them to meet other siblings of autistic people and share their experiences and emotions.

∗ Acknowledge the uniqueness of the sibling experience and their ongoing role in the life of their autistic brother or sister.

∗ Keep them informed and involved in decisions about their brother or sister. If you are looking at a special school or going to a SALT session, for example, bring them along.

∗ Try not to rely on them to help with caring, and involve the wider family instead if possible.

∗ Plan for the future, particularly if the autistic child is unlikely to live independently.

Look out for signs the sibling is struggling at school or emotionally. These include changes in behaviour, such as a child becoming withdrawn or having problems with anger.

Support groups

Sadly, there aren't many support groups for siblings, and what is available may come with long waiting lists. Contact your local disabled children's team – part of social services – to find out about groups in your area. YoungSibs, an online support service for siblings under 18, offers information about autism and coping strategies. There is also a chat room moderated by Sibs' staff. More information is available on the Sibs website (sibs.org.uk).

Telling a sibling their brother or sister is autistic

'It's about not making autism a taboo subject,' says Monica McCaffrey. 'Talk about it honestly and matter-of-factly. Say, "Everybody finds some things difficult and some things easy." Most kids under seven will take that information in their stride. At seven, most children start noticing *things that are different about other children, and parents often report siblings at this age asking a lot of questions about their brother or sister's behaviour or appearance.*

'At the same time other children in their peer group at school will be asking them things like, "What's wrong with your brother?" This is all normal at this stage of development. You should answer simply and straightforwardly when siblings bring these questions home, and practise role-playing how they'll answer questions in future. They could respond, "My sister has autism. This means she finds it hard to understand games but she's really good at gymnastics." It is important to help them feel confident when telling others about their brother or sister.'

A, who has an autistic sister and lives in London:

'I am the middle child of three – my younger sister, L, is 18 months younger than me and was born in 1969. She was diagnosed as having autism and learning difficulties when she was about two.

'L didn't sleep much and was prone to severe tantrums. She was also incredibly strong and caused quite a lot of physical damage to our home. Once, on an aeroplane, she was given some food she didn't like the look of and threw her tray in the air in a rage – God knows what the other passengers thought. It must have been exhausting for my parents, particularly my mother, and I guess it was probably pretty hard for my other sister and me to be around that all the time.

'At the time we didn't know any other families like ours. Looking back, I can see that this was very isolating for us as children, and I know that as a family we were always careful about who we drew into our close circle. It's hard to know how much it affected my older sister and me. I've always felt a bit different from other people and maybe that's why. I'm sure we missed out on a certain amount of attention, from our mum in particular.

'L is in her forties now, lives in a flat my parents bought for her about ten years ago and has a part-time job. She is able to mimic in social situations but she often misses the point a bit when it comes to conversation. She has a great sense of humour, though, and we do often have a lot

of fun together. We manage her finances for her and her flat is held in trust, as she could be vulnerable to someone unscrupulous taking advantage of her.

'She isn't really able to manage the maintenance of her flat and doesn't like having workmen in to fix things. She had a leak in her bathroom for over a year before she told us about it. It caused a lot of damage to her downstairs neighbour's property. She is quite resistant to being helped, particularly by family members, and can be quite resentful and unpleasant about it.

'It's a huge concern now that our parents are elderly and we are all getting older – I do worry about the future and how she would manage if we weren't around to sort things out for her when there's a crisis.

'Whenever anyone asks me for my thoughts about being the sibling of someone on the spectrum, I always say that I think it's important to give siblings the space to talk about their feelings and to acknowledge that it's hard sometimes. My older sister and I were often told how great we were and how understanding. I think that probably wasn't very healthy and it might have been good for us to have been given some space to talk about how difficult it was for us.

'I also tell them that they need to think very carefully about the future. They always say they don't want the siblings to feel responsible when they get older. I think it's probably impossible to achieve that – most people feel some sense of responsibility for a sibling who is vulnerable or finds life challenging. I think now my mother is 80 she is only just beginning to really acknowledge that my older sister and I will take on the responsibility in the years to come. I think it's important that the support network is as wide as possible and isn't too focused around the family.'

* * *

11

NURSERY AND SCHOOL

* * *

'If you understand that the autistic students in your class are just as complex and nuanced and intensely emotional and hopeful as you are, you'll do everything in your power to help them lead happier and more engaged lives.'
Author Steve Silberman

I'm not good at dealing with my son's school. I find it stressful and frustrating, and I sometimes get so upset over a discussion with the school that I end up begging my husband to take over. Then I micromanage him.

The stressful part stems from my overdeveloped fear of awkward conversations that may turn into confrontation. The frustration bit is that I'm often chasing people to do what they have said they are going to do but haven't, or compromising on what my son should be receiving when I don't want to compromise: I want him to get every single bloody thing on his EHCP, like the law says he should.

If I'm honest, though, the stress and frustration are also about my lack of control. A school is not a democracy, as my overeducated head teacher told me when I was young; it's a benign dictatorship. And when I really disagree with my son's school and am left with the option of liking it or lumping it, I retreat into a daydream of sending my son to a private school – which means I never have to lump it again. Instead, I pay extortionate fees so people have to reply to my emails, give me straight answers and support him properly at playtime.

Back in the real world, I am sure I drive my son's overworked SENCO mad by firing off emails before I find out the facts of whatever situation has got me particularly exercised. I'm also aware I'm not good at trusting the school – sometimes justifiably so, sometimes not. Every term I vow to cut down the rate at which I send these emails, but something important always seems to crop up that means I have to weigh in. Or I succeed in stopping myself, then I end up regretting it, because the thing I judged to be minor was actually pretty major. I then overreact when the next incident happens: it feels major, but it turns out to be minor. Why am I not better at telling major incidents from minor? I feel like everyone else around me is.

Luckily for me, the SENCO at my son's school is a mum too, and I think she gets that, even though my emails must be irritating, I'm doing it for my son. She's very understanding.

Schools aren't always easy to deal with, though. I'm guessing teachers can only find time to teach by employing ever-more subtle methods of keeping helicopter parents like me at bay. Which is understandable given the pressure they are under; it's just I wish schools could be more transparent. Parents tell me their child's school opts not to tell them certain things that would have been in the child's best interest to know – perhaps because they fear they will have to do something about it, or assume the parent will overreact.

Sometimes they feel lied to, but often it seems to be lying by omission: teachers not volunteering information.

I wonder if it boils down to confidence. Teachers are part of an education system where the focus is on keeping autistic kids in mainstream schools, yet no one has bothered to train them up about autism. How mad is that?

On the whole, teachers, head teachers and governors – even the governors designated to oversee SEN – know a lot less about autism than the parents they are having meetings with. That can't be a comfortable experience for them. They don't always feel they can say to you: 'I'm sorry I don't know more about this, but I'm here to learn more about your child. What do you think needs to be done?' How wonderful would it be if they did? Instead they hide their lack of confidence and knowledge, possibly even from themselves, by denying need. Some teachers are young and may not yet have developed that inner confidence that means not having to pretend you know everything.

Perhaps I over-empathise with my son. I struggled socially when I was at school. I think this is part of the reason I'm so drawn to autism and autistic people. I did not fit in at school and was always trying to work out the secret of being popular. I'm not good at waiting for my conversational turn and talk over other people; I'm not a natural listener. I can't always tell a story in a logical order and I still find it difficult to navigate the parental chit-chat at the school gate. I have had to pay a lot of money to a therapist to learn how other people tick.

I'm therefore not naturally equipped to advocate for my son and have to force myself to be assertive yet reasonable, when my natural instinct is either to pretend something isn't happening, so we don't have to have a tricky conversation, or to yell and shout until someone is forced to do things my way. My son's autism is equipping me with new skills of negotiating and I'm having to go out of my comfort zone – and it's bloody stressful. Now I come to think of it, learning to negotiate and stretching beyond your comfort zone are the exact two things I regularly ask of my son too. There's a fairness in that, at least: the whole family is learning hard lessons.

What are the responsibilities of schools and nurseries towards autistic children?

All maintained (i.e. state) schools, academies, nursery schools and state-funded special schools *must* follow the SEN code of practice (CoP), guidance that sets out their responsibilities towards SEN pupils, written by the Department for Education: www.gov.uk/government/publications/send-code-of-practice-0-to-25 #history.

The CoP states schools must use their best endeavours to ensure that special educational provision is made for children with special educational needs.

What does inclusion mean?

The principle of inclusion is that children with SEN or a disability have the right to be educated in mainstream schools alongside other children from their community rather than being educated in special schools. David Blunkett brought in the inclusion policy in 1997, when he was Education Secretary. He said at the time that it was inspired by his experience of feeling 'separated out' from society at a boarding school for the blind, where he was denied the opportunity to gain national qualifications.

Early years

The Department for Education has written this guide to early years settings' obligations around SEN: www.gov.uk/government/uploads/system/uploads/attachment_data/file/350685/Early_Years_Guide_to_SEND_Code_of_Practice_-_02Sept14.pdf

The introduction to the document makes it clear that early years settings, such as nurseries and play groups, have a responsibility to identify children with special educational needs and to involve specialists if necessary to either be part of the identifying process or to add support.

What different types of nursery are out there?

Broadly speaking, there are three types: maintained nurseries or playgroups that are funded by the local authority; specialist maintained nurseries that have experience of working with children with SEN, and private nurseries.

Specialist maintained nurseries usually have a limited number of places, which are allocated via the LA according to need. Playgroups are similar to nurseries but may be less formal, with less adult support.

Maintained nurseries, often attached to schools, can work out better for children with SEN than, say, playgroups, as they tend to be more structured and staff may have more knowledge of SEN issues. Maintained nurseries can be better than private ones as they have clear obligations; however, some private nurseries are good and fulfil these obligations on a voluntary basis.

Private nurseries come in different shapes and sizes. There are your traditional nurseries, which may be more structured, with adult-led activities, but they are often noisy and can have young teachers. Montessori nurseries, meanwhile, take a child-led approach to learning, with teachers facilitating learning rather than guiding play. (This is often the exact opposite of what a child with autism needs, which is adult-led structure.) Their nursery teachers can be older and more experienced, however, and some settings are calmer. Steiner schools incorporate a lot of free play, which again can be very difficult for the autistic child.

Identifying need early

While some nurseries are brilliant at this, many aren't. How good they are at spotting SEN will come down to training. And even if nurseries do spot a child who needs support, they don't always know what to do next. It may be that they don't know what their obligations are under the CoP, or how to deal with the local authority, or what money they can access to support a child. Nursery teachers often don't get the right support to know how to help the child best.

EHCPs and early years

Education, Health and Care Plans – EHCPs – can begin from birth. If your local authority tries to tell you your six-month-old will have to wait until she's two to get an EHCP, ignore it.

How does SEN funding work at nurseries?

To get funding, nurseries must apply to the LA. The onus is on nurseries to provide enough evidence, and their success in getting their hands on the money usually relies on them having observed a child for a term. If appropriate, the nursery can and should ask professionals who work for the local authority, such as a SALT and OT, to observe the child (the LA pays for their time, not the nursery).

If a child is due to start at nursery and they are already in the system – i.e. already known to the SALT or OT departments – then it's possible there will already be enough evidence for the nursery to apply for support before their first day. In reality, however, the vast majority of children, unless they have very complex needs, won't have had their needs identified beforehand, or the process of getting them support will not have begun. Most autistic children won't have an EHCP while at nursery for the simple reason that it takes so long to get one.

Nurseries with higher staff–child ratios – more teachers per class size – are more likely to be able to provide a child with one-to-one support until extra funding comes through, although they are not obliged to do this.

Parents may self-refer to the LA's educational psychology service – you can phone them up or email (you will find their details on your LA's website) or you can ask the head of the nursery to do so for you. You may also self-refer to SALT or OT departments, though not all boroughs are as good as they should be at making an early years assessment, usually because they don't have enough staff.

What does good support for an autistic child in nursery look like?

'We provide visual timelines and lots of visual prompts for the autistic children,' says Shapla Rahman, SENCO and manager of Jellie Tots preschool in Twickenham.

'If we suspect a child has autism, then in the first two weeks I'll be tracking them: where are they going? What's triggering their challenging behaviour and meltdowns? Every ten minutes I write down where the child is, and I can then look at what patterns emerge. Some nurseries are very rigid but we believe that labelling children "naughty" or putting them in the corner is wrong and doesn't work. Positive reinforcement is key for all children.

'We do lots of small-group work. One child in the group will be socially capable, someone who is a good role model, and the autistic child also gets to choose a friend to join in. We might have a small box with their name on it with items inside. We might blow bubbles together or pull funny faces or do some fine-motor work with a "find the peg" game, or look at stories together.

'We're working on their social communication, teaching them to communicate with the other children in the group: "Whose turn is it next?" It's easier for them to practise all this in a small group; they just can't do it in a big one. We might take them to another room where it's not so noisy, so they can concentrate.'

What to look for in a nursery

A suitable nursery might be somewhere small, calm and nicely structured. It's best to avoid the church hall-type nursery, which will amplify sound for noise-sensitive children. When you go to have a look try to gauge if the nursery staff recognise the importance of visual timetables, visual timelines and visual prompts. Try to get a sense of their knowledge of sensory processing disorder.

Take your child with you: I went to visit a nursery with my son, who couldn't speak at the time. He responded by anxiously handing me my bag several times, which was a pretty clear sign. We visited another, calmer, nursery and he sat down on the carpet and started playing.

'Every child should have a certain amount of structure; they should be warned before an activity ends or changes; and teachers should not automatically assume the child understands,' says Sarah-Jane Critchley, programme head of the Autism Education Trust (AET). 'Small things can have a big impact on a child with autism, for example if a teacher wears perfume or changes their washing powder, so they don't smell the same as they usually do. Nurseries can be noisy and sensorily overwhelming. There's a balance to be struck in providing appropriate stimulation and not overwhelming an autistic child.'

Finally, if your child is anxious around other children, you might find it easier to send them for mornings only, to see how they settle in. If they are very anxious, then it may be best not to send them to nursery yet but to focus on a different form of childcare (such as a nanny or childminder) or more specialist small-group work until they are better equipped to cope in a nursery setting. If a child is struggling, trust your gut instinct – if it's telling you to take your child out, then do so. I didn't when my son was small and I regret it.

Other things to consider:

✳ Nurseries that close during school holidays can be difficult for an autistic child to manage as it means a disruption of their routine.

✳ Good questions to ask a prospective nursery include what training the staff have done and whether they follow the SEN CoP.

✳ Also ask if they have had the setting and the way the nursery is run assessed for autism-friendliness by the Autism Education Trust.

✳ Are they open to working with parents to change things that aren't working or are causing distress? (For example, if a child finds it difficult starting the day with lots of kids already at nursery, can they arrive five minutes before the nursery opens?)

School

Mainstream state schools

The 'normal' school to which non-SEN kids go. In almost all cases, but to varying degrees, autistic children will need extra support.

PROS:

✳ The school may be close, so the commute will be easier.

✳ A mainstream school gives autistic children the opportunity to access a full range of qualifications, such as GCSEs and A-levels.

✳ Some mainstream schools try hard to differentiate the curriculum and make reasonable adjustments.

CONS:

* Some schools can be inflexible about accommodating the needs of autistic children, such as changing the environment to suit them, even if it involves no extra cost.

* Teachers often lack knowledge about autism, which may lead them not to believe parents, which leads to antagonism and parents feeling isolated.

* Pupils are largely expected to fit in with existing routines and structures. Children may be labelled 'naughty' if they aren't able to meet those expectations.

* Some children who need lots of one-to-one support to cope with a mainstream school can become overreliant on adult help, which can have an impact on their resilience and confidence.

* If a mainstream school doesn't support its autistic pupils properly, that can add to a child's anxiety and exacerbate mental health problems.

Private, non-maintained, mainstream schools

Independent schools that are fee-paying and not funded by the local authority.

PROS:

* Potentially smaller class sizes, so less overwhelming; the teacher has more chance to get to know your child.

* Some autistic children like the more old-fashioned structured school environment, with explicit and firmly policed boundaries offered by some independent schools.

* Bright kids get the chance to be stretched academically, though the emphasis can be on academic success and not on the child's emotional and social wellbeing.

CONS:

* As these schools don't have to abide by the CoP, what SEN provision is offered varies greatly. They have no obligation to accept pupils with SEN or in terms of how they support them.

✳ A small number of parents do get local authorities to pay to send their child to a private school, but usually these are extreme situations where a child has had a terrible time at other school placements.

✳ It's unlikely an LA will pay for support – say a TA or SALT – if a parent has elected to send their child to a private school.

✳ While some private schools allow parents to pay for the TA themselves, some charge more for SEN pupils, to cover the increase in paperwork. Some run a mile as soon as SEN is mentioned.

✳ Many private schools lack awareness of autism.

✳ There can be issues around parents who are unenlightened (to put it nicely) and paying high fees who have concerns about disruptive behaviour. They may not make SEN families feel welcome.

Mainstream schools with autism units

An autism unit – effectively a small school – attached to a mainstream school can be a good compromise. Here a child can receive more specialised teaching in smaller classes, then gradually move to the mainstream part of the school if and when they are ready.

PROS:

✳ Specialist teachers, smaller class sizes. Some offer the opportunity to play with a variety of children with and without SEN.

✳ Some children spend the morning in the unit and afternoon in the mainstream school. Others stay in the unit full-time then can integrate into the mainstream school if appropriate.

✳ Your child will have access to other autistic pupils, meaning they feel less different.

CONS:

✳ The idea is that staff in the mainstream school benefit from knowledge shared by teachers in the specialist wing of the school, but sometimes the former aren't given time to do this.

* Children can get stuck in the autism unit and not be integrated into the mainstream school when parents feel they are ready.

* Some parents find the mainstream school, despite its proximity to the specialist unit, is not as good on inclusion as they had expected.

Does a state school have to accept my child?

It's hard for them to say no. Section 43 of the Children and Families Act 2014 states that a school named on a child's EHCP must admit that child. This is true for independent schools and institutions approved by the Secretary of State for Education under section 41 of the act. (Search for the school on Edubase to see if it has received this approval.) As always, it is not quite that simple, however. Before a school is named on an EHCP, the local authority must first speak to the school. If the school feels it is unable to support them, then the child is typically placed elsewhere, though some local authorities force schools to take a child, sometimes with very unhappy results for the child.

Special schools

Schools specifically for children with SEN. Some specialise in autism; others may cater for children with a variety of conditions but who fit in the category of having mild learning difficulties or a learning disability.

PROS:

* Smaller class sizes, trained staff, an autism-friendly environment and a very flexible approach to learning.

* Social skills are taught more intensively. There will be more SALT and OT.

* Some kids who have had an awful time at a mainstream school can flourish once they are in an autism-friendly environment with other SEN children.

CONS:

* Specialist schools can be located quite a distance from the child's home, and if the LA is paying for the transport, cost-cutting exercises can mean drivers change frequently.

* Some more academically able children may not be able to access a broad curriculum. It is unlikely that they will do GCSEs at a special school; instead, they will pursue independent living qualifications, focusing on personal and social skills. Some special schools now offer 'dual placements', which means some lessons or exams are carried out at a local mainstream school with support. This can be extended to visiting the mainstream school for playtime, again with support.

* If you have a sociable child in a small class of children who are less keen to interact, they may feel hurt by having their advances rejected and may not be stretched socially. There are more boys in special schools, so girls may struggle to make female friendships.

Not in any school

Some school-aged pupils are at home because they have been excluded from school, they refuse to go, or their parents have taken them out as their child is very unhappy and/or their needs are not being met. This is a big issue: the latest figures show that 4,050 children with statements or EHCPs are without a school. These children are meant to be eligible for a tuition service offered by the local authority, but this is usually offered part-time and seen as a short-term measure. There is more information on home education later on in this chapter.

Kerry Sternstein is head teacher at TreeHouse School, a specialist school for young people with complex autistic needs, which was set up by the charity Ambitious about Autism. She has worked in both mainstream and special schools.

'In special schools you may have a maximum of ten pupils in a class supported by at least two additional adults. When you are talking about a school for pupils with more complex and severe autistic needs, similar to TreeHouse, classes will be considerably smaller, maybe a maximum of

six pupils in the class, with one-to-one support, additional to the teacher, and in extreme cases two-to-one support.

'In a mainstream school, pupils will generally follow the national curriculum, with some SEN pupils experiencing a modified version. They can be streamed into high, medium and low attainers for their learning.

'In a special school, the curriculum is more personalised. The teachers look at what the learning style is and interests to formulate the curriculum.

'At TreeHouse, pupils receive daily reinforcement in SALT and OT. In a mainstream school, a young person with autism may have anything from four to ten OT sessions a year.

'I see inclusion in terms of the modification of the environment to suit the pupils. Special schools are all about accessibility and inclusion. Mainstream schools have pressures and demands that make inclusion of SEN pupils more challenging.

'Mainstream schools may be more suitable for young people on the higher-functioning end of the autism spectrum, who can verbally self-regulate their anxieties, engage in learning and use higher-level social communication skills. They may be less stressed in social areas such as the playground and the canteen. They may be academically on a par with their peers, can focus in class with support and are likely to head to a computer room at lunchtime.'

Choosing the right school

Some mainstream schools are autism-friendly, some special schools get the basics wrong, so you'll need to check things out for yourself. Get advice from the professionals you are working with as well as autism parents in the area – they may be able to point you towards the most autism-friendly schools. If you are thinking of sending your child to a particular school, speak to another autism parent there for their thoughts.

It's difficult establishing the school's culture from a single visit. The attitude towards and awareness of autism of the head teacher is probably the biggest factor. You need a school that is going to be open-minded when things aren't working and work with you to find a solution, rather than one where the staff close ranks or one that doesn't involve you in decisions. This can be hard to gauge before you start school, of course, but asking some direct questions might help.

GOOD QUESTIONS TO ASK YOUR CHILD'S PROSPECTIVE MAINSTREAM SCHOOL

* What autism training have the teaching and support staff received, including the head teacher and governors?

* Are there structured activities during playtime?

* What adjustments has the school made for autistic children in the past year's intake?

* How has the school's environment been adapted for autistic pupils?

* What communication do they think is reasonable between parents and school?

* What is their behavioural policy and how flexible is it for autistic students?

* Is the SENCO part of the senior leadership team?

* Detail a few scenarios your child finds difficult and ask the school how they would deal with them.

QUESTIONS FOR A SPECIAL SCHOOL

* What is the staff–pupil ratio?

* How much time do the children get individually with the teacher?

* What is the curriculum and focus of the work?

* What is the peer group of your child's year likely to be?

* How does the school differentiate the learning of each pupil?

* Are there opportunities for spending time with pupils not on the spectrum?

* Which interventions are on offer and what resources are available?

* Are the interventions one-to-one or in a group?

* What teaching approaches are used?

The Autism Education Trust has a good guide to choosing a school: www.aet-traininghubs.org.uk/wp-content/uploads/2014/07/parent_carers_guide_A4_NEW.pdf

> **R, a 21-year-old autistic woman:**
> *'At primary school I remember that I was clever for my age, clumsy and not good at sports. I felt like the odd one out except at home. I was bullied a little bit and I trusted people way too much; I let my friends from sixth form use my money for their snacks, which they would promise to pay back and never did. Even after my parents told the school, "She doesn't talk at school even when she needs help – ask her if she needs help", they never really listened.'*

How to get your child into a special school

A child who applies to a special school will typically have an EHCP. However, it is possible to get a placement without one if the school agrees to it and the LA has given an indication that an EHCP will be issued shortly. If you would like to send your child to a special school and the local authority disagrees (potentially because mainstream schools are cheaper for them), then this is usually resolved through a tribunal.

'A local authority has to look at a special school as long as it doesn't amount to unreasonable public expenditure or it isn't unsuitable for a child's needs,' says Ed Duff, a senior associate solicitor at the Education Law Department at HCB Solicitors. 'However, LAs will typically operate their own policies in respect of which children they will admit. Typically they will need evidence of failure to progress in a mainstream school – usually this means at least a year of struggling in a mainstream school.'

If you want your child to go to or stay in a mainstream school, the law is on your side. There is a statutory presumption in favour of mainstream education, as set out in the Children and Families Act 2014. Unless there is clear evidence that the child's presence there is going to cause a problem for the other pupils, and it doesn't cost an unreasonable amount of money to adapt the school for them, to a mainstream school they should go.

How to get your child into an out-of-borough school

Plenty of parents achieve this, but not without a fight. You will need to convince the LA that no schools in your borough are able to provide an appropriate education for your child – perhaps your borough doesn't have an autism unit – and the out-of-borough school will need to have space for them. LAs usually oppose the request, meaning things are likely to be settled at tribunal. Don't be put off if you feel this is the right move for your child, though. It's easier than the agony of having to pack your child off each morning to a school you know isn't right for them.

The professionals you might work with

SENCO (SPECIAL EDUCATIONAL NEEDS COORDINATOR) The SENCO is based at school and their job is to support the identification of children with SEN, coordinate their provision, liaise with parents, liaise with professionals and keep a lot of records. An effective SENCO has clout – they will be a senior staff member and advocate for the child within the school. They will be confident enough to have transparent discussions with concerned parents and senior enough to tell class teachers what they need to do.

The school has an obligation to make sure the SENCO has enough time to carry out their duties. In theory, the individual will hold a national SENCO award. This is compulsory if they have been in post for three years or longer and were appointed after 2009. Some schools get round this by keeping SENCOs on temporary contracts, the result being that the role changes hands frequently and the SENCO's knowledge of the children is poor. If you are concerned, you could ask your school how the department's monitoring is done and ask to see any minutes of governors' meetings when SEN outcomes were reviewed.

TEACHING ASSISTANTS (TAs), ALSO KNOWN AS LEARNING SUPPORT ASSISTANTS (LSAs) The TA supports a child for a specified number of hours a week. How many hours and whether this support is one-to-one depends on what is agreed in their EHCP or what the school feels is necessary if the child is on SEN support.

TAs, overseen by the class teacher, earn the least money and hold the least status in the classroom, yet are dealing with the most complex issues and can have the biggest impact on the progress of your child. They deliver the OT,

SALT and physio programmes, help the child with their learning, work towards the goals set in meetings, foster their friendships and look after their emotional wellbeing. There's not really any limit to what you can ask from the TA if it's reasonable and your child needs it, but if the TA has too much on their plate there is a danger they can end up overwhelmed as everything can be heaped onto them.

TAs aren't always trained well enough by schools, so it's good to ask what training they have received or intend to undertake. Some parents pay for private professionals to train the TA in school (some schools are open to private professionals visiting, others aren't).

Current research suggests that having a TA velcroed to an SEN child doesn't do them any favours: other pupils are often unwilling to engage with them because they are with their TA. TAs who work closely with a child can often end up not allowing them to make mistakes, because they worry the child will feel bad about themselves. One head teacher of a special school reports seeing pupils recently joined from mainstream schools drop a pen on the floor . . . and immediately look to the teachers or support staff for help picking it up. Because they had such close one-to-one support from their TA, they didn't know they could and should be doing such things themselves.

TA support can also mean the SEN child receives less time with the teacher, meaning they are effectively being taught by the TA.

The wider point is that the wonderful work being carried out by TAs up and down the country is masking a bigger problem: teachers simply aren't trained well enough in autism.

AUTISM OUTREACH AND ADVISORY TEAM Many authorities now have autism outreach teams who can be brilliant and make a huge difference. They are specialist teachers who have experience of working with autistic children and can come into the mainstream school and advise, or exchange ideas and practice. Some teams also provide workshops for parents. They are likely to have a high caseload, however, so it's best to get in touch with them yourself. Be proactive rather than waiting for them to contact you. I use my fantastic autism outreach lady as a sounding board to work out how best to broach a particular issue with the school.

Who to raise issues with at school

If the issue is with a therapy – say, SALT or OT – then speak to the SENCO. Similarly, if it's a management issue about the TA or lunch-time support, e.g. you want them to get more training, or your child was left alone during lunch when they should be supported, then it's the SENCO.

If it's a day-to-day issue – you would like your TA to do something that day or from now on, or you are concerned something isn't working – it's best to go to the teacher. When my son was in reception I didn't understand who to turn to when, and would often go over the teacher's head straight to the SENCO on things that I didn't think were working in the classroom, which alienated the teacher.

If you aren't able to reach an agreement with the teacher, you could then approach the SENCO – colleagues usually support their colleagues, but sometimes they will take the point on board behind the scenes – and if that doesn't resolve things, speak to the head teacher. If the issue is serious, then you may choose to go to the head teacher straight away.

Meetings

ANNUAL REVIEW If your child has an EHCP, there has to be an annual review meeting – though actually this must take place every six months for kids under five. The meeting usually lasts an hour to two hours and the purpose is to discuss the progress they are making, and any issues or problems they are experiencing. The objectives of the EHCP are discussed – what's going right, what's going wrong? Is the provision working?

The SENCO is responsible for organising the annual review. It is good practice to give six to eight weeks' notice of the meetings, to allow professionals enough time to prepare their reports, but a minimum of two weeks' notice must be given. Any professionals who work with the child should be invited but there's no legal requirement for them to attend. They will still have to produce reports describing their progress against the objectives, though, and any changes needed to the provision or outcomes. These reports should be sent to you before the meeting.

The SENCO documents what takes place during the meeting and sends the paperwork and reports to the local authority's SEN team. The LA then reviews the meeting and decides whether the EHCP should continue and whether it needs to be updated. Either that or they ignore the paperwork entirely, which often happens too. Within four weeks of the review meeting, the LA should inform parents of its decision to maintain the plan or to cease it; if the EHCP is to be updated, then it must also send out the new version. Once parents receive the amended plan they have 15 days to comment, and if they are not happy they can appeal.

'The annual review is a good opportunity to get more support if you're unhappy with the current level,' says Liesel Batterham of the National Autistic Society. 'It's also possible to request an early review of an EHCP if things aren't going well. Using the annual review process, early or not, gives structure to any request for changes. There are legal deadlines that have to be met.

'If you're looking for big changes, like a change of school, you should get in touch with the caseworker to ask for someone from the local authority to attend the meeting. In most cases they don't attend but it's worth trying. It can create more influence if an LA representative can be there to hear the school's difficulties first hand, the emotion behind that, and how it's often affecting the whole family.

'Sometimes parents can feel bamboozled at these meetings, when all the professionals are talking. If you feel this way, you can contact your LA afterwards with bullet points of the things you didn't get a chance to say, and the LA should take these into account.'

Tips for the annual review:

* Be prepared. Print out a copy of your child's EHCP and edit it before the meeting. Highlight the bits you want to change, adding your amendments, or go with a list of bullet points you want to raise. Give a copy to everyone.

* Read the reports of the school and professionals before you arrive. Chase the school and the professionals for these reports two weeks before the meeting if necessary.

* Don't get sidetracked. The purpose of the meeting is to go through the EHCP, to check that it's still accurate and being implemented.

PROGRESS MEETINGS These are for children on SEN support as well as those who have EHCPs. The school should organise these meetings – it isn't stated in the CoP how often they should happen but once a term is good practice. Again, all the professionals who work with your child should be invited to the meeting, though sometimes you will need to check with a school that they have done this. The meetings offer a chance to discuss any issues and agree short-term goals – for example: 'Peter will play for five minutes a game that another child has chosen' – as opposed to the longer-term aims set out in the EHCP. You can decide a strategy to achieve these goals and how the goals are going to be measured. Schools should give you enough time to ask private professionals to attend if you want them to.

It is best to back up a request with evidence and information. Explain why you're asking for something so the school doesn't write you off as an overanxious parent. It's good to follow up the meeting with an email outlining what has been agreed and who is going to do what. In order to remember the points I want to raise in the meeting I use a Google Docs document to record things that occur to me over the term.

TRANSITION MEETINGS These take place at the end or beginning of the academic year and are designed to make your child's move to a different year or classroom smooth and stress-free. It's a chance for this year's teacher and TA to hand over to next year's, and an opportunity to build on the knowledge gained over the past year, such as who your child's friends are, good learning partners for them, where they like to sit in class, things that make them anxious. This is a reasonable request to make at the end of the academic year, but often you have to make it rather than schools offering it, and even then they don't always happen.

Here are some transition strategies:

* Take your child to visit their new classroom the day before term begins if the school is open. This allows them to familiarise themselves with the new classroom and to meet the teacher in a quiet, calm environment – though this could prove tricky for very literal children, who might expect the classroom to be similarly serene and kid-free the following day!

* If your child is likely to be using a new playground, ask if they can use it for short periods the month before they move. See if the school can assign them a 'buddy' from a higher year to help them integrate when they first arrive.

* Assuming your child has a new teacher at the start of the year, it's a good idea to write a brief guide explaining what strategies are working for them, what their trigger points are, any anxieties. Ask the TA to add his or her thoughts too.

* Ask the school to prepare a transition book, with pictures of your child's new classroom and TA, detailing any changes to expect the next year.

Extract from one parent's notes to a new reception teacher and TA

My son J is a really enthusiastic and cheerful little boy with a diagnosis of autistic spectrum disorder. His behaviour can sometimes be unusual and challenging, so I'm writing this guide to give you a heads-up.

Need for structure

PROBLEM: J really struggled with the free-flow environment at his preschool. He would flit from activity to activity without focusing on anything for more than a few seconds, often leaving chaos in his wake.

SOLUTION: His preschool imposed a structure on the free-flow environment by providing J with a timeline of activities when he arrived each morning. J can read and tell the time, so understands the concept of doing something for 15 minutes, etc. If he had trouble sticking with an activity, they would promise him a reward on completion (for example, two minutes playing with a spinning top).

Behaviour

PROBLEM: J can be utterly charming and well-mannered when receiving one-to-one attention from an adult but in a busy classroom environment, or any situation where he is not centre of attention, his behaviour can be very demanding. He is very self-directed, with his own agenda, and it can be hard to deflect him once he decides on a course of action. When in this state he will often completely ignore instructions and, if thwarted, can have a meltdown.

> SOLUTION: The strategy that gets the best results is rewarding him for positive behaviour and constantly reminding him the reward will be withdrawn if he doesn't behave as expected. At the beginning of each session, J's teacher and I would remind him that if he got through the morning without hurting another child he would be rewarded with a treat. This yielded really good results whenever J's behaviour looked like it was deteriorating.

Examples of strategies that might help at school

HOME-SCHOOL DIARIES A diary lets the school tell you about your child's day while you tell the school about their evening. Photos can be stuck in, which can help a child process their day, especially those with limited language or at nursery. It is also a place where parents can make observations to the TA or teacher about a child's learning and behaviour. It is particularly useful for children whose parents don't collect them from school and so have little contact with the teachers.

However, it is not a replacement for the email conversations and chats at the classroom door you need in order to get a full picture of how your child is doing. I ask to have a ten-minute catch-up with my son's TA each week, which we both find helpful. Some teachers agree to do this instead of the TA.

MAKING THINGS VISUAL Corinna Laurie, author of *Sensory Strategies*, a book published by the National Autistic Society, says: 'It should be remembered that anything auditory is transient. It cannot easily be referred to again. Visual, meanwhile, is non-transient. The visual prompt can be referred to as many times as is necessary to reassure the child what is happening next . . . no nasty surprises! Simple visual supports such as timetables, a list of who's working in the classroom today and a lunch menu will help. A simple whiteboard can work wonders as it can be updated easily if there are unforeseen changes throughout the day.'

Labelling the classroom drawers with symbols or pictures will help with organisation and also reduce anxiety around remembering where items are kept. Understanding the passage of time can cause extreme anxiety too. Simple visual supports can help with this: clocks and timers.

Here is an example of a visual timetable and a non-visual one:

Year 3					
	Monday	Tuesday	Wednesday	Thursday	Friday (LCP OT)
9.00am – 9.10am	Register	Register	Register	Register	Register
9.10am – 10.10am	Maths	Motor Skills United Maths	Science	Maths	Maths
10.10am – 10.30am	Whole School Assembly	KS1 Assembly		KS1 Assembly	Achievement Assembly
10.30am – 10.50am	Morning Break	Morning Break	Morning Break	Morning Break	Morning Break
10.50am – 12.00pm	10.50 – 11.10am Guided Reading	10.50 – 11.10am Guided Reading	10.50 – 11.20pm Handwriting	10.50 – 11.10am Guided Reading	10.50 – 11.10am Guided Reading
	11.10 – 12.00pm English	11.10 – 12.00pm English	11.20 – 12.00pm Spelling	11.10 – 12.00pm English	11.10 – 12.00pm English
12.00pm – 1.00pm	Lunch Break	Lunch Break	Lunch Break	Lunch Break	Lunch Break
1.00pm – 1.05pm	Register	Register	Register	Register	Register
1.00pm – 2.15pm	S & L	P.E Hall	ICT Ipads or Laptops	Music	Art/DT
2.15 – 2.30pm	Afternoon Break	Afternoon Break	Afternoon Break	Afternoon Break	Afternoon Break
2.30pm – 3.30pm	Talkabout Responding to Marking	PHSE	2.30 – 3.00pm Singing Assembly 3.00 – 3.30pm Spanish	P.E Hall	R.E

VISUAL THINKING AND VISUAL SUPPORTS Tempin Grandin, the autistic academic, believes that autistic people can be divided into three categories of thinking: visual thinkers; pattern thinkers (these people can be very good at maths and music); and 'verbal specialists' who are good at talking and writing but lack visual skills. Grandin is a visual thinker. She describes her mind as being like an Internet search engine that looks for photographs. She then uses language to relate the photo-realistic images that her imagination creates.

Most autistic children, but not all, will benefit from visual supports. In nursery and reception (the first year of primary school), this type of thinking is catered for as pictures are used a lot, but from Year 1 onwards, education becomes more language-based. Some children struggle to understand ideas that aren't concrete – if an idea can't be quickly translated into a picture, it can be difficult to understand. Others will be able to repeat an instruction, but they won't understand what is being asked of them.

Visual supports not only help understanding, they can also provide structure, predictability and encourage independence as they remove the need for a child to ask an adult for help. They can take the form of photographs, videos, real objects, symbols, written words, stick men and squares of coloured card (a green card on a desk means the child is fine; red means they need help). They can help a child feel heard and communicate – for example, they can choose a picture of an activity they want to do that day.

'Visual supports can provide a clearer channel of communication even for very verbal students with autism' says Barney Angliss, who works as a SENCO. 'But for these students, part of the pleasure in life comes from the rich variety of language we use, such as the word "exquisite" or "procrastinating". So, we shouldn't allow visuals to become automatic for students who would prefer language to be the default choice and visual support only to be used when they have lost focus or are unfamiliar with the context'.

STRUCTURE A structured activity has a clear start and finish, and children know what is required of them – a board game is a good example, as opposed to, say, playing in a toy kitchen. Free play is the opposite of structured play, and this can be intensely anxiety-provoking for pupils who thrive on predictability and rules. Now/next cards are good for structuring free-time play – basically two cards telling a child what activity they are doing now and what activity they are doing next. Visual timetables structure a day, as does a timer that signals when an activity is over – this can be helpful for children who find transitions from activities difficult. Structure can foster independence, meaning the child has to ask fewer things of other people.

PUPIL PASSPORT This is a condensed guide to your child, with an up-to-date picture, which fits on one side of A4. It's meant to be handed to supply teachers, TAs or anyone else who briefly/unexpectedly comes into contact with your child at school. It is the responsibility of the school to put this together, but you sometimes have to pester schools to do it.

Other good things to know . . .

WHAT IS A REASONABLE ADJUSTMENT? Schools are required by the Equality Act 2010 to make 'reasonable adjustments' for pupils with SEN. 'The school has a duty to take positive steps to ensure that disabled pupils can fully participate in the education provided by the school,' says Annette Williams of Express CIC, a not-for-profit organisation that supports autistic families.

Some simple but effective examples of this are: the creation of breakout or quiet areas; provision of fidget or sensory toys; allowing breaks during class; supplying pen grips; providing children with printed notes rather than expecting them to copy from a board; giving them a card to alert the teacher that they need assistance; and providing them with a laptop.

SENSORY DIFFICULTIES Corinna Laurie has some tips on getting the basics right for a child with sensory issues. All these are relevant to children in mainstream or special schools. The latter ought to have the basics right anyway, but you never know . . .

Addressing the environment
'The key is structure as well as addressing the sensory components of the environment and the individual student's sensory sensitivities. Simply reducing clutter, providing a workstation or privacy screen and ensuring adequate movement breaks along with visual supports can often be enough to remove barriers to learning.'

Key areas to address:

* **Lighting**: avoid flickering/humming fluorescent lights and where possible opt for natural lighting.

* **Seating type**: some children need to fidget to focus. See if the school can provide a wobble cushion or wobble stool, incorporate regular movement breaks into the day to ensure appropriate arousal states.

* **Seating position**: children should be seated away from sensory sensations that they find difficult. If a child has a sensitivity to light, they should not be seated by the window; if they are worried about being touched, then they should be at the back of the room so they can see everybody in front of them; if they are sensitive to noise, away from the whiteboard motor and the chatty girl in the class!

* **Movement**: starting the day with a movement break (see 'Glossary' for details on what this is) will help calm some children down and improve their alertness.

* **Emphasise personal space**: carpet squares or gym hoops on the floor are helpful so each pupil knows where they should sit. Explain that during certain activities there should be at least one arm's length between them and their friends sitting next to them. If a child is sensitive to touch ask them to go at the front or back of the line to prevent them being bumped.

* **Noise**: ask the teacher to be mindful of classroom noise and how uncomfortable this can be for children with sensitivity in this area. Use ear defenders but also see if the teacher can use a Chatter Tracker – a sound-level monitor that looks like a small traffic light, with red, amber and green lights to keep the noise in check. Red means too loud!

* **Time out/safe space**: absolutely essential for our overloaded children. Space to calm and unwind for ten minutes may allow a child that is disengaging completely to come back and pay attention for the rest of the day. A simple table with a blanket over it works, with a beanbag, and maybe some squeezy toys and music through headphones. Ask for regular timeout periods to be timetabled if necessary.

* **Teachers** should be mindful that many sensory sensitivities are exacerbated by our own behaviour. For example, clothing too bright/patterned, perfume/deodorant/aftershave too powerful, voice too loud, and too many words used when maybe just 'snack now, then maths' would be enough.

Get teachers on board

'If they can take ten minutes at the beginning of each day to address the sensory requirements of students by adding a movement break, for example, then the impact on focus and learning will be clear,' says Laurie. 'This will increase academic learning and create a calmer and more focused classroom. Learning won't happen without this foundation, but challenging behaviour might.'

Autism-friendly school uniforms

Marks & Spencer has a range of 'easy dressing' school uniforms, designed in conjunction with the National Autistic Society. Some of the adaptations include hidden velcro strips rather than shirt buttons and pull-up trousers, so children don't need to tackle zips or buttons.

Building independence

A child's independence must be built up in a considered way; it won't simply be magicked into existence when support is taken away by a school that has staffing issues. If a school suggests reducing your child's support to build their resilience and ability to stand on their own two feet, it needs to be cut back in a planned way rather than abandoned. As one parent tweeted recently, 'You don't teach maths by removing the teacher – why do this with independence?'

How to work well with schools and nurseries

It's best not to go to the school or nursery with a moan or a problem for them to solve, but rather with a request or a solution – something I've learned the hard way.

If something isn't working, state concisely and clearly what has gone wrong and either ask for something specific to be done or ask the school what they are planning to do about it. Stay positive, if you can, don't accuse anyone, and work out what are the key things that will make the most difference to your child. Your requests have to be achievable: if you produce a long list of things, chances are none will happen.

'The most successful parents are firm, know their rights, don't get angry and are charming,' says Elizabeth Archer, former policy director of Ambitious about Autism. 'If you get irate about something, people just see your anger, not that you are in the right. A better approach is, "This is not me being aggressive, this is me telling you this has to happen otherwise I will take steps to make sure it does."'

Some tips from the Autism Education Trust:

Make contact with staff early and make it positive
Contact key people before your child starts school and meet them regularly, as and when needed. Do not wait until your child has a problem. Parents who share relevant information help school staff to prevent problems occurring. Try to stay positive and calm, as discussions are easier and more fruitful when staff and parents are in this state.

Use an agreed method to communicate with staff
Agree with the staff the best method for contacting them and for them to contact you. This may be by email, by phone, by letter, by text or a combination of these. Before meetings it is helpful to write down a list of things you would like to discuss.

Keep your messages short and focused
Keep your written comments, emails or voicemail messages short and state your main issue clearly. Follow up with information about how and when staff can best reply to your message. If you think a short message will not work, ask for a meeting with staff to discuss your concerns in more detail.

Be clear about dates, actions and responsibilities
Parent–staff discussions often result in an action plan. You need to clarify who (teacher, child, parent, other professional) will do what (make an assessment, help develop friendships, check the arrangements for the school trip) and when

(every day, weekly, monthly). At the end of a meeting or discussion, it is helpful to confirm the list of actions and the date of the next review.

Be patient, but be persistent

Most school staff will try to acknowledge contact from parents within 48 hours, or sooner if the issue is urgent. If you do not get a reply, send a brief follow-up email or call the school secretary to ask to have a message delivered to the staff member. If you feel there is a lack of response from staff, then you can discuss this with the head teacher or principal of the school.

Ask staff to explain the reasons behind their actions and decisions

Allow staff the opportunity to explain the circumstances and reasons for their decisions about your child. If necessary, take time to think over the explanation and your response. If the explanation does not satisfy you, explain your reasons for this. Agree next steps for resolving any issues with the school.

Ask a friend, relative or a professional to attend meetings at the school

It is often useful to ask another person to come along to meetings at the school as it can be difficult to listen to what is being said as well as to think of the questions you might want to ask. Another person can remind you of what you wanted to get from the meeting.

Lucia Santi, head teacher at The Grove, an autism school in Wood Green, north London, and parent of an autistic ten-year-old girl:

'I've lived with autism every day for ten years and worked with it for 20 years. And still sometimes, a kid starts here and I think: "I don't know what to do." I think it's difficult for schools to admit they don't know. It takes a confident person to say that. I do sense schools sometimes go on attack and push parents away.

'Schools often treat what happens rather than looking at the cause of the behaviour. We get boys here who couldn't cope with big mainstream schools, the rigidity of rules and consequences. Some schools don't believe these kids have autism and the consequence of this can be awful. At the end of the day, how good a school is will come from the leadership – they are either inclusive or not.

'Some parents at the school I work in are difficult to engage. They *have had to fight all the time for everything. We tell them we are going to be open and transparent; they say, "We've heard all this before." Needing to fight all the time leaves you very sensitive – you don't know who to trust. People are quick to be opinionated about what you have or haven't done.*

'Dealing with schools is about picking your battles and looking at the bigger picture. There's a fine line between working with the school and being the parent whom the school rejects. You have to work with the school. You don't want to create ill feeling that will affect your child.'

Autism and education: the numbers

* There are at least 108,403 young autistic people in schools.

* 70 per cent of autistic children are educated in mainstream schools.

* 60 per cent of teachers in England do not feel they have had adequate training to teach children with autism.

* 35 per cent of teachers think it has become harder to access specialist support for children with autism.

* Autistic children are three times more likely to be permanently excluded from school than children with no SEN.

* In a survey of 1,100 schools, 82 per cent said they did not have sufficient funding to provide adequately for pupils with special educational needs or disabilities.

Autistic adult who was non-verbal for part of his childhood, writing on Twitter:

'I'm really grateful for my parents who kept insisting that teachers talk directly to me about what my goals were. Nobody spoke for me. If you're a parent of a kid who doesn't seem to be speaking for themselves very well, helping them to find their own voice is essential.'

Common issues

First off, it needs to be said that many teachers are brilliant and almost always well-intentioned, albeit overworked, meaning they are doing a lot of the things they need to do for SEN in their spare time. The lack of adequate funding pitches parents against local authorities and schools when really we are all struggling with the same issue: there is not enough money available to make what should happen, happen. Yet problems with schools are common. Here are a few of the typical issues you might face:

The school doesn't believe you

I am now used to teachers thinking I'm an overprotective or overanxious parent. It comes with the territory when you have a child who masks their problems. Teachers often don't believe in the phenomenon of the 3.30 time bomb – when a child behaves well at school then has a meltdown as soon as they get home, because the strain of holding it together all day is too much.

The answer to this is for teachers to receive adequate training – and on this score things are about to get better. Ambitious about Autism and the National Autistic Society have successfully campaigned for new teachers to learn about autism awareness as part of their initial training from this year. It's appalling it's taken this long.

Tracey Gaggiotti of autism charity Express CIC recommends that schools ensure each member of the teaching staff has completed the National Autistic Society's Making Sense of Autism training, a 90-minute session that is delivered face-to-face in schools, and those with direct teaching responsibility should be trained further. 'In addition, the school's best source of information on how a child learns is the parents – and schools should have half-termly updates to share expertise and work with parents,' she says.

Children who are passive or internalise their problems get less support than those who act out

Lucia Santi adds: 'You may have a child who internalises things, who isn't causing difficulties and, in a crisis, is introverted. You have another child in a crisis who shouts, hits and screams. Which one gets dealt with first, do you think? And are their needs any different? The first child's needs get overlooked because they are easy. If a child throws a chair, we'd all be in a meeting the next day, trying to work out what is going wrong, but the other child is doing exactly the same thing only invisibly, or at home.'

The school uses your child's TA for other purposes

This happens a lot. They might be asked to run a reading group elsewhere in the school, or provide cover for another TA who is ill. More subtly, they might be used as a whole-class TA, rather than dedicating themselves to supporting your child. Or it might be that the one-to-one TA who is supposed to work with your child on a permanent basis is also being used to deliver another pupil's SEN support.

If your EHCP states one-to-one support and that isn't being delivered, you need to raise it as an issue. The problem is often that within the EHCP local authorities have included a budget for the TA hours but haven't specified that this is for one-to-one support, usually in order that they can take it away more easily. This suits cash-strapped schools, which get to use the TA elsewhere. It's yet another reason to make sure everything is spelled out and nailed down in the EHCP.

Some situations where a TA is being used elsewhere are more acceptable than others. When it is not acceptable is when it leaves a child unsupported at a time they need support – potentially an unstructured time or lunchtime play – or if they are left for a long time and frequently. And it's totally unacceptable when a child is left in front of a computer while their TA is used elsewhere. SEN children who mask their difficulties and are more verbal than others are more likely to have their TAs taken away from them, for the simple reason that schools may not recognise their needs, despite the TA support being set out in their EHCP and the school receiving funding for it.

One mum, having found out that her son's full-time TA was frequently being used to run literacy groups, took to emailing the head teacher each academic year, asking to be informed when the school planned on using the TA in a role other than that of supporting her son.

If your child is able to tell you, ask them to describe their day, and note down the times they report their TA wasn't there. Once it has happened, say, three or four times, email the SENCO.

A broader problem is schools receiving money to support children with SEN and it being spent elsewhere. Speaking to schools and to parents, there is often a difference of view on how EHCP money should be spent. Worryingly, I spoke to a head teacher of a large primary school with a lot of SEN children who didn't seem aware or concerned that the EHCP top-up money – the amount budgeted for the child in addition to the notional SEN money – is ring-fenced for the individual child. Given the financial pressures schools are facing, it also seems very likely that money given to schools for their notional SEN funding – money that is not ring-fenced, so they are not in fact obliged to spend it on SEN – is being spent on plugging holes elsewhere.

Funding

School funding is complex, but it's helpful to know how it works so you know what you are entitled to. Here is a simplified version of how it works with SEN:

Early years funding

Unlike schools, nurseries do not have a notional SEN budget (i.e. a budget automatically given to them for SEN). However, if a child's needs cannot be met from the budget they receive from an LA, and an EHCP is not in place, early years providers can request a top-up from the LA.

Mainstream schools

Notional SEN budget: this is £6,000 per child annually. The school reports their SEN population to the Department for Education and the numbers are included in the following year's budget calculations. This means there is a year's lag in getting funding, so if a school actually has a higher SEN intake than anticipated the next year, there will be a funding shortfall (or surplus if the opposite is true). Heads and governors are free to make decisions about how the notional SEN budget is used within a school – it is not ring-fenced. However, the school should be able to demonstrate the effectiveness of their SEN provision.

Top-up funding: this is for children with higher needs – it is the money for EHCPs. The first £6,000 of the plan must be funded by the school from its notional SEN funding. The top-up amount is ring-fenced for your child and can't be spent elsewhere by the school, even for general SEN. Teachers and schools don't always seem aware of this – or if they are, it doesn't stop them spending the money elsewhere.

Special schools

Funding is £10,000 per place, and if the school is maintained, it can apply to the LA for extra funding.

The school assumes your child wants to play on their own at lunchtime

Do they really want to play on their own or are they unable to join in? As Alis Rowe, an autistic writer, points out in the 'What is it like to be autistic?' chapter, it can be very damaging for children who genuinely want to be left alone to be forced to socialise. If your child is socially wired, however, they need to be given the tools to do so.

You might assume that a school is the perfect place for your child to learn to socialise, and many people send their kids to mainstream schools for precisely this reason. Except, frustratingly, schools don't always have the skills to help children who aren't born knowing the social Highway Code. Two reasons why not: they are used to working with children who don't need to learn these skills, and they are incentivised to turn out children who can pass exams, rather than ones who are socially active.

Teachers can look at playtime through a neurotypical prism: that it's fun for kids to break free from the structure of the school day and run about like lunatics. They don't always understand that, for some autistic children, this chaotic freedom can be hell. It is the time of the school day with the least structure and the most social pressure – awful for anyone with anxiety and a need for predictability.

You shouldn't just assume the school has support in place over lunchtime, even if it is stated on your EHCP. Double-check someone will be with them during morning break and at lunchtime, as this is the time TAs and teachers take their breaks. Explain clearly to the teacher and/or SENCO why your child can't be on their own and why a vague promise of someone 'keeping an eye out' will not be enough to help your child integrate. Check your child can go somewhere inside and read a book if they want to, and that they know how to ask for this, either verbally or by using a visual prompt. (Also check that the lunchtime staff know they are allowed to go inside.) If the school runs structured games at lunchtimes, this can remove the need for a TA to be one-to-one with a child. But if you feel your child does need that one-to-one presence, be firm. Remember that many teachers have no idea what goes on during playtime as they are in the staff room. If your child doesn't have a TA, ask the school for someone to provide structured games (like duck, duck goose), even if only for 15 minutes.

There are ways you can help your child prepare in advance for lunchtimes. These ideas can be particularly helpful for children without support. Often children find it hard to initiate, so you could practise this at home (making sure you practise age-appropriate initiations, not the initiation of an adult with a child).

Giving your child a prop can help too. Certain toys and equipment can act as a sort of icebreaker with other kids – a cape or a sword or sand pit toys or a football.

The school/parent relationship – taken from the Autism Education Trust report 'Educational provision for children and young people on the autism spectrum living in England: a review of current practice, issues and challenges.':

The parent of a ten-year-old girl who attended a specialist school for pupils on the autism spectrum rated her relationship with the staff, school and the LA as not very good. Some of the ways in which they felt relationships might be enhanced were: to carry out the provision on the statement; to carry out agreements made in meetings; to be truthful at all times; to work with parents and child together to get a consistent approach; to allow parents into class occasionally and informally; to view parents as the expert on their child; to be respectful to parents. The barriers were felt to be high staff turnover, poorly managed meetings, failure to understand the parents' perspective, poor records of what was agreed, lack of focus and ambition for the child, and external advice not sought.

Bullying

This is the biggest issue affecting young autistic schoolchildren. 'It is the thing that worries parents and can break school placements,' says Sarah-Jane Critchley of the Autism Education Trust. 'Often because of the social naivety of autistic people, they may do something because a "friend" manipulated them and it gets them into trouble. There is also a lot of pushing, prodding and low-level bullying that can have an impact on the young person.'

According to Critchley, research has shown that the single best thing to protect a young person from bullying is to have a friend. You tend not to be bullied if you have a mate to stick up for you.

'Parents, schools and teachers need to be aware of what is happening,' she adds. 'Children don't hit and prod another child when the teacher is there, and sometimes a young autistic person might react to something that has happened earlier on and hit someone later in the day. They then get in trouble. Schools need to be aware if they see an incident that there may well have been an antecedent and examine what that might be.

'The main thing schools need to do is to believe the autistic child. Someone needs to listen to what they are saying and act upon it as soon as possible. If the young person is bullied and they come to you in a state of distress, that might not be the best time to talk to them. Verbal skills drop when the level of anxiety increases. Comic Strip Conversations, where you draw out what happened, can be good for this. Get the young person to draw out what happened, rather than relying on the intense eye-to-eye conversation.

'Lots of young people will not act out and may shut down instead – they may go very quiet. Schools don't always respond when a child has shut down; teachers are under a lot of pressure and they don't have time. If the class has learned about difference and a culture of acceptance of difference, it makes it much easier to accept that someone who has autism needs extra support or behaves differently.'

Dr Emily Lovegrove, known as 'the Bullying Doctor', formerly a research fellow at the University of the West of England, teaches anti-bullying strategies in schools and businesses.

'If you have a child who looks or sounds different in any way, we are all hardwired to pick up on that,' she says. 'For kids who are autistic, if they are not confident about who they are – and very often the system means they are not – their lack of confidence can be compounded by parents thinking their child is different, that they don't fit in and don't seem to make friends easily or like big birthday parties.

'It's one of the ways we judge our kids as successful: that they are popular and are invited to parties. You can then end up with a perfect storm: a child who is different and parents who are anxious. I deal with so many bullied children whose parents are beside themselves, because you can't protect your child at school. Parents make it worse for the child because of their own anxiety. It's totally understandable.

'When kids tell us about things, they want to listen; they don't necessarily want to us to act. The response should always be: "I'm so sorry to hear this.

What can I do to help?" Or you can say, "OK, so you got bullied – we've got to sort this out."

'For a parent whose child is different, it's all mixed up with the feeling that you've failed, you haven't produced a child that is perfect. In reality they are perfect; they are simply different from other kids.

'It is about giving your child confidence: "You are different from those kids but that's OK. What are you good at?" Things that contribute to a child's self-esteem include finding a skill they have. It's up to them to choose. They might say: "I'm very good at falling asleep quickly." Or it could be that they are a hard worker, though they find making friends difficult. It doesn't matter, as long as it's something they value about themselves.

'The other thing is finding something about their appearance that they value; to foster some kind of pride in how they look. Kids know how they look affects how people treat them.

'Being comfortable in your own skin is important. If you have a child who genuinely doesn't care about their appearance, that's fine; they will have the confidence to pull it off. But if they do care, it's counterproductive to say, "It's who you are inside that counts."

'Studies show that appearance is a common reason for bullying. If kids feel they don't look OK, then it translates into their behaviour and other children pick up on those facial and body clues. If you are going to a party and think, "Bloody hell, I've scrubbed up well!", it will totally alter the way you go into that party and the way others react to you.'

School trips

School trips must be appropriate for everyone in the class, including autistic children. Their right to access all areas of school life is set down in the Equality Act 2010 in Britain and under the Disability Discrimination Act 1995 in Northern Ireland. Teachers need to bear in mind the needs of children with SEN when they plan trips, and if a trip isn't suitable for your child they should not ask you to keep your child home – this is illegal exclusion. I opted to keep my son at home during one trip to a museum, where a 'Victorian teacher' was going to teach them how strict schools used to be – a nightmare for an anxious child who can't distinguish real life from pretend and is frightened of being told off.

If you are not happy with your school or nursery

The first port of call is usually to try to resolve things with the teacher or SENCO. If that doesn't work, speak to the head teacher, followed by the governors. After this, it's best to get in touch with the Special Educational Needs and Disabilities Information Advice and Support Service (SENDIASS), which is free and can help mediate between you and the school or nursery, and will let you know if they are fulfilling their duties towards your child. The SENDIASS is funded by the LA, and the advice it offers varies in quality.

If there is an issue, it's a good idea to keep notes documenting what the issue is, when you raised it, with whom and what the outcome was – something like the example on the facing page.

Home educating

Some children simply can't cope with the sensory bombardment or social pressure of schools. Others are just far happier at home, or have had such a negative experience of school it's put them off entirely.

'It is particularly common for parents of children with autism, compared with other SEN, to say: "There's nothing a school can offer that is appropriate for my child, so I'm home educating." And it's a valid choice,' says Barney Angliss, an SEN consultant who works as a SENCO in a mainstream school. 'There is that feeling that schools never understand autism properly, so why keep banging your head against a brick wall?'

It's surprisingly easy to take your child out of school. In England, Wales and Northern Ireland, you don't need permission to home educate. In Scotland, you must ask for consent from your local authority, which may not unreasonably withhold consent.

You do not need to have any teaching qualifications, follow a fixed timetable, work to school hours or have any set curriculum. It is very unlikely that the LA or education authority will provide financial assistance, however, or provide you with the interventions that an EHCP would have entitled your child to at school. If you live in Scotland, your LA has discretionary power to provide appropriate additional support for your child. It may also comply with a request made by you to establish whether your child has additional support needs or would be entitled to a coordinated support

	Contents	Comments
9	3/3/15 *Email to Sam Jennings, Class teacher* Dear Mr Jennings Would it be possible for us to meet after school one day next week? This is the second time I have asked – I appreciate you are busy but I am concerned about Annie and plan to see her GP next week. It would be good to talk to you about my concerns in advance of the meeting.	I received no response and saw GP 14th March. GP made a referral to the autism assessment team.
10	16/3/15 *GP letter to school* Copy of the GP letter to the autism assessment team sent to school.	School have not acknowledged the letter.
11	23/3/15 *Conversation with Gill Potts, TA* Mrs Potts asked to see me after school. She said that Annie had become 'a bit distressed' during the first lesson, shaking her hands, and had said that she was worried about assembly later that day. Annie has been in tears during playtime but had been 'fine' in assembly.	Annie later told me that she had been taken out of the first lesson and spent it in the medical room because her breathing went all funny.
12	22/4/15 *Planned meeting with Sam Jennings, Class teacher* Unknown to me, the SENCO, TA and HT were also invited to attend the meeting (which they did). They repeatedly advised me that Annie is 'fine in school' and perfectly happy there. They said that Annie's progress was satisfactory. I asked how her work compared to her peers of her ability 2 years ago. I didn't get an answer but all school staff made it clear she was 'fine' and did not require an assessment of any kind. I reminded them that Annie had been referred to the autism assessment team by her GP and that they had wanted her to also be seen by an occupational therapist. They said that she must not be allowed 'to get away with' not doing her homework and suggested that I considered attending a parenting course.	Annie scored very highly in her KS1 SATs and now seems to be in the middle sets. She is unable to manage her homework on most nights.
13	22/4/15 *Email to school office* Further to my conversation with Mr Jennings after school today I am writing to confirm that Annie will be seen by her occupational therapist tomorrow (24/6/15) at 10am.	I later discovered this appt was marked as unauthorised.
14	1/7/15 *Email to Sam Jennings via the school office* Dear Mr Jennings, Annie is exhausted after being awake most of the night and this morning she is very distressed and unable to get dressed for school. I think that the change in teacher yesterday, on top of her worries about sports day at the end of the week, has been too much to handle. Please can we meet to talk about how we can help her to find school easier to manage and how best we can prepare her for year 5?	Mr Jennings saw me after school and said that Annie could have an extra half-day with her new teacher as part of the transition.

Source: itmustbemum.wordpress.com

plan if the authority had been responsible for your child's education.

Some people do manage to get 'education other than at school' included in their EHCP, with the provision set out there delivered by the LA, but it's rare.

T, from London, mum of a five-year-old autistic boy, D, who has verbal dyspraxia and emerging language and is home educated:

'In the UK, it feels like only the extreme ends of the autistic spectrum are catered for. D falls between two stools and right now we feel there is no school that is right for him.

'He has significant sensory issues and is easily distracted, so a noisy classroom with 30 other children is not the right environment. The schools that cater for more complex needs are also wrong for D. We tried a special school last year and they completely underestimated his cognitive abilities. D had been able to recognise numbers from one to ten from the age of three, and yet a year later the school had listed in his set of targets the recognition of numbers one to three! Speech therapy was in groups, not one-to-one, which was totally inappropriate for a child who was non-verbal at the time. And this was a private special school, which was very expensive. D started to deteriorate in this environment and was desperately unhappy. We took him out of the school and decided to home-school him instead. We felt this was our only option.

'For me, self-esteem is as critical for children with autism as it is for anyone else. I won't have my son in an environment where he feels undervalued, underestimated or inferior to others.'

Some useful home education websites

www.educationotherwise.net (England)
www.he-special.org.uk/content/joinhere.php (England)
www.electivehomeeducationservice.co.uk (Wales)
www.schoolhouse.org.uk (Scotland)
www.hedni.org (Northern Ireland)

Exclusions

According to government guidelines, a child may legally be excluded only for a fixed number of days or permanently, and any exclusion must be formally recorded. Informal or unofficial exclusions – such as sending pupils home early or for 'cooling-off' periods – are unlawful, regardless of whether they happen with the agreement of parents or carers.

The Department for Education released figures in 2017 showing the rate of exclusions for autistic children doubled from 4,300 in 2014/15 to 9,190 in 2015/16. These figures reflect legal exclusions, but unlawful or informal exclusions are common too. Ambitious about Autism released some research in 2016 that suggested half of all pupils with autism have been illegally excluded from school. This commonly happens because the school can't deal with their behaviour. The research revealed that schools have asked autistic children to stay home during National Curriculum statutory assessments (SATs), Ofsted inspections and school trips without making a formal record.

The reason schools don't make them official is that any exclusion is supposed to trigger a process whereby the school and LA look again at whether the needs of the excluded child are being met. Children with SEN account for almost half of all school exclusions, according to Department for Education statistics; with autistic children it's often for hitting another child. Schools need to realise that this aggression is a symptom, a warning that the child's needs aren't being met, or that they are being put in a situation they can't cope with. It should be rare that it gets to a stage where a school feels it has to exclude a child with an EHCP. In reality, it's anything but.

Some parents feel schools are coming up with other reasons to exclude autistic children, to disguise the fact they don't have the money or desire to support them. One parent recommends that if a school calls you in for a meeting about the 'challenging behaviour' your child is displaying, you should ask them to replace those words with 'signs of distress'.

'Sending a child home from school illegally is not only a stressful and disrupting experience for the pupil and their family – it can also be incredibly difficult to challenge,' says Elizabeth Archer, the former policy director at Ambitious about Autism, a charity that has published new guidance on its website (see below). 'This new guidance aims to equip people with knowledge about their rights when illegal exclusions take place.'

Ambitious about Autism has very useful information on the subject: www.

ambitiousaboutautism.org.uk/understanding-autism/education/exclusions

It also has a guide and advice on illegal exclusions:

www.ambitiousaboutautism.org.uk/sites/default/files/AAA%20Unlaw-ful%20exclusions%20SPREADS%20LO%20RES.pdf

For advice, the National Autistic Society has a School Exclusions Service: schoolexclusions@nas.org.uk or 0808 800 4002.

Government guidelines on exclusions: www.gov.uk/government/publica-tions/school-exclusion?utm_source=

Suggestions from parents and autistic adults on effective support

* Lunchtimes need to be structured/supervised/in quiet places. 'Too much unstructured time with lots of other humans leads to meltdowns,' says one autistic adult.

* Ask the teacher or TA to keep verbal instructions short and to the point, then write them down. Also make sure things are explained in a concrete way, with no room for confusion.

* Allow opportunities for the child to succeed.

* When the child is looking lost, distract them by giving them a job to do – for example, delivering an envelope to another class.

* Check with the child what they want for lunch in advance. This way they can avoid having to make a decision in the dinner line.

* If the child struggles with transitions, use a five-minute sand timer and tell them 'Finish in five minutes'.

* Check if the child has colour sensitivity – they may not like certain-coloured dinner plates.

* Have an alert system on the child's desk: a red card means 'Don't talk to me'; amber is 'I'm confused'; and green is 'I need help'.

* Give them access to a winding-down zone where there is no stimulus and a comfy 'safe area' that is shielded from prying eyes. Schools should make it normal for the child to go to this quiet space for lunch if they want to.

* Allow stimming.

* Have sensory/stim toys readily available.

* Run a sensory gym before classes start.

* Give the child access to a separate 'workstation' in a quiet area when they need it.

* Be relaxed about uniform rules to accommodate their sensory needs.

* Have 'now and next' guides on their desk.

* If the child enjoys and is good at computing, offer them higher-level lessons.

* Let the child arrive 15 minutes before the others in the morning; they can help get the classroom ready. It means they can get used to the room when things are quiet and get to know the teacher better.

* Ask teachers and TAs to anticipate changes and keep surprises to a minimum. Get them to explain what is happening next – and to make expectations and rules very clear.

* To help build self-awareness, give the child the opportunity to reflect on things that have happened, as well as on their own behaviour and the behaviour of others.

* Print out a weekly timetable. The child and their teacher can then discuss how each session has gone and the child can colour each session in terms of how much they enjoyed it. This gives the teacher an opportunity to learn why others didn't go so well.

* Try to avoid social or academic overload.

C, from west London, autistic parent of an autistic son:
'I don't think the perfect school for a child with high-functioning autism exists. I'm the parent of a child who is in a mainstream state school with a full-time TA. The teachers don't properly understand him or his anxiety, though he enjoys learning and mostly copes, but it's tough-going for him socially. We fought for our EHCP so hard and now only half of it is delivered by the school. I've had to forego perfection for something more

realistic; to pick my battles and concentrate on the things that will make the biggest difference. That frustration of knowing that by law my son should be getting all these things but it somehow doesn't work like that is hard to live with.

K, a 20-year-old autistic woman in southeast England:
'Two key issues for me at both primary and secondary schools were bullying and study skills. For the bullying, the school essentially told me to ignore it and the bullies would stop. As for study skills, I was considered a gifted and talented student, which I feel meant my being autistic was ignored. Where everyone else seemed to "just know" how to revise and so on, I never understood that, and never got any extra help with it.'

Karletta Abianac, autistic adult based in Australia and the author of the blog musingsofkarlettaa.com:
'If I am interested in something, I will research it and talk about it. If I am not interested in a subject, my brain shuts off. If it is not relevant, there is no reason to learn it.'

⁕   ⁕   ⁕

12

SUPPORT IN EDUCATION

* * *

'A child in a wheelchair would not be asked to walk. Yet a pupil on the autism spectrum is often expected to manage in school without this equivalent support.'
Professor Rita Jordan, professor of autism studies,
University of Birmingham

I was in a boxing exercise class at the gym. My instructor told us to think of the person we hated most and imagine beating the crap out of them. But it wasn't a person that sprang to mind; instead, I wanted to hit an institution. I imagined myself beating the crap out of Haringey council.

How had it come to this? I'm pretty sure I was the only person in the class wishing violence on an entire local authority. I wanted to punch Haringey for causing me the stress of having to fight to get the right support for my son. It is dealing with the council, and not my son's autism, that causes me sleepless nights. My coping mechanisms are wine, antidepressants, working part-time and therapy, not necessarily in that order.

Part of the stress is frustration. Before, I had naively assumed that local authorities did what they ought to do. I understood they were slow and inefficient, but I never thought they would behave illegally. How could a local government body act outside of the law?

But then I started actually dealing with them on a regular basis, beyond simply paying my council tax bills. The efficiency local authorities demonstrate when collecting money disappears when it comes to supporting autistic kids.

Dealing with them feels like a constant battle, or like trying to solve a logic puzzle set by a crazy person. When it comes to the EHCP – the document that sets out what support the local authority will provide or fund – it often goes like this: Your local authority produces a document stating that black is white. You try to call them up to clear the matter up quickly, except no one answers the phone. After a few tries you give up and send an email. They reply and restate the facts: black is white – and they are not going to change their minds. No one speaks human or levels with you. You respond by saying: it's not actually true, is it? Furthermore, the law is very clear that black is black. You are feeling confident: they can't fail to realise their position is untenable. And yet you hear nothing back.

After much hounding, the local authority finally gets back to you to say it will take the decision to an SEN panel, where many of the decisions are made, in a month's time. You hound a little more to learn the outcome, only to be told the panel concurs that black is white. You are forced to go to a tribunal, a gruelling process that involves the local authority spending thousands of tax-payer pounds on lawyers to delay the case and trot out colour experts who can confirm that black is white. It's only settled when the two-person panel at the tribunal intervenes and rules in your favour. Black was always black, of course – it just turns out white was cheaper and the local authority was hoping you'd eventually give up.

It's a frustrating scenario, and far from untypical, but what elevates it to can't-think-about-anything-else stressful is the fact that what is really being negotiated here is the happiness of your child. The outcomes of these inter-actions will decide their learning or school experience; whether they integrate at school; whether they have positive social interactions. You are negotiating, in short, their future. It's as high as stakes can get – and it doesn't just happen once. The terms of support are constantly renegotiated, or the support isn't provided, meaning you have to restart the whole horrendous endurance test once again.

My anger with the local authority did not lessen once I realised it wasn't all their fault. I can now see that the overworked and demoralised SEN depart-ments of local authorities are also victims of the same crappy system that lets down vulnerable children, adults and their families. Recent reforms have in-creased their workload and responsibilities, while at the same time their budg-ets have been cut to the bone. For them to be able properly to support families will take money from central government, a plan for how to spend it most ef-ficiently and a radical culture change.

Some local authorities are good, but many of you who have already em-barked on the quest to get your council to stump up will know it is those who fight hardest and play the LA at their own game who get most support. The poorer kids, or the kids of parents who don't have the capacity for the fight, are getting less support or, increasingly, none. Meanwhile, the children of the middle classes are getting provision because their parents can understand and can play or afford to play the system.

I'm hoping this chapter will empower parents to know some of their rights and help people with less money and privilege to navigate this complex system. At first, I wanted to compile a list of every problem you might encounter, and provide a potential solution, but if I did, this book would become the SEN version of *War and Peace*. So instead, here are some of the common issues and some insight from people who work in this field.

The basics

What is the definition of special educational needs (SEN)?

A child has SEN, according to part 3, section 20 of the Children and Families Act 2014, if 'he or she has a learning difficulty or disability which calls for special educational provision to be made for him or her'.

The SEN code of practice written by the Department for Education adds that if a child's progress is 'significantly slower than that of their peers' or the child 'fails to close the attainment gap' separating them from their peers, they may have SEN. Four areas of SEN are identified, though it is possible to have SEN which do not fit neatly into any of these areas.

1. Communicating and interacting
2. Cognition and learning
3. Social, emotional and mental health difficulties
4. Sensory and/or physical needs

What are local authorities obliged to do?

They are obliged to identify which children and young people in their area have special educational needs. Then they have to assess those needs and ensure those children and young people receive a level of support that 'will help them with regard to achieving the best possible educational and other outcomes'. These are legal responsibilities, as set out in section 19 (d) of part 3 of the Children and Families Act 2014. If your local authority is not doing these things, it is breaking the law.

The 'will help them' and 'with regard to' are crucial bits of the sentence.

The local authority has no legal obligation to ensure that the best outcomes happen, it just has to aim for its efforts to be in that direction. Similarly, 'with regard to' has limited legal heft – it means that this is the general principle that LAs should be aiming for, but it doesn't mean they are legally obliged to ensure it happens.

Does having SEN mean my child has a learning difficulty or disability?

According to the legal definition, they do if they find it significantly more difficult to learn than the majority of children the same age, or if they find it difficult or impossible to use mainstream school facilities, which include the playground and lunch hall.

What are the different levels of support available?

There are two tiers of support in an education setting in England:

SEN SUPPORT which triggers a cycle of observation and support known as Assess, Plan, Do and Review. SEN support is funded by the £6,000-per-child annual notional SEN budget a school receives from the local authority – this is a budget that a school gets automatically and doesn't have to apply for, and the school is in control of choosing how and when it's spent. The majority of autistic children will be on SEN support. You don't need a diagnosis for this to apply.

EDUCATION HEALTH CARE PLAN often shortened to EHCP. This is typically for children whose support is going to cost more money than what a mainstream school can offer through SEN support. It is a legally binding document, based on an EHC needs assessment, that states what support the LA must arrange, backed up by a budget. Parents name a school they want their child to go to – they don't have to live within the catchment area – and the school usually takes the child unless they argue they can't (more on this on page 213).

What is SEN support?

Barney Angliss works as a SENCO and has worked as a local authority SEND manager. He wrote the list below of what should happen when SEN support is triggered. (This first appeared on the Special Needs Jungle website – the full post can be found at: www.specialneedsjungle.com/key-points-sen-support-schools/)

The SEN code of practice (2015) is guidance, much of it drawn directly from law, which schools must follow. It makes these points about pupils who are vulnerable and who may have special educational needs but do not have an EHCP:

* Schools should regularly and carefully review and, where necessary, improve teachers' understanding of strategies to identify and support vulnerable pupils and their knowledge of SEN (section 6.37 of the code of practice).

* For higher levels of need, schools should have arrangements in place to draw on more specialised assessments from external agencies and professionals (6.38).

* Schools should hold an early discussion with the pupil and parents. They should record and copy to parents the outcomes which are agreed together with the next steps to help achieve these outcomes. At this point schools should also tell children, parents and young people where to find the local authority's Information, Advice and Support Service (6.39).

* Schools should make it clear to parents whether the support their child needs can be provided from the school's 'core' (standard) offer or whether something different or additional is required (6.40).

* A clear date for reviewing progress should be agreed and the parent, pupil and teaching staff should each be clear about their role. If it is decided that a pupil does have SEN, this should be recorded and the pupil's parents must be formally informed that special educational provision is being made (6.43).

* Schools should then assess the pupil's needs, plan appropriate support, do what has been planned and review the pupil's progress in response to support (6.44).

* The school should obtain a wide range of evidence including the views and experience of parents, the pupil's own views and, if relevant, advice from external support services. Schools should take seriously any concerns raised by a parent (6.45).

* The assessment (and not just the support) should be reviewed regularly (6.46).

* Where outside professionals in education, health or care are not already working with school staff the SENCO should contact them only if the parents agree (6.47).

* Where it is decided to provide a pupil with SEN support, the parents must be formally notified and the teacher and the SENCO should agree in consultation with the parents and the pupil the adjustments, interventions and support to be put in place, as well as the expected impact on progress, development or behaviour, along with a clear date for review (6.48).

* All teachers and support staff who work with the pupil should be made aware of their needs, the outcomes sought, the support provided and any teaching strategies or approaches that are required. This should also be recorded on the school's information system (6.49).

Provision of SEN support – what might this look like?

A teacher may have to differentiate lesson delivery in some way for a child with SEN support or an EHCP. Some examples of what this might entail: extra equipment (e.g. sensory toys); advice to the school from professionals (e.g. SALT); small-group work (e.g. handwriting classes); some support during the school day (e.g. at play or lunchtime); training for classroom teachers or other staff (e.g. on teaching a child with autism); mentoring or supported social opportunities (e.g. Minecraft or Lego lunchtime club); staggered lunchtime break to avoid busy times; differentiated homework (e.g. using a computer to create a poster rather than having to draw one).

Is SEN support effective?

The reality is schools don't have the time or the money to do half of what they should be doing for SEN support. Research shows that these pupils are less likely to continue in education compared with those who have a statement (the documents pre-EHCPs), let alone those who have no SEN. Pupils with special needs who do not have an EHCP are more likely to be excluded from school and, if this hasn't depressed you enough, are almost three times as likely to drop out of higher education compared with those with no special needs.

One of the main problems is SEN support has little legal status, so it is hard for parents to enforce what should happen. Parents are therefore totally reliant on how good a school is.

'The gulf between what the Department for Education suggests should happen in a mainstream school and what really happens is widening all the time,' says Angliss. 'If I were a parent of a child being offered SEN support, I would settle for it only if the school writes down what my child is going to get. But schools don't write it all down as they don't want to be committed. Lots of parents then end up requesting an EHCP because the SEN support is not effective. There are some schools offering SEN support that is effective, because they know what they are doing and they are committed to training, but those schools then attract parents of children whose needs haven't been met elsewhere and they are drained of resources.'

What is an Education Health Care Plan (EHCP)?

An EHCP is a document that clearly states need and support that a child is entitled to. It can start from birth and goes up to the age of 25. The EHCP must include the views and interests of parents and children (if they can or are old enough). A good-quality EHCP will contain a 'golden thread', in the words of the Department for Education, that connects the aspirations of the child or young person, and/or their family, with their needs, provision and outcomes.

It is legally binding, obliging local authorities as well as social services and NHS health trusts to deliver the support stated. The look of the document and some of the wording will change from borough to borough, but all must have the same categories.

EHCPs were introduced as part of the Children and Families Act 2014, an Act of Parliament that aimed to bring about a culture change in the laws governing SEN. The intention was to put the child or young person at the centre of all decisions about their support, to involve families more and to reduce the fight that parents experienced trying to get the right support.

It was a piece of legislation that has been hobbled by austerity cuts, which happened at the same time as its implementation (thank you, George Osborne and David Cameron). EHCPs greatly increased expectations of what local authorities have to do and the number of children needing support – the cut-off went from 19 to 25 – while at the same time, budgets for day-to-day SEN delivery were slashed. The government has found money for creating new EHC plans, which have cost billions of pounds – money that would have been more effectively spent in nurseries and schools.

'The SEN reforms that brought in EHCPs happened because of an inquiry carried out by Brian Lamb, published in December 2009, when he said that the system of Statements of Special Educational Needs was too opposition-al,' adds education lawyer Ed Duff. 'Parents interviewed for the inquiry said they needed to battle to get the right support for their children and Lamb said there needed to be a massive culture change. So what the Department for Education said was: the way we are going to change the culture is to say in law there is going to be a culture change. Every judge in the world knows this doesn't work; you can't legislate for a change in behaviour.'

Very few EHCPs have meaningful input from health or social care and par-ents report they have to fight even harder now they have been phased in. The number of appeals lodged at tribunals has rocketed and education lawyers have never been busier. Many feel that the golden thread has unravelled.

The plan contains 11 sections listed alphabetically. Below is a summary of each section. For more detail, IPSEA, a charity that provides SEN parents with free legal advice, has produced a comprehensive document explaining each section and what should be in there: www.ipsea.org.uk/file-manager/SEN-law/ipsea-ehc-plan-checklist-september-2016.pdf

A – Views, interests and aspirations of the child or young person. The par-ent writes this if their child is young or non-verbal, involving them and re-flecting their views.

B – Special educational needs. What your child needs at school to progress.

C – Health needs. Your child's health needs, which are related to their SEN.

D – Social care needs. Your child's social care needs, which are related to their SEN.

E – Outcomes sought for the child. A set of short- and longer-term objectives that the EHCP is trying to achieve and the steps towards meeting them. Outcomes that will prepare them for adulthood should be linked to their aspirations in section A and should link up with the needs identified in B and C and the provision required in F–H.

F – Special educational provision. Support provided to help with the needs identified in section B.

G – Healthcare provision. Health provision to be provided by the NHS. This can include support and therapies, such as medical treatments and delivery of medications, nursing support, specialist equipment and wheelchairs.

H1 – Social care provision. Any support that your child needs in accordance with section 2 of the Chronically Sick and Disabled Persons Act 1970. This might include practical assistance in the home, adaptations of the home, help with travel and 'facilitating the taking of holidays', non-residential short breaks (these are day trips run during half-term or holidays to give parents a break) and support the parent may need.

H2 – Social care provision. Any other social care provision reasonably required to help with your child's development, i.e. residential short breaks and 'services provided to children arising from their SEN but unrelated to a disability'.

I – School placement. The name and type of school or other educational setting to be attended by the child or young person.

J – Personal budget. How much the LA will give the school or parents through direct payments to cover the support detailed in the EHCP. IPSEA says: 'Any amount of money specified in this section must be enough to secure the provision specified. It is, therefore, essential that type and amount of provision is adequately specified, e.g. as well as amount of time per week, the qualifications and experience and therefore grade of a specialist teacher.'

K – List of advice. The advice and information gathered during the EHCP needs assessment must be attached (in appendices).

KEY PARTS OF THE EHCP

Sections B and F: special educational needs and provision

It is important to have all your child's educational needs nailed down in section B. Every special educational need in B must be matched by provision in section F. Basically, if you want to ensure it is going to happen and the LA can provide it, then it must go in section F.

LAs sometimes try to put SALT, OT and physio in section G (Health), meaning it is the responsibility of the NHS – whose budgets are even more squeezed than local authority SEN departments – which will make it much harder to enforce.

Sections H1 and H2: social care provision

It's clear that, at the time of writing, this bit of the EHCP isn't working. LAs are allowed to take into account the cost and convenience of providing social care – something they aren't allowed to do for provision laid out in section F – which gives them a lot of wiggle room to not include it in the plan. And even if you do get provision included, it is delivered by notoriously understaffed social service departments. It has been estimated that only 40 per cent of EHCPs have any input from social services at all, and that is usually to say they don't know the child. Most people don't have the stamina to sort out the social care side of things as well as the education component.

Section E: outcomes

What the code of practice says about outcomes:

'EHC plans should be focused on education and training, health and care outcomes that will enable children and young people to progress in their learning and, as they get older, to be well prepared for adulthood. EHC plans can also include wider outcomes such as positive social relationships and emotional resilience and stability,' (9.64 of the code of practice).

An outcome can be defined as the benefit or difference made to an individual as a result of an intervention. According to the code of practice, outcomes should be SMART: Specific, Measurable, Achievable, Realistic and Time-bound. Outcomes should follow from the aspirations identified in section A.

The outcomes should be the guidelines for what the EHCP is hoping to achieve – a combination of short-term goals (as in the next 1–2 years), medium-term (end of the current school phase) and long-term (when your child is 18 or 20).

Ed Duff suggests people can get a bit too carried away with the SMART model, which can lead to parents concentrating on mainly short-term outcomes, as it's easier to specify and be realistic about things in the near future. 'A lot of LAs want to keep outcomes short-term so they can argue that, if the short-term goals are achieved, then the need for the EHCP has come to an end.'

There is no limit to the number of outcomes you can specify. If the LA tells you that you can only have three or five, that isn't true – or lawful.

Some examples of good outcomes, provided by the Council for Disabled Children:

* Mohammed (eight years old) will work independently for at least 50 per cent of each lesson period, by the end of KS2.

* By the end of year 9 William (12 years old) will be able to make his own way to school every day.

* By the end of KS1, Sheila (six years old) will be able to express her preference when offered a choice between two activities.

* Janice (nine years old) will be able to greet different people appropriately. This will include family members, her friends and unfamiliar adults. To be achieved by the end of KS2.

* Mason (three years old) will be able to engage in a play activity with another child and an adult on a daily basis by the time he is in reception.

Who can apply for an EHCP?

Parents, the school or a professional working with the child. Parents can refer the child themselves for an assessment by the local authority – it is not up to the SENCO to give the go-ahead. Parents have to be consulted when a school applies for an EHCP.

What is the legal threshold to trigger an assessment?

It's low. The legal test for when a local authority must carry out an EHC needs assessment is that:

* The child or young person has or may have SEN; and

* It may be necessary for special educational provision to be made for the child or young person in accordance with an EHCP (section 36 (8) of the Children and Families Act 2014).

How do I apply?

Write to your borough and request an assessment. IPSEA has a template letter: www.ipsea.org.uk/what-you-need-to-know/model-letters/model-letter-1

It's all about the evidence. The Special Needs Jungle has a useful blog on this, some of which is printed below (the full blog can be found at www. specialneedsjungle.com/get-prepared):

> Speak to your child's head teacher or the SENCO. Find out what level of support they are already on . . . Ask to be provided with a record of the educational and/or behavioural interventions used and comments about how they have worked or not.
>
> Gather together any reports or tests your child has ever had done. This means all their school reports and exam results, any referrals they have had to paediatricians, occupational therapists, speech and language therapists, educational psychologists, etc.
>
> The LA will argue that just because a child is achieving below average does not mean that they have special educational needs . . . Children in each class will have a broad spectrum of achievement according to their individual potential . . . So, how can you show that your child has a greater potential than their current achievements point to?
>
> The obvious way is to secure an educational psychology assessment for them . . . You may also need to consider a speech and language assessment or an occupational therapy assessment if this is indicated.
>
> If an educational psychologist assessment is not forthcoming, you could consider a private assessment, usually at great expense, although these are often regarded with suspicion by the LA that the report is biased towards the parents' views, even though it almost certainly isn't.

For further details of the advice and information that must be sought by the LA as part of an EHC needs assessment, see Regulation 6 of the SEN Regulations 2014.

What should happen

* After you make a request for the EHC needs assessment, the local authority has six weeks to decide whether to carry out the assessment. If it decides not to, you have a right to appeal at a SEND (Special Educational Needs and Disability) tribunal. See the facing page for more information.

* If the local authority does carry out an assessment and goes on to issue an EHCP, the whole process must take no more than 20 weeks from the date of the initial request for the EHC needs assessment to the issuing

Department for Education

SPECIAL
NEEDS
JUNGLE

Requesting an Education, Health and Care (EHC) Needs Assessment

An EHCP can be requested by parent, young person, teacher or anyone else concerned about the child's SEN

Where, despite the school having taken relevant and purposeful action to identify, assess and meet the SEN of the child or young person, the child or young person has not made expected progress, the school or parents should consider requesting an Education, Health and Care needs assessment.

When your initial request has been received, think about what help you might need with this, for example from an independent supporter who can help you through the process. Your LA will ask you about this. Independent Supporters can be supplied by a local non-profit organisation or by the IASS Network, depending on the area you are in. The IS can help to coordinate the process and/or provide help and support to your family while the process is underway. You can decide the kind of help, if any, that you think you will need

A full diagram of the process can be found in the Code of Practice p154.

Contact your local authority's SEN department and ask to start the SEN Statutory Assessment process.

You then have six weeks during which time the Local Authority should seek to gather school reports, old IEPs/ documentation from the Assess/Plan/Do/Review process, any other speech & language/educational psychology/ OT or other reports.
Parents may wish, if they are able, to gather together all the reports and information that related to their child's SEND themselves as well to ensure everything is considered by the LA. This will also assist as a timeline reminder when you are writing your child's story as part of the application.

You then need to write your child's story including any relevant information from the gathered reports. If you have an Independent Supporter, they will be able to assist you with all of these steps. Include how your child's difficulties impact upon your whole family and what support your child already has that really helps. Remember to think about their strengths as well!
Make sure you number the reports and include them in your application (only ever send copies). Any medical and social care needs should be included.

The local authority decides whether or not to conduct an assessment of SEND.

If an assessment is agreed, move to part 3 "Conducting an assessment"

If the response is no, the LA should advise you of other options short of statutory assessment that can support your child from the Local Offer on the Assess, Plan, Do, Review process. Your LA should never just say 'No' without looking at what provision can better help your child from the Local Offer

If you are not satisfied with this decision or any other help sourced from the Local Offer help you can seek mediation and/or appeal to the SEND Tribunal

Move to part 4, Disagreements"

of a finalised EHCP. (According to the Department for Education, LAs are only managing to stick to this timeframe just over 58 per cent of the time.)

* The LA prepares a draft EHCP and is supposed to work closely with families during this drafting process. The draft plan is sent to families to check, suggest further changes, and name a preferred school. Families are given 15 days to do this but can ask for more time if they need it.

* The LA then finalises the EHCP and issues it. If a parent or young person is unhappy with certain parts of it (the description of the SEN needs, the special educational provision to meet those needs or the school or college placement named in the EHCP), they have a right of appeal at a SEND tribunal.

* The LA should have obtained professional reports as part of the EHC needs assessment process.

* Regulation 6 (1) of the SEN Regulations 2014 sets out the people from whom the LA must seek advice and information on the needs, provision and outcomes for a child or young person. These include an educational psychologist, someone from the LA's social care team, a healthcare professional, the child or young person's educational setting, and anyone else from whom the parent or young person reasonably requests advice.

Alison Worsley, Director of External Affairs at the charity Ambitious about Autism:
> *'Just under three-quarters of parents who responded to a survey we did stated they had lost sleep trying to get the right support for their child.'*

The SEN system in Wales, Scotland and Northern Ireland

The system in Wales is similar to that of England pre-EHCP, with three different options. They are: School Action, School Action Plus and Statement of Special Educational Needs. Children have Individual Education Plans and a statutory assessment determines if a child is going to get a statement or not. For more information go to www.hcbgroup.com/sen-aln-in-wales.html

The Scottish system is different. Most autistic children have Individual Educational Programmes (also known as learning plans or additional support plans), which are not statutory. Children with more complex needs who require support from health as well as social services are given Coordinated Support Plans, which are statutory. There is a higher threshold of support for Coordinated Support Plans compared with EHCPs. More information can be found here: www.enquire.org.uk/

Meanwhile, Northern Ireland operates a five-stage approach to SEN. Schools have funding to support children through school-based help at stages 1–3 of the five possible stages. Stages 1 and 2 would not involve any external agencies to the school; however, at stage 3 the child can be receiving support from external specialists. Stages 4 and 5 would be for those children with more moderate to severe special educational needs involving statutory assessment and a Statement of Special Educational Needs – www.senac.co.uk

What is the Local Offer?

The Local Offer is information a local authority gives on its website outlining what services and support are available to young people and parents, alongside descriptions, contact details and how to access them. The Local Offer includes services from birth to 25, across education, health and social care. It describes state-funded, charitable and private services, and is meant to include services outside the local area, such as schools, that are used by local families.

LAs are obliged to do this under the code of practice, and the intention is to provide clear, comprehensive and accessible information about the available provision and how to access it. Also LAs have to involve the people who use the service in the development and review of the Local Offer.

What should be included in the EHC plan?

* Make sure every area of need and every element of provision in the EHCP is specified and quantified: who will deliver the provision? How often will, say, SALT sessions take place? How long will they last? The law requires this – and if the provision isn't specific and quantified, it's harder to enforce.

* Make sure all the recommendations from all the professionals who assessed your child are included in the plan. If the SALT report is woolly and unspecified, go back and request specified advice from the therapist.

* LAs sometimes do not quantify provision for children in special schools. In a 2003 appeal case brought by a local authority, a court accepted that a lower level of specificity was appropriate in certain situations, but that doesn't mean there should be no specificity.

* The level of special educational provision included in the plan will be dependent on evidence. A parent simply saying that their child needs something is unlikely to be enough.

* If your child needs it, there is no limit to the level of special education provision that can be specified within an EHCP, but the need for provision has to be backed up with evidence and there is no legal entitlement to the best possible provision.

* If you do not agree with the findings of a professional report prepared as part of your child's EHC needs assessment, consider seeking further professional evidence in the form of an independent report – for example, from an educational psychologist or a SALT.

* Most children with autism will need support during unstructured times, such as lunchtimes or breaks. If this applies to your child, make sure the need for structured activities during these times is specified in their EHCP.

* If your child needs one-to-one support from a TA, make sure it is clearly stated within the EHCP and how many hours' support are needed.

* Make sure it's stated in the EHCP that the school has to provide cover if the TA is away, undertaking training or unwell.

Catriona Moore of the National Autistic Society:
  'One of the keys to a successful EHCP is to draw up a list of the right people to give their fullest knowledge possible. They need to define what the child's needs are and what support is needed.'

What is the personal budget?

A personal budget is essentially how much the EHCP costs the local authority. A direct payment is an amount taken from the personal budget that is paid directly to the family so you can control how it is spent. When EHCPs were first devised, the intention was for families to be able to easily request direct payments from LAs, but LAs successfully argued this was unworkable. You cannot get the whole EHCP budget in one lump sum.

At the start of 2017, there were 175,000 children with EHCPs across England and, according to the Department for Education, just 6,400 EHCPs contained a personal budget component. One parent successfully argued that they should receive a personal budget for OT as their child was already working with a private OT and wouldn't engage with the LA's OT. You can't appeal if the LA refuses to grant it, however – you can only take it to a judicial review.

To lawyer up or not?

Despite the intention for EHCPs to reduce the need for families to hire lawyers it seems clear that the opposite is true. Ed Duff of HCB Solicitors reports that, 'Every education lawyer I know is struggling to keep up with demand – and each of these cases is a family going through a nightmare. It's not a good reflection of how things are going.'

Catriona Moore of the National Autistic Society adds: 'When we have done surveys of parents' experiences, what comes across is how much some parents have to fight – and not everyone has the same capacity for that fight.'

Whether you are able to hire a lawyer or not will likely come down to how much money you have, how your local authority treats you and how desperate you are. Be careful to get a recommendation and go with someone experienced. You could also try an 'advocate': a specialist in helping parents access support for their children and dealing with LAs. They are not trained solicitors but know the law around SEN provision; this makes them cheaper but sometimes less experienced than a lawyer. Some get very good results, however. Two advocates I have used and can recommend are Fiona Slomovic (www.advocacyandmediation.co.uk) and Barney Angliss (www.adlzinsight.org).

Common problems

Our EHCP assessment request has been turned down

These days it is rare for someone to have their request for an assessment agreed first time. Some LAs refuse *all* requests the first time round, as a way of managing their workload. They know that not everyone can or will persevere. Figures published by the Department for Education in 2017 showed a 35 per cent annual increase in local authorities refusing to assess.

LAs give parents a variety of reasons why they won't assess a child – many of them unlawful – or ask parents and schools to jump through hoops they shouldn't be expected to. Parents may be told to go through three cycles of Assess, Plan, Do, Review before the LA will consider an assessment; that their child has to be a certain number of years behind in their progress at nursery or school; that their child doesn't qualify because they are not in the bottom 2 per cent of the class academically; that they have to see an educational psychologist first; that their child has to have more complex needs; that their child is too young. All of these are wrong.

The first thing to do if your request for an assessment is turned down is to talk to your local authority. Ideally, you will be able to meet with a representative or speak to them on the phone, to ask them for more information on why they came to their decision and to explain why you think they got it wrong. If that doesn't get you anywhere, or you don't get a reply, the next option is to go to tribunal – you have two months after the local authority's decision not to assess to register your appeal, or you lose the right to appeal – or gather more evidence and request another assessment (there is no limit to how many assessments you can request).

Before you can go to tribunal, you must either enter mediation or get a certificate from a mediator to show you have considered the option – you have two months to start mediation from the day the LA makes its decision not to assess. If you choose mediation and it fails, you have a month to lodge an appeal.

For refusal-to-assess cases, tribunal judges can now reach their decision simply by looking at the paperwork; parents don't have to be there, though they still have the option to request an oral hearing if they prefer. You will need to include any evidence contained in your application letter – a diagnosis or a professional report – and your view as well as the school's, if they agree on why your child may need a plan.

If you do launch an appeal, particularly if the school is supporting you, the tribunal judges are likely to agree with you, as the onus is on the LA to prove your child doesn't have SEN or that their needs are being fully met and always will be.

Local authorities must pay for impartial advisers from the Information Advice and Support Service, also known as SENDIASS, to support you through some of this process. Most SENDIASS services don't support parents through the appeal process, but all offer advice / support in the stages prior to appeal. If you google your borough and SENDIASS, you will find the organisation that can help you. The quality of the advice is variable – an issue raised in a report commissioned by the Department of Education and Social Justice. Many parents feel uncomfortable that local authorities fund the service, meaning it isn't truly independent – sometimes SENDIASS staff work in the same building as an LA – and there have been claims that some SENDIASS services aren't trained well enough to know the finer points of the law.

The charity SOS!SEN has an information sheet for appealing a refusal-to-assess decision: www.sossen.org.uk / information_sheets.php

T, from London is the mum of M, an 11-year-old autistic boy:
   'The school we were hoping M would go to is in another borough, but it was not named on his statement. The LA had a duty to consult with the neighbouring LA to see if there was a place, but, unknown to us, they didn't consult with them at all; they just said he couldn't go.

   'It feels like the local authority knows they have to ask for your input, but it's just a formality and they take no notice of your amendments. One time I was absolutely frantic, as we needed our EHCP transferred so we could get M into a secondary school. They didn't give a damn. I spoke to everyone at the LA, and my local MP, local charities were phoning the LA up about it, but they didn't get back to them. The only thing that did work was when I lodged an internal complaint with the council and was told the complaint would be investigated within 15 days. On day 15, at 5.50 p.m., I got a response: our EHCP had been transferred.

'My experience is that LAs don't approach things in a sensible way. They just run around thinking they are going to fight everything. It's a knee-jerk reaction. One time we were asking for something that was cheaper than what we were currently getting and they still refused! I don't think it's a new situation. I was reading a book about autism provision in the 1970s and it talks about the fights among local authorities and parents. It's always been this way.'

My child has been assessed and the LA has refused to provide an EHCP

You must be informed of the reasons and you have the right to appeal within two months of the date of the letter informing you of the LA's decision.

The EHCP is vague

One thing local authorities excel in is producing vaguely worded EHCPs. The LA only has a duty to secure the provision specified in a plan. A plan could stipulate that a child is entitled to support from a teaching assistant, for example, but that TA could have a responsibility for a number of children, unless it is stated explicitly that they are dedicated to providing one-to-one support for a particular number of hours. Beware woolly phrases such as 'would benefit from' or 'regular'.

IPSEA has a brilliant document on its website entitled 'The Duty to Specify': www.ipsea.org.uk/download-resource?id=0b418248-3925-4648-827e-0691643f30fa

If your child's EHCP contains vague or otherwise inadequate provision, you should tell the LA or tribunal what should be altered or inserted. Here's what the document recommends you do:

* With the help of the IPSEA plan checklist (see earlier in this chapter), first check that each and every need for provision is there, in the right section and adequately described.

* Delete phrases such as 'access to', 'opportunities for', or 'up to' (as in 'up to X hours').

* Go through all the reports attached to the plan and extract any useful advice which actually quantifies provision.

✳ If the advice is vague (e.g. talking about the necessity for 'high levels' of something or 'small groups' without any size), speak or write to the professional who wrote the report to see if they can be more specific.

✳ If the people who wrote the reports aren't helpful, try reminding them of what the SEN code of practice says about their advice, that 'the evidence and advice submitted by those providing it should be clear, accessible and specific'.

Liesel Batterham, education rights coordinator at the NAS:
'It is important that SALTs, OTs and other professionals assessing your child observe them in lessons and unstructured time. Parents are sometimes concerned that the assessments are carried out only in a room with just them and the professional. If this happens and you don't believe the resulting report is a true reflection of your child, it's possible to contact the professional and explain. If that doesn't work, it's important that you write a counter report and explain that because of the environment in which the assessment was undertaken, it doesn't accurately reflect how your child is in a busy classroom or playground.'

My LA doesn't want to specify how many hours of one-to-one support my child is to receive

LAs are often very resistant to stating on paper how many hours' one-to-one support a child should get. Schools often prefer it vague too. As a result, a budget for a TA is often given without the ECHP stating how many hours a week the child should receive TA support. If your child needs one-to-one support, you could point out that provision must be quantified, detailed and specific, as per the code of practice, and see if it does the trick; if it doesn't, this is often an issue resolved at tribunal.

We have an EHCP but the LA still isn't providing the support detailed on it

It's at this point the system seems rigged, but don't give up, says Lorna Pape, the former head of legal at IPSEA. 'It is the local authority's absolute responsibility to secure the special educational provision specified within an EHC plan, and if this is not happening, a parent can complain to the LA or ultimately take action such as bringing a claim for judicial review. Such actions are rare and, in an appropriate case, the threat of such action would often be sufficient.'

IPSEA has a model letter that you can use: www.ipsea.org.uk/what-you-need-to-know/model-letters/model-letter-6

I can't afford private reports and need legal aid

Parents often seek private reports, particularly when going to a tribunal. These reports are expensive – the going rate in London is £400–1,300 at time of publication. If you don't have access to this kind of money, you can seek help from legal aid, but be aware that it's difficult to get. The income thresholds are very low – as a rough guide, you need to be earning below £18,000 to qualify – and if your home is worth more than £208,000, you will be ruled out automatically.

Even if you do qualify, only two firms in the whole of England and Wales offer legal aid in education law, at the time of writing, and they aren't coping with the workload. Legal aid lawyers are juggling about 80 cases each at a time.

'The worst thing about legal aid in education law is that while there is funding to prepare for an appeal, there is no funding for a lawyer or experts to go with you to your appeal,' says education lawyer Ed Duff. 'If you remove the lawyer, it can be managed, but remove the expert, and you have a parent facing a LA that has brought in an expert for every discipline – SALT, OT, educational psychology and physiotherapy – and they will probably send a lawyer too. And the lawyers they use are notoriously brutal. Some of these lawyers are awful to parents and deliberately frustrate the process.'

The notorious Baker Small

Baker Small, a law firm that works with a number of LAs, had to apologise in 2016 for a series of tweets that appeared to gloat about victories over SEN parents. One of the tweets said: 'Crikey, had a great "win" last week which sent some parents into a storm!' The tweets were subsequently deleted and the firm made a donation to charity.

'Probably not that funny on reflection?' one person tweeted in response, to which Baker Small replied: 'Whenever someone thinks they have won and they have conceded 90 per cent of their case, it does make me smile.' The law firm is notorious among parents for its aggressive tactics, so much so that some SEN parents refer to its director, Mark Small, as 'the Terminator'.

The LA has produced a draft EHCP that we don't agree with

You have 15 days to respond and/or request a meeting with the LA, which must consider your requested amendments but does not have to incorporate them into the final EHCP. If you are still unhappy, the next stop is a tribunal.

I want to change my child's EHCP

You want to move your child to a different school, or amend EHCP outcomes that were too unambitious or short-term. The best way to make changes is at the annual review after having discussed them with the school. If the LA refuses to make such changes, then – you guessed it – it's a tribunal. If you have serious concerns that cannot wait for the annual review, you can request an early or emergency review.

We're moving to a new home in a different local authority

Joy of all joys, you will now have to deal with two LAs. Write to your new LA on the day of your move or soon after to let it know that you are now resident in the area and you have a child with SEN. It will contact your old LA and ask it to send all records relating to your child's EHCP and must let you know within six weeks that the plan has been transferred. However, the new LA has the right to carry out a new EHC needs assessment, which does mean your child's provision might change. The time limit for this is six weeks, though you won't be surprised to hear that this deadline is regularly missed. When we moved from one LA to another the transfer took nine months and only came after intervention from our local MP.

Conflict of interests

The EHCP system has two major conflicts of interest. The first, most glaring instance is that local authorities must both assess need and pay for it. You can see the problem: cash-strapped LAs are unlikely to conclude that money is no object when it comes to supporting your child at school; there is an inbuilt pressure on them to minimise need and deny provision. Sometimes it is cheaper for them to spend money on expensive lawyers to challenge the support your child needs than simply to pay for it.

Another conflict is the role of the LA's educational psychologists. 'They are employed by local authorities to carry out an initial assessment of a child's needs, but within the context of what resources are available from the local authority,' says Catriona Moore.

At the moment there are no meaningful consequences for LAs that break the law or give parents 'facts' about their rights or how the system works that are either untrue or unlawful. In fact, they gain by saving money if they win and they spin the process out if they don't – the tribunal appeals process usually takes many weeks and months, and this is weeks and months that the local authority doesn't have to pay for provision. For specialist provision this can save tens of thousands of pounds per case.

Ed Duff, senior associate solicitor, Education Law Department, HCB Solicitors:

'Within a LA you have a SEN team. That team will be staffed by people who have most likely worked in the role for no more than five years. They leave because it's a horrendous job: they are trying to do their job with no time, no money and constant pressure. Mostly, SEN officers are not trained in the law, but they are trained in LA policies.

'How disadvantaged are parents if they don't have a lawyer? Massively, particularly at appeal. If you are looking for, say, a change in school placement, and parents say we want a specialist school that is going to cost £300,000 a year, the LA will throw every expert, every barrister at the case and totally ambush the parents.'

Tribunal

There are two tiers of tribunal. Your first port of call will be the first-tier tribunal. If you are not happy about its decision – and there is a legal basis to challenge – you can then go to the upper tribunal.

'The number of appeals being brought is going through the roof,' says Ed Duff. 'Tribunal staff are now working weekends and before 2017 it would be rare to find a panel of fewer than three members. Now two-member panels are the norm. The upper tribunal is also bursting at the seams – because of the first-tier tribunal's workload they are having to rush decisions and are falling into error more.

'The reason the tribunal staff are struggling to cope is because LAs are making errors everywhere and the system is flawed. Also there has been a growth in parents informing themselves, and as soon as you are aware of what should be happening, you are aware of what isn't.'

The tribunal itself is tough. It's a long day – sometimes you get a half-day hearing, but usually it's an eight-hour day – and it's upsetting for parents, who will spend that time listening to their child's difficulties being laid out before judges.

'It requires a detailed knowledge of the facts and the law,' says Duff. 'One judge will be a specialist – say, working in education – while the other will be a lawyer. You must address the legal points as well as the factual, education-based questions. You can have a very experienced autism teacher grilling you on a number of things, and parents need to be able to question experts in a purposeful way to build a case. The judges will usually pose questions gently to parents but the questions from the LA's lawyer can be very intense.'

Some parents, particularly those without legal representation, have felt bullied and threatened by the LA at tribunal. It is not uncommon to hear of LAs that are in charge of getting all the evidence to the tribunal (the parents' as well as the LAs own) withholding crucial evidence that would support the parents' case. One woman received a letter from the LA the day before the appeal warning that she would have to pay its £15,000 legal fees if she didn't pull out. She went ahead and found the tribunal judge unsympathetic and that the witnesses – the LA-employed therapists that in theory are working for the child's best interests – had been coached on what to say by the LA's barrister.

She lost (and didn't need to pay the fees in the end), but in 85 per cent of cases where parents challenge an LA decision and go to tribunal, they win, according to Ministry of Justice data. This means that, in 85 per cent of cases, parents have been forced to go through horrible stress and to waste money and energy to get something to which they were entitled. LAs often behave unlawfully until it gets to the tribunal stage, when they have no choice but to follow the rules.

For an example of the horrifying way one local authority behaved around a tribunal with tips on how to protect your case, read here: www.itmustbemum. wordpress.com/2017/07/24/education-tribunal-and-local-authority-games/

Tips from parents

* Whatever you ask for, back it up with reference to SEN code of practice/law.

* Be very focused about what it is you want and evidence everything – this is the Achilles heel of the LA. At a tribunal, it will come down to who has the better quality evidence.

* If you feel that section B of your EHCP [the special educational needs section] doesn't describe your child's needs because the existing reports are too poor, provide evidence from the school: reports, medical history, behaviour incidents, log of communication with school.

* According to insiders at the panels that decide on the support a child gets, some decisions are made on the back of the likelihood of a parent going to appeal and what their case is – so giving the impression you know your legal rights from the off will help in these situations.

* Keep notes of all interactions with the LA and school, which you may need if you go to tribunal.

* One parent asked her private OT to write a report and cost it out, detailing what it would cost to implement, thereby proving the money involved was over the £6,000 threshold.

* Stay strong. It is worth the stress. There are charities providing support.

S is a mum of a 20-year-old autistic man, E, who was diagnosed when he was nearly four. E has been to five different schools.
At one secondary school, S saw her son being shouted at for not making eye contact with a teacher as well as for being too scared to enter a room. Fellow pupils swore at him. The school also used his TA for general class teaching, leaving E in front of the computer for long periods of time. Despite her pleas to help her son make friends, the school didn't do this.

S took her son out of school and the LA failed to find a suitable alternative, telling her she should put him back in the school where he was being bullied. She tried different schools, but they didn't work out. The LA gave up on placing her son at a suitable school and, in total, he lost four and a half years of education.

In the end S went to a tribunal to ask the LA to pay for her son to go to a small private school for one term to finish his GCSEs. The LA was represented by a legal firm that she says fought 'tooth and nail' to oppose her and delayed proceedings at every stage, hoping she would give up. All she was asking for at this stage was one term at the private school – the LA almost certainly spent much more money fighting the case.

S is not from the UK, English is not her first language. 'I didn't know my rights at first,' she says. 'My son's experience at one of the schools left him crying all the time and I hate myself for allowing it. I feel I let E down and I feel I let the schools and the LA bully me. I don't like conflict, so I found it very hard.'

In the end, S, with a lawyer's help, won the case, and her son E is going, far too late, to finish his final term.

Useful websites

www.gov.uk/government/publications/send-code-of-practice-0-to-25
www.ipsea.org.uk
www.hcbgroup.com/special-educational-needs-faqs.html
www.hcbgroup.com/special-educational-needs-in-england.html
www.hcbgroup.com/sen-aln-in-wales.html
www.specialneedsjungle.com
www.mumsnet.com/Talk/special_educational_needs
www.expresscic.org.uk

* * *

13

PLAYDATES

* * *

There's no two ways about it: playdates can be hell for autistic children and their neurotypical parents alike. I certainly know I have invested way too much emotion in them. A playdate that went well would fill me with hope that my son would have a rich social life; one that went badly, as they sometimes inevitably do, would leave me despairing.

For many autistic kids, they hold zero appeal – they may in fact cause a great deal of anxiety – so if your child doesn't want to have or go to a playdate, don't make them. Let home be the place where they get to escape all social demands.

I remember what it was like when I was young, arriving at the house of a friend of my parents and being taken almost straight away to the room of their kids, whom I didn't know. I recall that feeling when the door closed; of being trapped and forced to socialise with strangers. I was shy and found it very difficult, even without being autistic.

Some autistic children do want to go on playdates, however, so below are tips to make them more autism-friendly, as well as some creative ways to make them more appealing to children who aren't initially so keen.

For neurotypical kids, playdates usually go something like this: one child arrives at another child's house and the pair quickly scamper off in search of toys. Meanwhile, the mums head to the kitchen for a cup of tea, a biscuit and a chat. One child reappears as there is a disagreement over who gets to play with the monster truck. This is quickly resolved and the parents go back to their chat. Playdate over, the first child goes home. Everyone happy.

This is not always what it's like on an autistic/neurotypical crossover playdate.

An autistic child arrives at a neurotypical child's house and is immediately freaked out as they've never been there before. They can't settle, nothing is familiar and the choice of toys is completely overwhelming. They start stimming or zone out to protect themselves, not engaging with the other child at all, despite their neurotypical mum's encouragement to go and play. Finally, the kids are in the same room together and the mums are in the kitchen, but the autistic child's mum can't relax and focus on her tea, biscuit and chat because she's nervously listening out for trouble. The child whose house it is reappears to say the autistic child has the monster truck upside down and won't stop spinning the wheels around. Playdate over, neurotypical mum and autistic child go home, both thoroughly demoralised. Horrible.

One solution is to have an autistic/autistic playdate, which may go better, or simply to anchor any playdate around a structured activity. Head to the swimming pool or a trampoline park – somewhere where success is more likely.

We now have a playdate routine: one of my son's friends comes over for two hours – I'm no longer shy about telling their parents when to pick up. We make a cake mix, they play a board game while it's in the oven, we then ice the cake and eat it, they play another game then it's home time. Short and structured. My son often regroups in front of the TV after, while I try not to spill my celebratory glass of wine as I pat myself on the back.

You may not exactly be batting away invitations to playdates every weekend, and playdates may happen because you instigate them and often they aren't reciprocated. This is the reality and it hurts. But you just have to focus on what you can do and not let it get you down. Things may change.

And if the playdate is miserable – if your child is having an awful time and so, for that very reason, are you – you know what? Don't do it. Make your excuses and just leave. Give your kid a kiss and tell them you love them. Let them do something they enjoy to get them back on an even keel. Take a break and try again when the time feels right.

Tips for a successful playdate from other parents

Parents who have gone through the playdate mill so you don't have to. Heed their words!

* If the playdate is at the other child's house, ask the parent to send pictures of their home and the rooms your child is likely to play in – as well as any siblings or pets – so you can show them in advance and they know what to expect.

* Playdates at other people's homes can be tricky, as on the whole they tend to involve more free play than you might indulge in at yours. Take along a board game or another toy your child enjoys that can be played with by two people. A familiar game can help reduce anxiety, while having something to show the other child can help smooth those potentially nervous initial stages of the playdate.

* Work on the rules beforehand – so waiting their turn, listening to what the other child wants to do, watching what the other child is doing. It's about unpicking those subtle things they struggle with and practising the give and take needed to join in with play. Practise the games your child might play beforehand.

* Stage your home – put the best toys out; hide the ones your child only likes to play with on their own or that will cause them to tune out.

* Pages 86–95 of the book *My Social Stories* by Carol Gray covers playdates, explaining issues such as, 'What can I say when my friend arrives?', 'Who decides which toys we play with?' and 'How can I get my toy back?' She also details a Play Plan, which is basically an agenda for the playdate that you and your child's friend can fill in together (but with an adult refereeing).

* Don't expect to be able to chat with the other parents the whole time. It's likely you'll need to be supporting the play – without intruding if your child is coping. It's a knack working out when your child needs you and when they don't. At the very least, you'll be needed at the beginning of the playdate. Immediately offer some structure – say, by suggesting a game of hide-and-seek – which allows both children to relax. It can be easier to host playdates, so you can get more involved in directing the play.

- Basing the playdate out of the home and around a non-social activity can work well until they are ready for more social interaction – watching a film together, for example, or a small show. Activities where the social demands aren't too heavy but your child has shared an experience with another child.

- Start with inviting just one other child, so the social rules don't get complicated by numbers, then work up from there.

- Forewarn your child before the playdate ends. Offering 20-minute, ten-minute and five-minute warnings is less likely to result in a meltdown.

- Support and, if necessary, interpret for your child, but don't embarrass them. I find asking questions is a good way of doing this, for example: 'How should we decide who goes first?'

- If they find losing difficult, think about collaborative games, or something like musical chairs where nobody is out – they just have to squeeze onto the last chair together.

Fun, structured activities to try on a playdate

- Conversation cubes can be a good icebreaker. You roll the cube and ask the question printed on the top.

- Board games.

- Mosaic sticker boards and stickers. They can do these side by side.

- Puzzles: one child provides the pieces, the other fits them in.

- Colouring-by-number books. Buy two and let the friends colour in the same pictures at the same time. Only provide one set of pens, so they have to share and ask each other for them.

- Baking/icing biscuits. If you're not much of a Delia, you can buy packs of ready-made cookie/biscuit dough that come with cutters and icing pens.

- Building something together using a map or a plan can be a good option – for example, Lego building blocks or Play-Doh. The website of London's Science Museum has some great kitchen science experiments.

* Play in the garden: see who can jump the highest; who can do the most star jumps; who can hop on one leg for the longest; fill up water balloons and explode them.

* Make a magic potion – use glitter, food colouring, flour, Lego people, lentils . . . pretty much anything – then pour into bottles so the kids can shake them up. Not one for neat-freak parents!

* Cranium Hullabaloo. You can buy this game second-hand on eBay for about £15. The kids press a button and it instructs them what to do – stand up, sit down, dance – allowing you to sit down and drink your tea (bliss).

J, a mum of an eight-year-old autistic girl, living in north London:

'We have found that trips to "neutral" and unconfined spaces where there are things to look at and plenty of space (for example, the zoo, parks, the RAF museum) are more successful than having other children round or visiting them.'

Things you can work on at home

My child won't take turns

It may seem straightforward, but turn-taking is a surprisingly complicated business when you look at it in detail. Mastering it means getting to grips with the four Ws:

1. An understanding of **why** we share

2. The ability to patiently **wait** your turn – that is, self-regulation skills

3. Knowledge of what to do **while** you are waiting

4. The ability to work out **when** it's the right time to take your turn

Turn-taking is vital when it comes to playing games, developing friendships and communicating with others – a monologue is not conversation, no matter what the opinionated pub bore believes. Some parents of autistic children don't insist their child takes turns in the same way as other children, believing they are not able to. This does them no favours.

Some ways to teach turn-taking:

* If your child is older, start with a Social Story, such as this one: 'I will be playing a game with my friends today. During this game, we will have to take turns and wait while others are having their turns. Taking a turn means that I can play, then my friends will have a chance to play. While I am waiting for my turn, I can count to 20 in my head or watch my friends play out their turn. When it is my turn, I will take my turn and then wait again while the next players take their turns. This will help the game to be fun and everyone will enjoy playing the game.'

* Model what good turn-taking looks like in lots of everyday ways: take turns to listen to a station on the radio; choose a TV programme; decide what's for dinner. Even standard daily events can be used, such as dressing ('You put on one sock, then I'll put the other sock on') or eating ('You take a bite, then it's my turn to take a bite').

* A variation on this theme is to have a tin and a container full of little objects. Throw an object into the tin, then hand an object to the child to do the same. Continue until they're all gone. Do it quickly so the child doesn't lose interest. If it goes well, try it again, this time throwing two objects.

* Make it visual. Have a card with the words 'Jack's turn' on one side – and a picture of Jack if your child isn't reading yet – and 'Mummy's turn' and a picture of you on the other. Use a timer to show how long each turn lasts. A kitchen timer might be better than one on your smartphone or tablet, as it's unlikely Jack will give two hoots about turn-taking if the iPad comes out.

Birthday parties

We went through some miserable birthday parties before I came to a decision: no more. Between the ages of three and five, we didn't go to any. At that point, there was nothing in it for my son. When he started reception, his first year of school, he was invited to a party. We asked him if he wanted to go and he said yes. It was difficult for him at first – he spent more than half the party, held in a school hall, hovering in the foyer, but once the disco started and the cake arrived, he plucked up the courage to join in. The bigger parties are still a challenge but he enjoys the smaller ones. I always give him the option not to go.

'A lot of kids who are autistic don't want to go to the huge parties – if they could have the bouncy castle to themselves, that's heaven, but fighting for your place is really not,' says psychologist Dr Emily Lovegrove. 'At the parties, parents tend to demand of their children, "Go and say happy birthday", and at the end, "Say thank you very much for having me." Well, often the autistic child thinks, "Why would I say thank you for something I haven't enjoyed?"'

My son's fifth birthday party triumph:

'My son struggled with his own birthday parties as well as other people's, so I tried to create a party he would enjoy. We kept it small – there were ten kids including him – and the location was a treasure hunt outdoors, so not so many sensory issues, with an entertainer dressed as an elf leading the treasure hunt around the local woods.

'We also kept it very structured: the children arrived, the elf arrived shortly after – he started off with games then the treasure hunt. After the treasure hunt there was the meal in a hut in the woods, then we played musical statues, cut the cake, then it was home time. There were adult-led activities at all times.

'I was organised to the max. I wrote him a timeline for the day: 1. Your friends arrive. 2. The elf arrives. 3. The elf, you and your friends play games. 4. The treasure hunt. 5. Pizza and chips. I stuck it next to my son's bed two days before the party. He knew the order by heart. The day before the party we visited the wood and talked him through everything that was going to happen, so he could visualise it.

'The result? Success! He loved it, interacted with his friends, albeit briefly, and didn't seem stressed. Yay!'

Dealing with parents at school – to tell them if your child is autistic or not?

This is a personal decision and there are pros and cons on both sides. I've opted for honesty – with the people I know and trust, at any rate. For me it's the least stressful option, and I'm lucky that the parents at my son's school have been brilliant. You may need their support, and if they don't know, they can't help. I've heard people say that the moment another parent has found out their child is autistic, the playdates stop. I'm sure it happens, but if that's the case, I wouldn't want my son playing round theirs anyway.

✳   ✳   ✳

14

GIRLS AND AUTISM

* * *

'Why should I cry for not being an apple,
when I was born an orange?'
Autistic writer Donna Williams

I know a woman who I'm going to call Jane. I love Jane. She's a friend of my cousin's and whenever we meet, she greets me with a tight hug, almost squeezing the breath out of me. She is fiercely bright, warm and talks a lot.

Now 50, Jane explained to me recently that she is beginning to think she's autistic. She has never understood what emotions she's feeling, she says; she thinks she can empathise but isn't sure it's in quite the same way as other people do – she either feels overwhelmingly sad for someone, a feeling that takes over her day, or oddly detached. When someone eats next to her in a restaurant she has to walk away as the sound feels so aggressive.

She spoke to me about this because she knew I was writing this book. I was initially surprised. Despite learning about the false assumptions the world makes about autism – that it's a male condition; that autistic people always struggle to communicate effectively; that they can appear aloof – I instantly ruled her out. This warm, chatty woman could not possibly be autistic. And yet it dawned on me soon after: she probably is.

The knee-jerk reaction we have, excluding women from our narrow definition of autism, is best typified by the experience of Sarah Hendrickx. Sarah has written six books on autism, completed a master's degree in autism, taken nearly 1,000 training/conference sessions and worked with several hundred autistic people – and yet with all her experience of the condition, she didn't realise until she was in her early forties that she too was on the spectrum. The reason? 'I had been doing what most of the experts had been doing: comparing myself with autistic males,' she explains.

I've been asking autistic adults a lot of questions and I have noticed something: while some of the women I've interviewed have asked me not to identify them as autistic, no autistic man has said the same. This reveals something, I think, about the extra courage women have to pluck up to tell the world they are autistic; they sense the world doesn't understand, or isn't ready, for women to be autistic too.

I feel awkward writing about the difference between autistic girls and autistic boys – it's problematic in the same way that all generalisations based on gender are. I look at my son and think how he fits in with the female presentation of autism more than the male (he tends to mask his problems, he internalises things, he's never disruptive in class and is very anxious). If the world were more gender-neutral, it would be interesting to see whether the difference between autistic boys and girls lessened. Maybe then Jane would be able to tell people about her thoughts and receive instant acceptance.

What we know about autistic girls from academic research

* Officially there are four autistic boys to every autistic girl at the time of writing.

* Girls experience more barriers to diagnosis than boys with similar levels of difficulty, and girls without learning difficulties are not being picked up so easily. They have higher levels of misdiagnosis, delayed diagnosis or no diagnosis.

* Girls are diagnosed three years later than boys – at the age of eight, on average, compared with five for boys.

* Some academics believe there may be two autistic boys for every autistic girl. Once autistic girls are better identified, some believe the true rate will be equal to boys.

* Autistic women on the whole have fewer obvious stims, such as hand-flapping, and fewer repetitive and rigid behaviours.

* Special interests can appear more similar to neurotypical interests compared with boys, but what will be different compared with neurotypicals is the intensity of interest.

* Girls are more inclined to seek out friendships than boys.

* They have better social skills than autistic boys in childhood, yet comparatively worse social skills by their teens.

* At school, girls are more likely to receive support for learning than they are for building friendships.

Source: Girls and Autism: Flying Under the Radar, *a guide published by the National Association for Special Educational Needs (Nasen); Sarah Hendrickx.*

Male bias in autism

Judith Gould, lead consultant at the Lorna Wing centre for autism:
'I think there may still be more boys on the spectrum than girls because boys tend to have more developmental disorders in general, but I don't think it is as biased towards males as the figures suggest.'

Hans Asperger initially thought that autistic psychopathy, as he termed it, was an exclusively male condition, although he later revised his opinion. While it used to be treated as a fact that autism is more common in boys than girls, this assumption is now being challenged. In a piece she wrote for the online magazine *Standard Issue,* Sarah Hendrickx writes: 'If you're essentially looking for the components of a boy, you'll find a boy. So, you can see that if your starting point is skewed, with the subsequent decades of research producing an increasing evidence base, along with generations of diagnostic clinicians who have been taught using this skewed evidence base, this leads us to an inaccurate autism diagnostic ratio of males and females.'

Laura James, author of *Odd Girl Out,* a book about being given a diagnosis of autism at the age of 45, also discusses the invisibility of autistic women in society. 'If I asked you to name one well-known autistic woman, would you be able to?' she asked a journalist interviewing her for the *Irish Independent* newspaper. 'You could probably think of Saga [a character from Scandi-noir TV series *The Bridge*] but that would be about it, whereas with men you could kind of list them and list them.

'There's this weird resistance to women who get diagnosed with autism, for some reason. I think it's partly because we don't project the view of autism that other people think is real.'

For many people, the 'extreme male brain' theory put forward by Professor Simon Baron-Cohen, director of the Autism Research Centre at Cambridge University, is the basis of their understanding of autism. Baron-Cohen proposed that men (non-autistic and autistic) are better 'systemisers' and (non-autistic) women better 'empathisers'. Autistic women, the theory suggests, are better systemisers than empathisers. This research is controversial within the autism community, however, with many claiming the extreme male brain theory has resulted in autistic women struggling to get a diagnosis.

Why is it hard to spot autistic girls?

Because of the male bias in what we perceive autism is and how we identify it. If SENCOs, teachers and parents still consider autism in girls to be rare, they may be less likely to refer girls for assessment. And even if they do take it further, there are still GPs and professionals who advise parents that their daughter can't be autistic because she can make conversation and hold eye contact, when some girls on the spectrum can do those things (or fake it more convincingly).

Early years

The stereotypical autistic child is one whose imaginative play is either reduced or absent. This may not be true for autistic girls, who can create intricate fantasy lands of imaginary friends, animals and creatures.

While autistic boys line up their Thomas the Tank Engine toys in size order, autistic girls may have a massive collection of cuddly toys and be very specific where each teddy must sit every time. Autistic girls at primary school may play pretend schools a lot, though what they are really doing is running through the script of their day and re-enacting it as a way of processing it.

The consultant clinical psychologist Judith Gould has found that girls are just as likely as boys to exhibit other signs of autism in early babyhood, such as a lack of social curiosity, late or non-existent pointing, poor eye contact and late smiling.

Social differences

Michelle Dean, assistant professor of special education at California State University Channel Islands, has researched social behaviours in autistic girls and boys in school. She found that autistic girls are less likely to be alone at break time than autistic boys, though the interaction is likely to be shorter than for a non-autistic girl, and the quality of the interaction may be different.

Far from aloof, some autistic girls can be clingy; they want someone around them all the time who makes them feel safe; they are very close to their mums; they are afraid to be alone. Either that or the social difficulties can see them labelled as shy.

Though they may prefer their own company, they feel they ought to be in a group or risk being teased. In their pre-teen years, girls' social skills can appear similar to those of neurotypical kids, but their social understanding is only surface-level. They are confused a lot of the time but cover it up. The autistic girl at school may be bossy, or, conversely, may be friends with a maternal friend who bosses them about. Frequently, they align themselves with a friend with good social skills to try to copy them, possibly to the point of wanting to be exactly like them. In effect, they are camouflaging their difficulties. When their relationships get more complex in teenage years, the gulf in skills widens and they are less able successfully to conceal what is going on. This can be a difficult time.

Communication

Felicity Sedgewick, a researcher at King's College London, adds that autistic girls are often better at picking up on social cues than autistic boys, although parents may feel that they've had to teach these skills, rather than them coming naturally to their daughters. Girls are also said to act out less when dealing with hurt, anger and confusion, instead internalising these feelings.

'She may look as though she's making eye contact but is actually looking at a dot between your eyes, or to the side or above. Autistic girls are likely to know that this is what is required socially, but direct eye contact can be overwhelming, so they develop compensatory strategies to help them appear more "normal",' Sedgewick adds.

Far from having communication delay, autistic girls can be early or even precocious speakers, as Sarah Hendrickx was. 'We can be fooled by speech ability,' she says. 'They may talk a lot, but the social understanding or reciprocal communication is not there.'

Imitating others

These girls aren't just fooling teachers into thinking they are like their neuro-typical peers – they can fool professionals too. 'Because girls tend to learn the social rules and imitate others, they can come across as not having problems in the structured clinic setting,' says Judith Gould. 'They may do well on the Autism Diagnostic Observation Schedule [a tool used by clinicians as part of the diagnostic process] as they are being observed on their own, rather than inter-acting with other children. If you have a girl on the spectrum with a learning disability, they may well have a more male profile of repetitive activities, such as spinning, but the more able girls who are missed tend to have less obvious obsessions.'

The psychologist Professor Tony Attwood adds that girls can have stylised gestures and phrases they've learned through imitation, so sometimes parents think: who is the real you? 'The autistic girl may change depending on who she's talking to and what she thinks they want to hear from her,' he says. 'She may have selective mutism [when someone is able to talk but only in particular settings] when she's overwhelmed by a social situation.'

They may be constantly doing things that aren't intuitive or easy for them. They are trying to be someone they aren't. 'It's mentally exhausting to continually suppress your natural social reactions,' says Sarah Wild the head teacher at Limpsfield Grange secondary school in Surrey for autistic girls. 'Understanding, regulating and managing their emotions is absolutely crucial to autistic girls' happiness in adult life.'

Special interests

Girls' special interests tend to be similar to those of non-autistic girls rather than the more technical hobbies and facts more common in [autistic] boys, says Gould. Autistic boys tend to be more object-related, commonly playing with trains or cars or taking things apart. Animals are a common special inter-est for girls, or fantasy worlds involving witches and princesses. Their fantasy worlds can be elaborate but solitary and rigid – there's no flexibility and they don't get symbolic representations, such as a banana for a phone. It may not include other children, or they may want to dominate and be in charge.

While Asperger-type boys are often referred to as 'little professors', girls may be known as 'little psychologists'. They are people-watchers, observing and trying to copy behaviour that is baffling to them.

To the untrained eye some autistic girls' special interests can look like non-autistic behaviour, but the difference is the intensity of that interest.

'One girl I worked with loved horses,' says Sarah Wild. 'Nobody thinks twice about a ten-year-old girl who loves horses, but she'd memorised the dressage handbook. Their special interests tend to have an unusual focus and intensity.'

Helen, an autistic woman who lives in Kent:
'I wasn't diagnosed until I was in my thirties, so at school I was labelled as thin-skinned and shy. I had very few friends. I think I would have liked there just to be awareness of the fact that autism can affect girls too, and that the presentation can be very different [to boys]. I went to an all-girls grammar school and I was perceived to have no problems because I was academically fine. My brother is also autistic and was diagnosed at the age of ten. There was no doubt that he would need support as he had a typical high-functioning male presentation.'

The end result of these differences is . . .

A lack of support. Even with a diagnosis, still schools often don't see a problem or recognise the girl's needs. Research shows that teachers tend to view the support needs of an autistic girl as far less than the parents do.

'Autistic girls commonly use masses of energy trying to hide any difficulties at school, trying to fit in, and then release an explosion of emotion at home,' says Ruth Moyse. 'It is really important that teachers take seriously any parents who are concerned about their daughter's behaviour at home, even if the school thinks the child is a model pupil, and not dismiss it as poor parenting.'

And . . .

Misdiagnosis. In a survey of more than 8,000 autistic people and family members in the UK, the NAS found that 42 per cent of autistic women had been diagnosed with another condition on assessment – frequently a mental health condition, caused by difficulties surrounding their autism – compared with 30 per cent of autistic men.

Autistic woman and journalist Nicky Clark started the Twitter hashtag #SheCantBeAutistic to gather some of the dismissive responses women have received from clinicians, friends and family. Women talked about being told that they or their daughter couldn't possibly be autistic, because they were able to make eye contact, had good verbal skills, showed empathy and weren't violent. This shows the misunderstanding of autism in women, but of the condition in general too. 'If they've gone under the radar until puberty, the difficulties may appear when their peer interactions become more complex and difficult at secondary school, where they can be bullied, experience high levels of anxiety and depression, OCD or eating disorders,' says Judith Gould. 'In this instance, eating disorders may not be to do with body image but a special interest relating to counting calories or needing a special routine around eating and keeping fit.'

School and friendships

'An Aspie girl is the most delightful friend you could ever wish for,' says Tony Attwood. 'She is incredibly loyal and doesn't do bitchy. She may be the victim of bitchiness, but she doesn't get it. You may find she actually prefers to play with boys.

'She will have a propensity to have one good friend – two's company and three's a crowd. At school there may be one girl who acts as an unpaid teacher's aid and who mothers her in the nicest possible way. She may be able to socialise but only for a particular amount of time. She can manage for half an hour then loses it. I call it "Cinderella at the ball at midnight".'

In the playground, if the autistic girl is teased or not included, there is a danger she will retreat into her own world, he adds. 'Schools need to have zero tolerance of meanness towards her because she needs to be encouraged to engage with others rather than escaping into her imagination. My concern is that her rejection by the neurotypicals will lay down the foundation for depression in her teenage years. Rejection can lead to low self-esteem and the basis of depression in adolescence.'

'It can be very difficult for autistic girls to keep up with lots of friendships because it is such hard work for them,' says Felicity Sedgewick. 'They have to think about what their friends like, remember to talk to them regularly, think about how they feel all the time, play what they want to play and navigate the unspoken rules of wide-ranging playground games or complex group situations.

'It's also important to remember that an autistic girl's friendships might not necessarily be what her parents expect, but if she's happy, that's OK. One mum I worked with always took her daughter and a friend to a trampoline park, where they jumped, giggled and fell over but didn't really talk to each other at all. To her, it didn't look like friendship at first, but they were having fun. It's about supporting the friendships your child makes rather than the ones you want her to make.'

Sedgewick recommends that schools and parents need to find structured environments where friendships can develop, such as a lunchtime computer class, craft or reading group. It takes away the pressure of having to make eye contact because everyone is working on the project, and it gives them something concrete to talk about.

Sarah Wild, the head teacher at the Limpsfield Grange, the only state (secondary) school for autistic girls, adds that in about year 4, at the age of eight or nine, the differences between autistic girls and their neurotypical friends will become more apparent. Girls' friendships start to move away from just activities and games and become more about social interaction; they become conversation-based friendships.

'Those conversations tend to be about other people,' says Wild. 'When that switch happens, autistic girls can't keep up. Boys will still be playing football and have friendships that revolve around shared interests. But the girls really want friendships and they're reaching out and trying to connect with their peers. From about year 4, autistic girls are just getting it wrong. They instinctively know "My experience is not the same as everyone else's, I'm different", but they don't know why.

'Year 6 can be a hideous year for them, with SATs and the prospect of transition to secondary school. Things can get really bad at home – they have meltdowns or simply shut down. Mum goes into school and is told, "We don't see any of that here, maybe it's the parenting." So the family become isolated.'

Meanwhile, special schools can be limiting for girls' social potential as they often have a small number of girls, meaning limited opportunities to develop appropriate peer relationships.

How to help an autistic girl with friendship – advice from by Sue Moon, a speech and language therapist who specialises in working with autistic girls:

* Girl friendships are very fluid – they fall in and out of friendships all the time. Often the girls I work with are possessive; they need someone to be their friend and their friend only. If their friend is also friends with someone else, that can be really hard.

* I use the social thinking approach, created by an American woman called Marcia Garcia Winner (www.socialthinking.com). You draw Comic strip Conversations: one stick figure to represent your daughter and another to represent her friend, with speech bubbles. You could ask: 'Why do you think they said that? What other explanations can there be?'

* Use visuals. You may not get her to respond to a question about what she likes about school, but she might rate lunchtimes or teachers out of ten.

* Personal identity is also a big issue. I'm working with an eight-year-old who has a best friend who is very social and confident. She watches her all the time; she's always close to her, sitting so close their legs are touching on the carpet. She is trying to become her, using her as a social guide. I do a lot of work helping these girls work out who they are, what they do and don't like, so they can develop their own identity.

* Assertiveness is also important: getting young people to be their
  own advocates. We unintentionally raise girls to be obliging. I use
  the 'I' message for this. You encourage the child to say: 'I feel X
  when you X because X.' It gives you a framework to say these
  things and then you don't have to act out.

* Not all communication has to be verbal. The parents of an
  11-year-old I'm working with have just bought her a phone. It's
  been amazing. She finds it hard to speak clearly and pauses a lot,
  but on text, where she's in control of the interactions, she can tell
  them concisely what she's feeling.

Carrie Grant, a vocal coach and TV presenter, is the mother of three
daughters – Talia, 15, and Imogen, 11, who have autism, and Olivia,
22, who has ADHD with autistic features – and an adopted son,
Nathan, seven, who has ADHD, dyspraxia (also known as Developmental Coordination Disorder, or DCD) and attachment issues. She
describes what life is like for her two autistic daughters:

'I learned on the same day that my two youngest daughters are autistic. I
had taken them to be assessed by the same doctor and he confirmed within
minutes that Imogen was autistic and Talia had Asperger syndrome.

'We never grieved, as the label doesn't change who they are. I saw them
both as creative. I love their difference and that their characters weren't
made in a sausage factory. So I thought, "They are going to be like those
people. More complex, a bit moody, quirky – that's OK." We felt almost
like, "Wow, we've got these special kids." We felt very positive about it.

'Then Talia got to the age of nine and started to have mental health
problems. Adapting to the mental illness was far harder than receiving
the autism diagnosis. The school didn't help. They were in absolute
denial that she had a diagnosis even though I showed them the paperwork. I told them about the meltdowns after school; that she doesn't
understand why the teacher tells the class to read and some people keep
talking; that she doesn't understand that when the whole class is being
told off, it's not only her the teacher means. But they didn't get it.

'Part of the reason why is Talia blends in and masks her difficulties.
Blending in is wanting to fit in; where you think: "I'll copy what my

friend next to me does." Masking is different – that comes out of high levels of anxiety. Masking is when Talia leaves the house in her make-up and looks a million dollars. She goes to school and pretends she's OK, only she comes home and it all comes tumbling out. She tells me, "That person doesn't like me, this teacher shouted at me."

'Imogen will get told off more and say, "This lesson is boring, why are we learning it?" We used to tell Imogen not to say these things, but then I realised we were teaching her how to mask, and that if we carried on, we were going to give her mental health problems, so we stopped.

'Things have been very tough for Talia but I'd say she's in a good place now. She's a deep, complex and gentle person. Everyone who meets her loves her. She gave a speech recently at the House of Commons and I was so proud of her – it was better than the Speaker of the House! It's a building block for her self-confidence. She's now a 15-year-old woman who has been through so much. Those things are going to shift her towards success.'

Eating disorders

Research carried out at the eating disorders unit at the Maudsley Hospital in London in 2005 reported that 23 per cent of its patients have Asperger syndrome.

Autistic adults highlight the sensory impact around food – some textures may feel impossible to eat. Mothers can become extremely anxious when their child doesn't eat and see it as a rejection of them and their care. Yet more stress is piled on the child. Some autistic adults have told me that as soon as they become stressed, they can't eat.

While anorexia is often about control for girls, whether autistic or neurotypical, the issue of control is intensified in autistic girls, particularly the perfectionist autistic girl. When your world feels out of control, counting calories may be calming (the numbers providing a structure). 'Routines are easy to get into and comforting to maintain. And there are sensory issues,' says Jen Leavesley, an autistic woman who lives in Birmingham.

She adds: 'As an autistic woman it is very easy to see how the "orthorexia" mindset could easily go too far and how healthy eating could easily become pathologised. Think about how a rigid teenage girl, pressured with the stress of fitting in at school, not understanding peers, being called fat by someone, then interprets the food pyramid literally. She won't eat "junk" food and becomes preoccupied with healthy eating – for example, avoiding all fat (which is perfectly fine). It becomes a rule she won't ever break.'

Exclusion from school

It's likely that a significant number of the children who find it difficult or impossible to attend school are autistic girls. But there are also girls who are in school but not participating – they may be so anxious they can't learn, or aren't being taught in a way that is appropriate for them – as well as persistent absentees or those who have been excluded. Their absence from school will have a significant and negative impact on their education, mental health and future life chances.

Lucia Santi is mum to a ten-year-old autistic girl who has been recently diagnosed as autistic. Her daughter stopped being able to attend school for a year and has only recently returned. Santi is the head teacher of The Grove, an autism school in Wood Green, north London:

'I knew my daughter was most likely autistic from the age of two but I thought she would manage without a diagnosis. Then she stopped coping at school – she started having tummy aches and panic attacks – and wouldn't go.

'I asked the GP for a referral to CAMHS, then got hold of the education social worker and attendance officer, so they knew why my daughter was off school. I got the attendance officer to contact the tuition service. Three months after stopping going to school, we had tuition at the house.

'I think the school thought it would pass, but I knew it wouldn't. She wanted to go to school but just couldn't cope.

'She was away for nearly a year but is now back full-time apart from Friday mornings. Her dad brings his laptop to school and works in the reception area, so she knows she has someone there – it's a separation anxiety and trust thing. He rents an office close to the school and is at the reception area in case our daughter needs him at 10.30 a.m., before lunch and after lunch. It means she has the security of knowing he's there if she needs him.'

Bullying and abuse

Because autistic young people have difficulty reading other people's motivations, they are more vulnerable to abuse. Dr Catriona Stewart, co-facilitator of the Scottish Women's Autism Network, says autistic children will tend to assume the best until proven otherwise. While boys can be vulnerable to being sucked into a gang or taken advantage of, girls can self-harm, be sexually promiscuous and be vulnerable to other high-risk behaviours when they get older.

'Children mature at different rates,' says Stewart. 'The autistic girl may be developing or outstripping her peers in some ways, but her emotional development is likely to be quite behind. You get this situation where a group of girls has a wee matriarch and there is a lot of power play and manipulation. The matriarch is finding she has the power to manipulate people; an autistic girl is not going to be able to understand everything and will be easily led. She will be vulnerable to being marginalised and to bullying.

'Bullying is important in terms of vulnerability to abuse. That sense of loneliness, confusion and the huge anxiety it causes; the assumption that it's down to them, it's their fault – all this makes them more susceptible to someone flattering them.'

Some autistic adults report feeling bullied by teachers when they were young. It's likely that these feelings of inadequacy kick in early – at the age of eight or nine – but the child can't articulate them. Professionals sometimes describe the signs of autism as subtle, yet the effect of these differences on girls' sense of self and their self-esteem is profound.

'The experience of bullying may be generic but the way it plays out is gendered,' Stewart adds. 'Boys are more likely to beat each other up – it's out in the open. The kind of mental cruelty meted out in films like *Mean Girls* kicks in a lot earlier than we are prepared to recognise, and when the girls mature it becomes more intense.

'It's about being your best friend one day then dumping you the next without any explanation. That kind of cruel manipulation and exclusion, with sometimes a big show made of those rejections and exclusions, is very difficult to deal with.'

Personal safety

Marianthi Kourti is an autistic PhD student at the University of Birmingham, researching autism and gender. As part of her research project, she focused on the childhood experiences of women whose autism was identified in adulthood. It became clear that many had been in unhealthy relationships.

'Autistic girls need an honest and detailed conversation on how to keep themselves safe and how to recognise danger,' says Kourti. 'It is important that the information is detailed and no euphemisms are used. One participant of my research group told me, "The subtle talks that teachers had during the 'sex education' at school, using innuendo and indirect references, were completely lost on me. I had no idea what they were talking about, and no one to ask, so wasn't prepared for anything."'

She adds: 'Recent research seems to focus on girls "masking" their autistic habits in order to fit in, and ignores the fact that masking may lead to them being scared of speaking up for themselves in dangerous situations, or being so concerned with not standing out that they agree to anything and compromise their own personal safety.'

This is uncomfortable reading if you are the mum of an autistic girl, but the women Kourti interviewed struggled to have their needs met or recognised. Our children are in a much more fortunate position – their parents will be clued up about how to help them.

*   *   *

15

AUTISM IN BLACK AND MINORITY ETHNIC COMMUNITIES

* * *

'Many families I have spoken to within the BAME community say their children were given the "naughty" label, or schools and professionals were quick to question what was happening at home.'

Venessa Bobb, mother of an autistic boy and
co-founder of the charity A2ndVoice

While the term black, Asian and minority ethnic (BAME) may be shorthand for a wide variety of non-white cultures and communities, BAME parents face similar issues when it comes to seeking help for their autistic children. The struggle to access appropriate support or get a child's needs recognised is harder than for non-BAME families, and the lack of support can have awful consequences.

Dr Ken Greaves is one of the few black specialist consultant psychologists working with autistic children, and is a member of the diagnostic team at the National Autistic Society's Lorna Wing Centre. He reports that only a 'minimal' number of children who come to the centre for an assessment are from BAME communities, suggesting there are many children who are not getting identified and falling under the radar. 'I see them as adults,' Greaves says. 'They've ended up in mental health institutions, chemically coshed, and it's destroyed them.'

Very few studies have been undertaken to establish what BAME autistic children and their parents need in terms of support, and their experience of the system. In research terms, finding out how to help them get what they need and deserve as citizens of this country seems not to be a priority at the moment.

As part of my research for this chapter, I looked for newspaper, magazine and online articles exploring the issue and found pretty much nothing.

One notable exception is the 'Diverse Perspectives' report, compiled by the National Autistic Society (NAS) to identify some of the challenges facing BAME autism families in England. It canvassed the views of 130 participants in focus groups around Britain who identified themselves as variously Indian, Pakistani, Bangladeshi, Chinese, black and Middle Eastern, and was launched in February 2013 at an event in the House of Commons, hosted by the Labour MP Diane Abbott.

It highlights how parents can experience an increased isolation, shunned by those around them and judged at school and in public. Some families are being failed at every stage: by their family, community, school, local authority and professionals.

What the research tells us about autism in BAME communities

* People with autism from BAME communities are less likely to be diagnosed, receive benefits and access appropriate help.

* Bangladeshis have the lowest uptake of disability living allowance of any ethnic group.

* Services are not meeting people's cultural needs.

* There is a lack of awareness of rights and relevant services in some communities.

* The prevalence of diagnosed autism in pupils of Asian heritage was half of the prevalence in white British pupils, as of 2012.

    Source: 'Diverse Perspectives' report, from the National Autistic Society; research from Lindsay et al; The Equalities National Council and Scope.

Autistic not naughty

Schools are not as good at picking up the early signs of autism in children from ethnic minorities as they are in white children. Some teachers see behavioural differences as misbehaviour. Black families say their children's difficulty with eye contact and their inability to sit still has been put down to sullenness and non-compliance, for example.

Assessments and diagnoses of autism can take far longer for BAME children than for their white peers. And even with a diagnosis, families report still having to work hard to convince teachers their children are autistic.

There are concerns that black autistic children who haven't been diagnosed are more frequently excluded from schools and placed in Pupil Referral Units – separate local authority-maintained schools that accommodate troubled and disruptive pupils who have been kicked out of mainstream education – with some eventually ending up in the criminal justice system.

Two pieces of research carried out in the US and presented at an autism research conference in Baltimore, Maryland, in 2016 offer some depressing statistics. They found that children from high-income families are just under 81 per cent more likely to receive an autism diagnosis than those from lower-income families. Black and Hispanic children are also less likely to get a diagnosis of autism than are white children.

The black children studied had lower verbal intelligence scores and were more likely to have lower IQs and poorer language and communication skills than white children. These differences were put down to the fact that black children tend to be diagnosed later than white children, and so often do not receive early interventions.

Low awareness of autism and child development

Awareness of autism is not as widespread in some BAME communities and can mean a delay in parents seeking an assessment – or not seeking an assessment at all. They may hope their child will grow out of it; that life will become more manageable for the child and family alike with more love, faith, space or, more worryingly, discipline.

'They may not have heard of autism and so when someone comes along and talks about it their emotional journey might take longer than someone else who knows more,' says Ken Greaves. He adds that, 'many people, particularly fathers from Afro-Caribbean cultures, are resistant to the diagnosis and may feel that the child can be disciplined into "correct" behaviours'.

Venessa Bobb, the mother of an autistic boy and co-founder of the charity A2ndVoice, a voluntary group that bridges the gap between parents and professionals, says a lot of BAME families do not understand that having a diagnosis will help their child get support. 'They don't realise that having a diagnosis doesn't mean their child is bad. They may not attend meetings, consultations or workshops or engage with teachers and professionals. The child may be missing out on their educational rights as a result.'

Some BAME parents who have heard of autism assume it's a condition that affects only white children. This could be down to the fact that it's mainly white kids getting diagnosed.

Shame and blame

These were recurrent themes in the focus groups that took part in the NAS's 'Diverse Perspectives' research and appeared in the context of discussions about family as well as the wider community. According to the report: 'Shame was felt when a child's autism was thought to reflect badly on a family or a parent. Participants felt that their families were judged by other people for not being "normal". Blame was commonly experienced as a view that the child's condition was not natural, and therefore was the result of something wrong that someone had done.'

While the role of religion can be of benefit – with faith giving strength – some parents perceived that they were being judged by members of their faith groups or places of worship.

Cultural stigma and
negative views

Some languages don't have any words to describe autism – there's no word for the condition in Somali or some Asian languages, for example. One Somali mum of an autistic girl reported that family members and friends from the community would refer to her daughter as 'crazy girl'.

Venessa Bobb says BAME families can struggle when a diagnosis of autism has been given. 'Many seem to be embarrassed by the label, language barriers can delay the process of seeking help and as a result behavioural problems can escalate to the point that social services get involved.

'Parents fear that their children will be taken away. They would rather rely on their friends, the church or mosque for help. Autism is often taboo in these cultures; they aren't able to accept that anything is wrong. Autism is invisible. The child can walk and talk, so people either can't or don't want to believe it.'

Mothers from BAME communities often feel as though they are doing most of the heavy lifting when it comes to overseeing the practicalities involved with having a child on the spectrum. On top of this, they are also more likely to have to deal with denial, frustrations and blame from their husbands or wider families.

'Female participants speculated that men are more likely to feel that an "abnormal" child reflects badly on [their] own status and identity,' the NAS report said. '[Men] may therefore feel threatened by the situation, and less willing to accept it. For instance, fathers had blamed the mother for having done something wrong in pregnancy, such as having an affair or not living and eating healthily.'

Working with professionals

Some families report that professionals do not fully involve them in decisions on what support their children need. Professionals can also struggle to know when a family does and doesn't want their help.

'The professionals need to be sensitive to working with culture-diverse families,' says Greaves. 'Too often a professional says, "I think your child has autism – there you go", and leaves it at that. These families need more support.'

Many BAME cultures have a very high level of respect for the medical profession and this can lead to parents feeling intimidated, or lacking confidence, which stops them asking questions and seeking more information. Yet Greaves acknowledges too that some of those coming into contact with BAME children and their families can lack the human touch, making them less approachable: 'In my experience, there is a certain type of professional who, for whatever reason, has an air that is more theoretical than caring.'

Language differences

Problems with language can include:

* Information may not be available in their native tongue for BAME families and they don't always have access to a translator when it comes to meetings.

* Not everyone is literate, so written information is not always appropriate.

* When it comes to conversations with, say, an educational psychologist or a paediatrician, even those who do speak English well can struggle to understand professional jargon.

* Interpreters don't always give accurate information. They may misunderstand what a professional has told a family, or insert their own cultural assumptions.

* Some families are forced to rely on a family member to act as their informal interpreter, but sometimes these helpful middlemen or women – in some cases even children – are only capable of partial comprehension and translation.

Support

'Some families believe everything the local authority tells them and don't know when to fight things, which means they're more likely to have delays in accessing support,' says Venessa Bobb. 'I had to go through four tribunal appeals to get the right educational support for Nathaniel. How could you do that if you don't speak the language or cannot read or write in English?'

Currently, accessing help from a support group is something of a postcode lottery. Venessa Bobb reports that when such groups have been run by white middle-class mothers, for example, it has been difficult to get BAME parents to attend.

Venessa Bobb on her autistic son Nathaniel, 14, who was diagnosed with autism and ADHD at the age of five. Bobb is co-founder of A2ndVoice for BAME parents and carers of autistic children or adults and is also chair of the Lambeth branch of the National Autistic Society:

'When Nathaniel was non-verbal, many blamed it on the fact his father was Jamaican and said the cultural differences had caused him to act the way he did. No one accepted that there was anything wrong, but looked at me as a bad parent, like I was trying to seek attention.

'When Nathaniel finally got the diagnosis at the age of five, many of my family members and friends asked: "Why are you accepting this label?" They didn't want to talk about autism and just saw his behaviour as that of a typical boy. I have chosen not to have contact with my family any longer.

'Looking back, I was on my own with a child who just seemed to be constantly getting in trouble and being judged by other parents. The professionals gave up on him. I grew up in a disciplinarian household, where I was smacked. If anyone told me to smack Nathaniel, I would say no.

'Smacking a non-verbal child, this is the most damaging thing anyone can do, but this happens across all communities. He is 14 years old now and very verbal when it comes to letting me know how he was treated by others as a child.

'I attend a Pentecostal church. My previous church didn't recognise my son as having a condition but rather viewed me as not caring for him properly. Nathaniel struggled with the long services; looking back, he had severe meltdowns and was very direct in his words. The majority of the congregation did not accept his autism. The church I attend now has been a great support in recognising autism and other related conditions.

'There is a lack of understanding among the BAME community, whether that's a fear of yet another label for black boys or that autism is a demonic spirit that needs to be exorcised. The autistic child or adult, whether black or white, needs to be accepted in society and given the respect and understanding to live their full potential life. When we all come together we have to remember that autism affects everyone the same.'

* * *

16

HOLIDAYS

✳ ✳ ✳

*'I have never gone on a real trip, never taken a holiday.
The best holiday for me is spent in my workshops when
nearly everybody else is on vacation.'*
Enzo Ferrari, racing driver and founder of the sports car
manufacturer

If visiting somewhere new and escaping your routine for a week or two sounds like heaven, you are probably neurotypical. Most autistic children will choose staying at home and sleeping in their own bed over lying on a beach any day.

Does that mean holidays and autism are incompatible? Not necessarily, is my answer, but possibly. I look back at the breaks we took before my son was six and think: why on earth did we bother? I suspect we were blindly trying to copy everyone else. What we should have done is stay at home and take day trips to the park. My son would have loved it and my husband and I could have blown the money we would have spent on flights and accommodation on a fortnight of babysitters and meals out.

Holidays with young children are always hard because, in a triumph of hope over experience, you always anticipate getting a break and never do. But it is more intense with, and for, young autistic children, for whom all the security of structure, routine and predictability has been taken away. Some feel as though they are never going to get back home.

If holidaying causes your child massive anxiety, then clearly don't do it. But there are ways to mitigate and decrease anxiety through arch-organisation and preparation. One mum describes below the steps she took to help her severely aviophobic son not only board a plane but also to (almost) enjoy the flight. If it's just possible autistic children may derive some sliver of pleasure from doing something or going somewhere new, then it will have been worth the effort of encouraging them to overcome their fears and doubts, since this is an invaluable lesson to learn.

And you, the parents and carers, certainly deserve a week or two where you get to exercise your basic right to eat and drink too much, to take time off from the dishes and housework, and forget, if only for a few minutes, the whole world of SEN.

Tips for school holidays

We're talking about time between terms here – Easter, summer and Christmas breaks – rather than jumping-on-a-plane, going-away holidays.

End of term at nurseries and schools can be tough. Teachers ease off on the teaching, the timetable goes out of the window and there may be class parties, free play, lessons outside. Kids without SEN love this loosening of rules, but autistic kids just want their routine back. A bigger disruption awaits, however: the final bell rings and suddenly school's out. Everything stops for a few weeks – no uniform, no bus, no classroom, no TA or structured timetable. You can see why it might be distressing to suddenly find yourself outside that secure routine, floating out of the confines of your predictable life.

Here are some ways I've found to help my son through what can be a difficult time for him, and I'm sure many others:

* Create a wallchart at the beginning of the holiday, showing each day and what you are going to do and with whom. Make the chart visual if you can, with photos of people and places/activities.

* Create a structure so school holidays are predictable. My son, for example, always does the same tennis camp and cooking classes, which are small, organised and by now familiar. I coordinate with the mums of some of his friends from school, so sometimes his little buddies are there with him.

* The week before the end of term or half-term, I go to the Book People website (thebookpeople.co.uk) and order a stack of activity and sticker books to keep my son amused – for a bit at least – in order to minimise the times I feel I have to resort to TV (though don't get me wrong – the TV still gets used plenty).

Tips for going away

And this bit is about the actual planes, trains and automobiles-type holiday – those regular bag-packing, fridge-clearing, passport-forgetting, crack-of-dawn-departing, are-we-there-yetting events that we put ourselves through every year. If your family is anything like mine, you come home feeling like you need a holiday to get over the holiday, or simply looking forward to getting back into the office.

Here are some tips to help your autistic kids cope with holidays away from home, anyway. How you keep your own body and mind together is up to you!

* If you can, book a holiday out of season – you're more likely to avoid queues and there will be fewer people around during those inevitable restaurant meltdowns.

* Don't go for a family resort during school holidays – it will be a crowded and noisy hell.

* Rupert Isaacson, author of *Horse Boy*, a book and film about going to Mongolia with his wife and autistic son, recommends camping. 'It's a kind of therapy for a kid to be free of bad sensory triggers, such as loud industrial noise, fluorescent lights and the smell of cleaning products. Choose places where they can run at will and make as much noise as they need, and where all the attention and focus can be on them. Don't take family members who will get annoyed if it's all about your child – it needs to be that way, because autism and new places don't always go so smoothly.'

* Self-catering holidays can work well too: there are only the family rules to conform to.

* Jamie Knight, an autistic programmer who works for the BBC, recommends Center Parcs. These holiday villages offer self-catering flats and houses to rent in woodland locations around Europe; there are no cars and everyone cycles or walks. Knight says the staff are very autism-friendly and the swimming pools and activities worked well for him.

* Get photographs of all the bedrooms, living spaces and facilities in the place where you'll be staying (either from the website or ask for the owner/travel agency to send them to you). You can make them into a scrapbook for your child to look at before you go.

* Think about what situations they may need to understand (such as delays or unavoidable changes to travel plans) and use Social Stories to help them prepare. You can do this via your smartphone or iPad with apps like Social Stories Creator & Library.

* If by some miracle you find a holiday that half-meets everyone's needs, go there every year! You might not see as much of the world but you will have a less anxious child on holiday.

Flying

One mum, Karen, compiled a document of how she managed to encourage her son, O, to get over his fear of flying. Every time the family flies, she carries out three stages of preparation.

Stage 1: prepare at home in advance

This begins six months ahead of a flight. Put together a visual Social Story that talks your child through all of the stages of your journey, from getting to the airport to coming home again. 'It was only when we did this you can appreciate how many stages there are and daunting scenarios,' Karen says.

Make a book of photos of the different parts of the airport you'll encounter – the customs queue; the moving walkway – and the planes, inside and out. Read through it every day for six weeks before the flight and use it as a 'now and next' on the day. 'We also watched videos – carefully selected, calm ones – of airplanes, inside and out, and role-played putting on seatbelts, being the captain, air stewards – you name it.'

Stage 2: enlist some help

Some airports, such as Heathrow, have passenger experience managers who help autistic families (it can be hard to find their contact details, so phone the airport's switchboard). 'We emailed the Heathrow lady our details in advance and she met us in departures – do bring your diagnosis form with you the first time. We were super-fast-tracked at check-in and again through security – it took 15 minutes,' says Karen.

Stage 3: rewards, reassurance and relax

'Our son loves magazines, so at the airport we choose magazines he knows he can look at only once we are on the plane. This gives him something to look forward to. He also has his own pull-along luggage – the proprioceptive input calms him and he can sit down on it if he gets tired. On the plane, we give him noise-cancelling headphones and a fully charged iPad loaded with films he finds funny. We have learned that he needs to focus on something to deal with everything going on around him. A couple of weeks ago he actually looked out of the plane window for the first time and didn't freak out.'

Autism-friendly UK airport initiatives

Most airports offer some kind of help for autistic children who struggle with airports. It's best to google 'autism' and the name of the airport to find out what is available, but here are some examples:

Stansted has a special assistance page with a short video about its autism provision: www.stanstedairport.com/at-the-airport/ guides-to-travelling/special-assistance

Autistic children can be fast-tracked through security at **Manchester**: manchesterairport.co.uk/at-the-airport/special-assistance

Gatwick has a visual guide for autistic children and adults: gatwickairport.com/globalassets/documents/passengers/prm/ autismguidetogatwick.pdf

Edinburgh has an impressive additional needs assistance team that meet you on arrival at the airport and escort you through check-in and security: www.edinburghairport.com/prepare/travelling-with-additional-needs

Belfast has a special email address for autistic families – autism@bfs. aero – and a special book, *Suzy Goes on an Aeroplane*, which it sends to families to prepare them.

Eating out

It's likely to be during your first meal out that you'll begin wondering why you're putting yourself through this – and paying for the privilege. Your child will probably be struggling to cope with the distractions and sensory bombardment of a restaurant environment, let alone managing to eat their veg, while the tut-tutting or side-eye being dished up by fellow diners may leave you hissing swear words in the wrong language.

If these sorts of occasions are often fraught, try going to eat slightly earlier or later than usual, when things are quieter. Book lunch for 2.30 p.m. or 3 p.m., say, or be the first people there at 11.30 or noon. Let your child use ear defenders or an iPad with headphones, or buy them a kids' magazine to distract their attention. Ask for the bill as soon as the food has arrived, so you can just munch and run, with none of that hanging around at the end waiting for busy waiting staff to notice you, which, if a meltdown is underway or brewing, is when things can get stressful.

Christmas and family get-togethers

Family gatherings can be tough enough for neurotypicals, let alone autistic people. Though he copes much better these days, my son can struggle with feeling overwhelmed when there are too many of his relatives in the same room, usually at Christmas time. Though he loves them all dearly as individuals, all together they become simply another crowd of people, a collection of noise, movement and demands for attention decked out in silly hats and reindeer jumpers. I dread to think how he'd have coped at a *Godfather*-style wedding.

Here are some tips I've picked up over the years about managing these family occasions:

* Your child's sensory difficulties should trump almost all other issues. Decide things like venue and seating plans around their needs. Seat them next to a door, for example, if they are likely to want to escape somewhere quieter, and as far away as possible from the loudest member of the family.

✳ Try not to have too many in the same small room, or at least don't force your child to stay there the whole time. Find a room where they can retreat to for regular breaks if it all becomes too much. Have their iPad, music or books there, anything to help them decompress. Put a sign on the door saying 'My chill-out room', so they feel they have permission.

✳ Don't require them to greet relatives with hugs and kisses if they don't want to.

✳ Keep social interactions short and with a clear ending.

✳ Put up pictures of family members on the fridge or wherever. This way you can remind your child who is who and let them know a little bit about everybody.

✳ Email the family before the event and remind them of your child's needs and that they may require extra patience. Advocate on their behalf.

The author David Mitchell on taking a recent trip to Japan with his autistic son, 11:

'We have reshaped our lives around our son's abilities and likes, as far as we can – to stay inside the comfort zone of the 'Known Do-ables', if you like. There have been times, however, when we can't, and we've had to go outside the comfort zone. Surprisingly often, these experiences go much better than I'd feared, because I haven't noticed the growth that's been happening in my son. For example, we had to fly to Japan in 2016, for reasons connected with my wife's family. I was very anxious about how our son would handle being on a long-haul flight – he hadn't flown once since diagnosis, years earlier. But it turned out that he loved the flight – two fully-charged iPads, earphones, magna doodle boards, and he was fine. He not only coped with the cooped-up-ness of the 12-hour flight better than his neurotypical family, but the stimulation he hoovered up in Japan lifted him a couple of developmental steps. His curiosity about the world was both fed and expanded. I could see it. He grew more responsive and expressive, as well as making the memorable discovery that you can eat ramen by sucking it up through a straw. Why not?'

✳ ✳ ✳

CONCLUSION

*   *   *

*'Normal is an illusion. What is normal for the spider
is chaos for the fly.'*
Morticia Addams, of *The Addams Family*

When I started writing this book, shortly after my son was diagnosed, I was depressed but didn't realise it. I felt our family had received a devastating blow. As time went on I kept thinking I was over it, only for something to happen that would floor me again. I also felt isolated from my friends. Weirdly, despite being a writer and a chatterbox, I couldn't find the words to describe what we were going through.

Things were tough. My son seemed in a fog; it was hard to connect with him. Professionals commented on how anxious he seemed and we didn't know what the future looked like for him.

Thinking about how far we've come as a family since then makes me feel weepy. My son is now seven, in year 3 at a mainstream school, with a TA. In the past few years I have felt – known – for the first time that he's happy. He is doing well at school and has friends. He can be anxious, and I find dealing with the school and the local authority very stressful at times, but that aside, I think life is throwing us the usual ups and downs.

I've been writing this book for over five years and approached Orion, my publisher, two years ago. It's fair to say it took them a long time to commit to the book. Thank God for that – had they said yes straight away I would have written a book about coping with an autistic child, looking at autism as an impairment, without realising how wrong that is or that it's often a two-way process.

My outlook has changed totally, which annoyingly meant I had to completely rewrite the book when I finally did receive a commission with a rather short deadline. If I were able to go back in time and choose whether my son was autistic or not, I would be tempted for a minute to choose not, just because you know being an autistic person living in a neurotypical world is not going to be plain sailing. But in the end I would choose autistic, because I love him and I would miss him if he were someone different. In his place would be someone less funny, less clever, less sensitive and caring. Less *him*.

Now I think of autism as being common; the one in 100 official rate doesn't ring true for me. Writing this, I have lost count of the number of family friends, or people I know, who have come up to me to say they think a family member is autistic.

Through writing this book I have identified some autistic traits in myself. I can be very literal, and this sometimes stops me understanding sarcasm or jokes. I don't think I intuitively had theory of mind (cognitive empathy) and had to learn this via seeing a therapist. I struggled socially at school. My husband says I try to control our conversations and I am aware that I feel frustrated when he's talking about something I don't want to talk about. I find it strangely difficult to understand the Sally-Anne test.

I showed my husband, whose job relies on having an attention to detail, the weak central coherence test (page 21) and he saw the smaller letters before the big ones (which is the way most autistic people see it). He hyperfocuses on noises.

This book was written primarily for selfish reasons: I was sick of seeing journalists write about autism when they had very little knowledge of it. I read an interview with a celebrity who was described as being almost autistic in their lack of sensitivity. I fired off an email to the journalist telling them their statement was exactly wrong: autistic people can be overwhelmed by other people's emotions. Reading that interview was the final straw – I didn't receive a reply to my email, so instead I've written a book. Take that, ignorant journalist who I probably would have been like if my son weren't autistic!

But I hope I'm also writing it for the right reasons, too. When I interviewed TV presenter Alan Gardner, of Channel 4's *The Autistic Gardener* fame, he told me about a visit he made to an autistic school. When he arrived, kids came running up to him proudly telling him: 'I'm autistic too!' That they were so proud of their autism made him cry, and this story means a lot to me too. Let's hope this is the future.

At times, I've felt like I'm writing a love letter to my older son, as he's been in my thoughts much of the time. I love him so intensely it can feel painful. Our bond has been strengthened by how much we've both had to work for it.

He didn't have an easy start to life, but I'm excited to see where he ends up. My mother is convinced he's going to be an inventor who changes our world. I act embarrassed when she says this, but secretly I agree.

I'll settle for him leading an unexceptional life and being happy, though. That would feel like a wonderful achievement. I hope he grows up knowing how brilliant he is, and being proud of his autism, and knowing how proud I am to be his mum.

*   *   *

GLOSSARY OF TERMS

✳   ✳   ✳

Adaptive skills – Skills a person needs to look after themselves.

Affective empathy – Responding with appropriate emotion to what someone is thinking or feeling.

Asperger syndrome – A form of autism, where people have average or above average intelligence and no learning disabilities.

Auditory processing (difficulty) – When people can't process what they hear because their ears and brains are not coordinated.

CAMHS – Child and Adolescent Mental Health Services.

Clinical psychologist – A professional who helps with behaviour and distress.

Code of practice (CoP) – This is a document that explains the duties of local authorities, health bodies and schools towards SEN children.

Cognitive behavioural therapy (CBT) – Talking therapy that can help manage a problem by changing the way you think and behave.

Cognitive empathy (also known as theory of mind) – The ability to imagine someone's thoughts and feelings.

Cognitive intelligence – Intellectual ability.

Developmental coordination disorder (DCD; formerly known as dyspraxia) – A condition that can affect planning of movements and coordination.

Disabled – Having a physical or mental condition that limits a person's movements, senses or activities.

EarlyBird – Course run by the NAS offered to parents of newly diagnosed children.

Education, Health and Care Plan (EHCP) – This is the document stating what support the local authority is obliged to provide the child.

Educational psychologist – A professional who looks at a child's learning in school.

Ehlers-Danlos syndrome – A group of conditions that affect connective tissue.

Executive function – The mental skills you need to get a task done.

Fine-motor skills – Small movements, such as picking up small objects and holding a spoon.

Gross-motor skills – The bigger movements our body makes, such as walking.

Hypermobility (often referred to as joint hypermobility) – When a person's joints have an unusually large range of movement.

Inclusion – The principle is that all kids with SEN have the right to be educated with their peers at a local school if they so wish.

Learning difficulty – When a child finds it harder to acquire new knowledge and skills compared with those of the same age.

Learning disability – A difference in the way a brain is formed that can make it more difficult for a person to read, write, spell, reason and organise information.

Learning support assistant (LSA) – See Teaching assistant

Local authority (LA) – The local government body that looks after the services in an area.

Mainstream school – Not a special school. Mainstreaming is the practice of educating some kids with SEN with their non-SEN peers.

Maintained school – A school that is funded and controlled by the local education authority (state schools).

Meltdown – An intense feeling of despair, powerlessness or being overwhelmed by sensory experiences which causes a child to act or lash out.

Mindfulness – A therapeutic technique in which you focus on keeping your awareness on the present moment.

Movement break – Time in the classroom where a child or the class does physical activity.

Neurodiversity – The range of differences of brain function as part of normal variation in the population. (Usually used in the context of autism.)

Neurotypical (NT) – Someone who is non-autistic.

Non-verbal – When someone has little to no spoken language.

Obsessive-compulsive disorder (OCD) – A mental health condition in which a person has obsessive thoughts and compulsive behaviours.

Over- or under-stimulation – When the senses are over- or under-reactive to stimulation.

Physiotherapy (Physio) – A person who helps people with functional movement.

Psychiatrist – A clinician who diagnoses and treats psychiatric conditions and can assess the need for medication.

Psychotherapist – A person who treats low mood or anxiety by talking.

Self-stimulatory behaviour (also known as stimming) – The repetition of a physical movement, sound or objects.

SEN casework officer – A person employed by the LA to carry out the administrative duties relating to pupils with an EHCP.

SEN support – A support framework offered by schools for children with SEN which is not legally binding.

SENCO (special educational needs coordinator) – This is the person in a school overseeing the support for SEN kids.

SEND tribunal – This is the body that you can go to if you want to challenge the contents of the EHCP or an action of the LA.

Sensory processing disorder (SPD; also known as sensory differences) – When the brain organises information from the senses in a different or disordered way.

Sensory-seeking – When a child is under-responsive to sensory input and so is looking for more sensory stimulation.

Social communication – Language used in social situations.

Social Story – A concept devised by Carol Gray to help autistic kids with social skills. It is a cartoon or written story that models a situation, explaining relevant social cues, others' perspectives and a suggested response.

Special educational needs (SEN) – When someone has learning difficulties that make it harder for them to learn than most people of the same age.

Special educational needs and disability (SEND) – The same definition as above, but for a child with a disability.

Special school – A school for kids with special needs.

Spectrum – Used to classify something in terms of its position between two extreme points.

Teaching assistant (TA; also known as learning support assistant) – A person who assists a teacher by providing additional support to children with SEN requirements, often working on a one-to-one basis with those children.

Theory of mind – The awareness that other people have different beliefs, intentions and perspectives to your own.

Theraputty – A play-dough-like substance which can be used to build strength in the hand.

Transition – The process of moving from one thing to another.

Visual processing (difficulty) – When people struggle to make sense of information taken in through the eyes.

Visual timetable – Using pictures to break down steps of a task or show what is happening throughout the day.

* * *

ACKNOWLEDGEMENTS

✳ ✳ ✳

Thank you to the amazing journalist Eve McGowan, who helped me research the book, interview people and came up with some brilliant ideas. Eve, I couldn't have done it without you.

I would also like to thank Amanda Harris, Olivia Morris, Virginia Woolsten-croft and Ru Merritt at Orion for your faith in this book, your editing skills, patience and for being a pleasure to work with. Also Barney Calman for getting the ball rolling.

Also Charlotte Lore, Catherine Ferris and her team at Ambitious about Autism for supporting me in this book at an early stage and working with me throughout. Also Virginia Bovell, thank you.

To the NAS press team: Louisa Mullan for your brilliant advice and Piers Wright.

To my team at *The Times*: Anne Ashworth and the Bricks and Money crew.

To Jasmine El-Doori, who has encouraged me to do this book when I wanted to give up. And for suggesting the format and helping me in so many ways over the years.

To the people who read chapters of the book to sense-check it and lend me their expertise: Matt Keer, Barney Angliss, Sarah Hendrickx, Georgia Harper, Robyn Steward, Ruth Moyse, Elizabeth (Ed) Archer, Dr Ken Greaves, Monica McCaffrey, Dr Julie Maxwell of the Royal College of Paediatrics and Child Health.

And to the brilliant contributors: Ian Bellamy, Alis Rowe, Alex Marshall, Jamie Knight and especially Isobel Pierce.

Thank you to all the autistic people who spent their time talking to me. Especially Laura James, who helped me in more ways than I can express given the word count I have left. I wish, Laura, that you could travel round the world and meet everyone (though I'm guessing you would hate it) – that would achieve more for autism awareness than anything else.

To Debora Elijah who has given us a happy son. I can never repay you for that.

Also my friends Hannah and Caroline – I'm lucky to have you. And Francisca Kellett for being the best bestie I could hope for.

To my wonderful dad, stepmother Noelene, in-laws Ann, Richard and Mary-Anne a heartfelt thank you for your support. To my beautiful sister, I love you Abs! And the same to my brilliant sisters and brothers-in-laws: Catrin, Gareth, Jessica and Aled. My lovely aunt Margaret, I appreciate all your help very much. To my wonderful mum for looking after me and my children with such love, thank you thank you thank you.

Finally, my loves: to my darling younger son Morgan, thanks for being patient with your mummy who rushed off to write this book all the time. I love you so much. Promise to write a book around something to do with you next time. And Ellis. You are the best. Never forget it.

Most of all to Eifion, who helped write this book. I really love you, penguin. There's no one else for this fox.

*   *   *

AUTISM INDEX

✳   ✳   ✳

NAMES/GENERAL INDEX

✳   ✳   ✳

*　　*　　*